THE BODLEY VERSION OF MANDEVILLE'S TRAVELS

EARLY ENGLISH TEXT SOCIETY

No. 253

1963

PRICE 40s.

cete þat tyme But af
terward cam᷒ þe kyng
of pers wiþdrow þe
watyr & distropede þe
cete & al þat contre þer
aboute for þey depryu
the grete rener of Eufra
tes & sodyn it renyth cet
el sundery weyes for he
hadde mad his grete oth
& swer his grete oth & so
greuosly þat be cause
þat so manye noble
haddyn ben drenkt þer
in þat he shulde bryn
gyn it to swich a stat þat
wom̄e schulde wadyn
þer ouyr & not wetyn
here kneis & so he dese˞
uyt it standyth in þat
degre ffor babylonye
where þat the sondon
dwellyth for to pase to
þe grete babylonye arn
xl iurneis thõ desert
& it is not vndyr þe sub
iection of þe sondon b᷒
w᷒ mine þe lordshepe
of þe kyng of pers &
it is holdyn of þe gre
te cane of tartarye þe
whiche is a gret ple of
cathan & of manye othe
re contreis & of a gret

tre of pride his son is
wytheborgh & marchid af
preter Jon is cond And
he hath so gret lordshep
þat he wot neue whe˞
his lordshepe endyth,
he is myghtiere w᷒ outy
coriсoū þan the sondon
of which gret stat & maies
te I thyṅke to spekken of af
terward whan I haue
tome þerto ∵ ffor de ter
ra egipti

Egipt is a strong contre
& manye psions haue mys
ben þerin for þere siþ
meche heuene ton gret
rychees in þe entre of þe
hauene toward þe est
is þe rede se þat renyth
right to þe cete of cos
tantyn þe noble. The
contre of egipt is in
lenthe v iorneis but not
b᷒ iij in brede for desert
þat aryn þere. Be twy
egip & þe lond þat is
callyd Nvndrea arn
xij iourneis in deserties
The folk þat wonyde
in þat contre armoris
tene mon but thy aryn
blake of cols for the on
gret hete þat is þere

Þus vndurstande þat this Babiloyne þat I speke of where is
þe Babiloyne where þe Sowdon dwellys is seuen daies Iourney
whan men passyth the confusion and diuisite of tungis whan
is þe Tour of Babiloyne. þat Tour þaȝt þe toucke is in desert
of Arabie. for it is long tyme sithenes þat any man durste gon
forto visite þat ilk wrecched place. for it is full of dyuyne and dragouns
and nadurs. and indude oþur dyuerʃe byftys for the vengaunce of god
tof. the bygynnyng of þat tour. for þat noo man dar come þer. Nyt
the circle of þat tour ys couȝte of the cite of Babiloyne þᵗ ys
was ʃomtyme contenyng xxvij. Myle. aboute. But neuertheles yit þe
was a tour yit þer was ʃomtyme in þat cercle nyndys fair. ftep
ayenys þat now is dysused and bronnen. of Babarus and þat the ʃite
of Babiloyne ffounded the kyng þᵗ hyte Nembroȝ þat was kyng of þᵗ
lond. and there he was þe fifte kyng þᵗ eù was in erþe. And þat
Ml. Babiloyne was ʃomtyme sitte on afair plaȳ feyld upon þᵉ ryue

Bodl. MS. Rawlinson D. 99, f. 8ᵛ (top portion)

THE
BODLEY VERSION
OF
MANDEVILLE'S
TRAVELS

FROM BODLEIAN MS. E MUSAEO 116
WITH PARALLEL EXTRACTS FROM
THE LATIN TEXT OF
BRITISH MUSEUM MS. ROYAL 13 E. ix

EDITED BY

M. C. SEYMOUR

Published for
THE EARLY ENGLISH TEXT SOCIETY
by the
OXFORD UNIVERSITY PRESS
LONDON   NEW YORK   TORONTO

UNIVERSITY PRESS

Great Clarendon Street, Oxford OX2 6DP
United Kingdom

Oxford University Press is a department of the University of Oxford.
It furthers the University's objective of excellence in research, scholarship,
and education by publishing worldwide. Oxford is a registered trade mark of
Oxford University Press in the UK and in certain other countries

© The Early English Text Society 1963

The moral rights of the authors have been asserted

Database right Oxford University Press (maker)

First Edition published in 1963

All rights reserved. No part of this publication may be reproduced,
stored in a retrieval system, or transmitted, in any form or by any means,
without the prior permission in writing of Oxford University Press,
or as expressly permitted by law, or under terms agreed with the appropriate
reprographics rights organization. Enquiries concerning reproduction
outside the scope of the above should be sent to the Rights Department,
Oxford University Press, at the address above

You must not circulate this book in any other form
and you must impose this same condition on any acquirer

Published in the United States of America by Oxford University Press
198 Madison Avenue, New York, NY 10016, United States of America

British Library Cataloguing in Publication Data
Data available

Library of Congress Cataloging in Publication Data
Data available

Original Series, 253

ISBN 978-0-19-722253-9

TO
MY MOTHER

PREFACE

IT is my pleasant duty to thank those who have made this edition possible. The University of California at Los Angeles gave me the opportunity to prepare a preliminary study, and the Principal and Fellows of St. Edmund Hall, Oxford, made possible its completion. Mr. Bob Campbell, the American bookseller, and the late Malcolm Letts, F.S.A., generously enabled me to acquire books not easily obtainable elsewhere.

Professor G. V. Smithers and Professor J. R. R. Tolkien gave me much help and encouragement in arranging and improving my material. Professor N. Davis and Professor E. J. Dobson read an earlier draft and made many invaluable suggestions. To the latter, indeed, I owe much more, a debt which only those who have had the good fortune to be his pupils can fully appreciate. Mr. R. W. Burchfield has generously given me much time and help in preparing this edition for the press.

Bodley's Librarian has kindly allowed me to print the English text and to reproduce the frontispiece, and the Trustees of the British Museum have kindly given me permission to print the Latin text. The staffs of the British Museum, the Bodleian Library, and the libraries of the University of California at Los Angeles and the University of the Witwatersrand, Johannesburg, have been unfailingly helpful.

It has been my pleasure to meet and work with these people, and their many kindnesses are gratefully acknowledged.

M. C. S.

5 December 1961
King's College, London

CONTENTS

BODLEIAN MS. E MUSAEO 116, f. 15ʳᵃ and BODLEIAN MS. RAWLINSON D. 99, f. 8ᵛ *Frontispiece*

INTRODUCTION

The affiliation of the manuscripts	xi
The date of the Bodley Version	xi
The origin of the Bodley Version	xii
The origin of the Latin text	xiv
A description of the manuscripts of the Bodley Version	xvi
A description of the manuscripts of the Latin text	xvii
The texts	xix
The language of MS. e Musaeo 116	xx

ITINERARIUM IOHANNIS MAUNDEVILE 2

MANDEVILLE'S TRAVELS—THE BODLEY VERSION

Prologue	3
The way to Constantinople	5
The Cross and the Crown	7
Constantinople and the Greek faith	9
The Lady of Lango	17
Cairo and the Sultans	27
Egypt	33
From Cairo to Mount Sinai. The Monastery of St. Catherine	37
The Desert. The Dry Tree. Bethlehem	45
Jerusalem and the Holy Sepulchre	51
The Temple at Jerusalem	57
The Dead Sea	61
Galilee. The Christian Sects	65
Mahomet and the Koran	67
Armenia. The Legend of the Sparrowhawk	79
The Land of the Amazons. Diamonds	83
Ethiopia and India	85
St. Thomas	91
Strange Customs in Ethiopia	95
Prester John	99
The Valley Perilous	103

CONTENTS

The Virtuous Heathen and Alexander the Great	113
The Gold-digging Ants	117
The Great Khan and his Court	123
The History of the Khans	129
Heathen Peoples and their Customs	137
Epilogue	145
COMMENTARY	149
GLOSSARY	177
INDEX OF NAMES	185

INTRODUCTION

The affiliation of the manuscripts

THE abridged Bodley Version of *Mandeville's Travels* is extant in two manuscripts in the Bodleian Library, MS. e Musaeo 116 and MS. Rawlinson D. 99. Each of these manuscripts was written in the first half of the fifteenth century, and each contains numerous unique minor variations from the common substance which prove that each descends independently from a common ancestor, now lost. Thus, to mention the two most striking differences, MS. e Musaeo 116 gives a fuller account of the Valley Perilous (107/11–24), which is abridged in MS. Rawlinson D. 99; and the latter manuscript gives an account of the Phœnix (37/29) which is omitted in the former. A mass of other minor variations, which support this claim of independent derivation, is recorded in the critical apparatus below the printed Bodley Version.

MS. e Musaeo 116, written by the scribe of Cambridge University Library MS. Gg. iv. 27, gives a better text than MS. Rawlinson D. 99, which hitherto has been the only manuscript of the Bodley Version to be printed.[1] This latter manuscript is noticeably shorter and contains more serious scribal contaminations, as distinct from elementary copying errors, than the other, and parts of it have been deliberately rearranged, thus distorting the nature of the missing archetype.[2] For these reasons MS. e Musaeo 116 has the better claim to be considered as representing the original text of the Bodley Version.

The date of the Bodley Version

The date of the making of the Bodley Version cannot be determined with precision. From the linguistic and palaeographical evidence it is clear that both extant manuscripts were written before 1450, and both derive independently from a common ancestor which was not the archetype of the Bodley Version.[3]

---

[1] M. Letts, *Mandeville's Travels. Texts and Translations*, Hakluyt Society (1953), series II, vol. cii.   [2] See below, note to 9/23.

[3] Both manuscripts contain identical scribal errors which could not have been present in the archetype; e.g. *Iaynes* 5/11, *pleyinge* 11/11, *vs* 13/23.

The lost English version of *Mandeville's Travels*, of which the Bodley Version is an abridgement, was in existence before 1425, since parts of it were incorporated in the conflated Egerton Version, made before that date.[1] The Latin version from which this lost English version was translated was being copied *c*. 1400 and was probably made in the decade previous to 1400.[2] It seems therefore that the lost English version was translated between 1390 and 1425.

It is, of course, impossible to determine without further evidence how soon afterwards the abridged Bodley Version was made from this lost English version. The state of scribal contamination in the two extant manuscripts suggests that a considerable scribal tradition separated them from the lost archetype, but this information is of little help in fixing a precise date. All that can be surmised is that the Bodley Version was made at some time after 1390 and before 1450.

The origin of the Bodley Version

The relation of the Bodley Version to other versions of *Mandeville's Travels* was first examined by Vogels, who thought that the two extant manuscripts derived from a slightly fuller but still abridged translation of the Latin text contained in MS. Royal 13 E. IX.[3] This view of the interdependence of these two versions was subsequently challenged,[4] but a detailed examination of the Bodley Version and the cited Latin text confirms Vogels's belief that the two texts are related. Not only does the Bodley Version follow the Latin text in every detail, apart from the major transposition of the accounts of Prester John and the Great Khan,[5] where the abridged nature of the former allows comparison; it also contains numerous readings which are explicable as derivatives of the Latin text. Some of

---

[1] G. F. Warner, *The Buke of Iohn Maundeuill* (Roxburghe Club, 1889), p. xii; M. C. Seymour, 'The Origin of the Egerton Version of *Mandeville's Travels*', *Medium Ævum*, xxx (1961), pp. 159–69.

[2] The oldest manuscript of this Latin version, MS. Royal 13 E. IX, was written *c*. 1400. Its degree of scribal contamination suggests a considerable scribal tradition.

[3] J. Vogels, 'Handschriftliche Untersuchungen über die englische Version Mandeville's', *Jahresbericht über das Realgymnasium zu Crefeld* (1889), pp. 47–51.

[4] M. Letts, op. cit., p. 416.   [5] See below, note to 97/20.

these are direct borrowings from the Latin (e.g. *Latynys* 15/9, *Surrany* 67/15, *Castrum Nisi* 79/28); others are either mistranslations (e.g. *in diserd* 17/16, *contynuel frost* 85/24) or translations of corrupt Latin variants (e.g. *ferme pes* 81/21, *Doras* 103/30, *lyere* 113/11); others are scribal contaminations which can be corrected only by reference to the Latin text (e.g. *pleyinge* 11/11, *helful weyes* 25/22). These and other similar readings, recorded in the Commentary, form a corpus of evidence establishing a connexion between the Bodley Version and the Latin text which cannot be denied.

However, Vogels's claim that the extant manuscripts of the Bodley Version are only slightly more abridged than their missing archetype requires some qualification. Further investigation of the origin of the Egerton Version (which, Vogels believed, was based on the Defective Version[1] and only used a manuscript of the Bodley Version at *one* critical point to fill the lacuna in the Defective text known as the 'Egypt Gap') shows that Egerton is a thorough-going conflation of the Defective Version and the text incorporated at the 'Egypt Gap'. Not merely there but at many other places the Egerton Version incorporates passages that either are found, almost word for word, in the Bodley Version or, omitted in that abridged text, are demonstrably translated from the Latin text.[2]

An analysis of the manner in which the redactor of the Bodley Version made his abridgement[3] shows that in the early stages of his work (i.e. until the beginning of the description of Egypt at 24/16) he made no important omissions. Comparison of the Egerton Verson and the Latin text at the 'Egypt Gap' shows that the former gives unabridged an account of Egypt which is clearly a translation of the corresponding passage in the latter. Thus, there exists in the extant manuscripts of the Bodley and Egerton Versions irrefutable proof that the lost English translation of the Latin text was, at least in its first quarter, complete and unabridged.

When the redactor of the Bodley Version reached the account of Egypt, he begin to abridge his work noticeably by

---

[1] i.e. the earliest English translation. [2] M. C. Seymour, op. cit., pp. 161–5.
[2] M. C. Seymour, 'A Medieval Redactor at Work', *Notes and Queries*, ccvi (1961), pp. 169–71.

systematically shortening or excluding any passage, such as detailed itinerary, which struck no general note of wonder.[1] This method of selection, when considered with the evidence of the unabridged state of the first part of the lost English translation extant in the Bodley and Egerton Versions, strongly suggests that the redactor worked from a complete English text.

This suggestion is further strengthened by the discovery in the Egerton Version of passages, other than the account of Egypt, which are demonstrably translated from the Latin text yet omitted in the Bodley Version. Unhappily, it is not possible to reconstruct from the Bodley and the Egerton Versions the lost English translation of the Latin text in its entirety, but more than half of such a text is recoverable.[2] On this evidence it seems certain that the lost English translation from which the Bodley Version was made was completely unabridged.

The origin of the Latin text

The relationship which the Latin text is thus shown to have with these two English versions of *Mandeville's Travels* makes desirable some inquiry into its own origins, and as a necessary preliminary the affiliation of the six extant manuscripts of this version has to be determined.

Four of these manuscripts, British Museum MSS. Royal 13 E. IX, Harley 175, Cotton Appendix IV, and Glasgow University Library, Hunterian MS. T. 4. 1, have in common a number of scribal errors and omissions (e.g. they omit *et numerosi* 44/23 and give a corrupt reading *in dente* 98/2).[3] As each of these four manuscripts has unique scribal contaminations,[4] they clearly

---

[1] M. C. Seymour, in *Notes and Queries*, loc. cit., p. 170.

[2] A detailed listing of the relevant passages in the Egerton Version is recorded in my thesis, 'A Study of the Interrelations of the English Versions of "Mandeville's Travels"' (Oxford, 1959), vol. i, pp. 150–8.

[3] In passages not printed below, MSS. Royal 13 E. IX (ff. 44va and 50va), Harley 175 (ff. 14^v and 36^v), Cotton Appendix IV (ff. 64^r and 73^r), and T. 4. 1 (ff. 275^r and 289^v) omit *Abelussum*, the Arab name for balsam, and *murata*, i.e. walled, and have blank spaces in their texts to mark the omissions.

[4] MS. Royal 13 E. IX gives a contaminated account of the Koran (see below, note to 66/24); MS. Cotton Appendix IV, f. 59^v, omits 8/5–8; MS. Harley 175, f. 67^v, has a blank space to mark the omission of *assuefaciunt*; MS. T. 4. 1, f. 270^r, omits a reference to Beyrout.

derive independently from a common ancestor which originally contained the contaminations common to them all.

Further investigation reveals that three of these manuscripts, MSS. Harley 175, Cotton Appendix IV, and T. 4. 1, are characterized by two other lacunae, avoided by MS. Royal 13 E. IX and the two remaining manuscripts; they omit *Lempnam* 10/9 and *quia res in se naturalis est* 14/4. Thus, they must derive from an exemplar copied from the common ancestor of the four manuscripts mentioned above.

The two other manuscripts of the Latin text, Durham University MS. Cosin V. iii. 7 and Jesus College, Cambridge, MS. Q.B. 18, lie outside this line of descent, since they avoid all the scribal contaminations noticed above. Moreover, each contains unique scribal features which preclude the possibility of their being directly related to the other manuscripts or to each other. MS. Q.B. 18 omits on f. 53ᵛ part of the account of the barnacle geese, and MS. Cosin V. iii. 7 omits on f. 68ʳ one of two quotations from the Psalms, besides giving an interpolated story of 'Mandeville's' visit to the Pope (see below, note to 146/7).

On the evidence of these otherwise trivial variations the affiliation of the manuscripts may be determined and expressed most conveniently in a stemma:

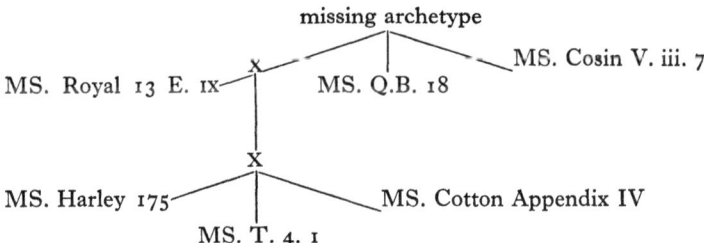

It is thus possible, on the basis of this stemma, to attempt a reconstruction of the missing archetype by taking what seems to be the oldest manuscript, MS. Royal 13 E. IX, and correcting it after collation with the five other manuscripts.[1]

---

[1] Such a text, with critical apparatus, is given in my thesis, vol. iv. The epitome extant in British Museum MS. Cotton Otho D. 1 derives independently from the lost archetype.

The French manuscripts of *Mandeville's Travels* fall into two broad groups, the Continental Version and the Insular Version.[1] The latter, written in English hands and mostly extant in English libraries,[2] is distinguished by a shorter account of the Valley Perilous than is found in the former.[3] As the Latin text (see below, 106/12 and note) gives the shorter account, it seems reasonable to assume that it was translated from a manuscript of the Insular Version.

This assumption is confirmed by the discovery in the Latin text of readings which are demonstrably traceable to corrupt variants in one sub-group of the Insular Version; e.g. *quandam villam* (4/12), *responsum Christi* (note to 58/4), and the omission of the Persian, Chaldean, and Saracen alphabets.[4] There is much similar evidence, but it is useless to seek farther for the Insular manuscript from which the Latin text was made. None of the twenty-one extant manuscripts of the Insular Version has the corrupt variants which gave, in translation, all the idiosyncratic readings of the Latin Version, although British Museum MS. Royal 20 A. 1 offers a very close parallel.

A description of the manuscripts of the Bodley Version

1. MS. *e Musaeo 116*. ff. iii+152+i. Parchment. 265 × 190 mm. Formerly two manuscripts, in hands of the fifteenth century, bound together before 1600 and owned by Sir Kenelm Digby.

First MS. (ff. 1–64) Double-columned, frame measuring 170 × 50 mm. and containing 30 lines. A change of hand occurs at f. 57. Collation: 1–8⁸.

Contents: f. 1ra Chaucer's Treatise on the Astrolabe (imperfect).
         f. 6rb Mandeville's Travels.
         f. 49vb 'Godfridus super palladium.' A treatise on fruit-trees, especially vine-trees, in English.
         f. 62ra Latin recipes for making wine.

---

[1] Guy De Poerck, 'La tradition manuscrite des Voyages de Jean de Mandeville', *Romanica Gandensia*, iv (1956), 125–58.

[2] J. W. Bennett, *The Rediscovery of Sir John Mandeville*, M.L.A. Monograph Series XIX (1954), pp. 265–71. The manuscripts nos. 11 and 12 of Mrs. Bennett's list are not of this version.   [3] De Poerck, op. cit., pp. 140–54.

[4] M. C. Seymour, 'The Scribal Tradition of *Mandeville's Travels*: the Insular Version', *Scriptorium*, xvii (1963).

INTRODUCTION xvii

Second MS. (ff. 65–153) Frame measuring 200 × 125 mm. and containing 42–45 lines. One hand until f. 148ᵛ. Collation: 9–19⁸, 20⁸ (lacks 8).

Contents: f. 65ʳ Henry Daniel, O. P., Liber Uricrisiarum. A treatise on urines, in English.
  f. 148ʳ Some notes on astrology.
  f. 149ʳ Miscellaneous items, in various hands of the sixteenth century.

2. *MS. Rawlinson D. 99.* ff. iii+32+many blank sheets bound with the manuscript in the eighteenth century to make a volume of convenient thickness. Paper, without watermark. 280 × 190 mm. Frame measuring 220 × 155 mm. and containing 32 lines. Rounded hand of the latter half of the fifteenth century. Collation: 1–4⁸.

Contents: f. 1 Mandeville's Travels. Sixty-nine numbered chapters, divided into five numbered parts.
  f. 32 blank.

This manuscript was printed by M. Letts, op. cit., pp. 416–81.

A description of the manuscripts of the Latin Text

1. *British Museum MS. Royal 13 E. ix.* ff. iii+326+i. Parchment. 350 × 315 mm. Double-columned, frame measuring 310 × 85 mm. and containing 58–61 lines. One hand, apart from f. 52 and f. 63, which form the outside sheet of a quire of 12. Written at St. Albans *c.* 1400 (the death of Sir Hugh Calverly, *ob.* 1394, is recorded on f. 253ᵛ). Collation (ff. 1–75): 4+1¹², 2¹² (wants 12), 3–6¹².

Contents: Twenty-five items, mainly historical and geographical, in Latin and French. *Itinerarium Iohannis Maundevile* item 12, ff. 40–71.

2. *British Museum MS. Harley 175.* ff. iii+106+iii. Parchment. 145 × 105 mm. Frame measuring 105 × 80 mm. and containing 23–25 lines. Collation: 1–12⁸, 13¹⁰.

Contents: f. 1 *Itinerarium Iohannis Maundevile*, in eighty-eight numbered chapters and two books, *liber secundus* beginning at ch. xli, f. 48ᵛ.
  f. 106 blank.

3. *British Museum MS. Cotton Appendix IV.* ff. iii+124+iii. Parchment. 270 × 180 mm. Frame measuring 180 × 110 mm.

and containing 39–43 lines. Written in first half of the fifteenth century. Owned by Oliver Nayler, 1596. Collation (ff. 59–102): 1–5^8+4.

Contents: f. 2   Guido, de arte dictandi epistolas.
           f. 59 *Itinerarium Iohannis Maundevile*, chapters numbered as far as ch. xlvii.
           f. 102 Prophetia Merlini Silvestris.
           f. 103 Philobiblon. Ricardus de Aungervile, completum in manerio de Aukeland, 24 Jan. 1344.
           f. 120 Provinciale catholicorum Cristianorum virorum.

4. *Durham University MS. Cosin V. iii. 7.* ff. ii+102+ii. Parchment and paper, with watermark of chalice found in English sources *c.* 1477–85 and listed as figure 70 by E. Heawood, *The Library*, series 4, vol. x, p. 282. Probably written after 1485 by William Ebesham. Collation: 1^{14}, 2^{16}, 3–7^{14}, +2. 225×160 mm.

Contents: f. 1   *Itinerarium Iohannis Mandevill.* Eighty-eight numbered chapters.
           f. 84^v de compositione chilindri.
           f. 88 story of the Holy Cross, in Latin.
           f. 94 verse summary of the Book of Judith.
           f. 95 sequences (in a different and later hand).
           f. 99^v Latin poem on monastic life.
           f. 102 two prose passages about the Psalms.

5. *Hunterian Museum MS. T. 4. 1.* ff. viii+340+viii. Parchment. 273×185 mm. Frame measuring 180×115 mm. and containing 36 lines. Written by Richard Frampton in the early fifteenth century. Owned by Mary Southwell (seventeenth century) and Thomas Martin, d. 1771. Collation (ff. 266–337): 1–9^8.

Contents: f. 1   historia de destructione Troie.
           f. 127 liber de gestis magni regis Alexandri.
           f. 165 liber domini Marci Pauli de Veneciis.
           f. 254 liber fratris Oderici de Foro Iulii.
           f. 266 *Itinerarium Iohannis Mandevill.*

6. *Jesus College, Cambridge, MS. Q.B. 18.* ff. v+151+iv. Paper, with watermark of crossed keys. 225×155 mm. Frame measuring 170×115 mm. and containing 35–36 lines. Written in latter half of the fifteenth century. Given by Mr. Man, a fellow, 1674. The end fly-leaves contain two rejected pages of the

Itinerarium corresponding to f. 24^r and f. 56^r. Collation (ff. 1–66): 2+1^{18}, 2–3^{16}, 4^{14}.

Contents: f. 3   *Itinerarium domini Iohannis de Maundevill*. Eighty-eight numbered chapters.

f. 68   Gesta Romanorum.

The Texts

The Bodley Version is printed from Bodleian MS. e Musaeo 116, ff. 6rb–49va. The scribe's corrections to the manuscript have been accepted, and his contractions expanded, without notice except in cases of doubt. Editorial corrections are shown by italicizing altered letters and by placing additions within square brackets. No attempt has been made to restore the forms of the lost archetype, but where evidence contained in other manuscripts shows the one now printed to be contaminated, correction has been made. Punctuation and word-division follow modern usage, and the scribe's initial *ff* has not been preserved. Latin rubrics, written in the manuscript in a distinctive red ink, are printed in capitals.

The critical apparatus below the text contains readings of the manuscript which have been emended and collated readings from Bodleian MS. Rawl. D. 99 (designated *R*). In this collation, synonymous and syntactical variants, variations of word-order not affecting the sense, and differences of rubrication are not recorded.

The Latin text is printed from British Museum MS. Royal 13 E. IX, ff. 40ra–71vb. Where the sequence of the printed Latin text departs from that of the manuscript, either by omission or by rearrangement, in order to present an exact parallel to the printed Bodley Version, the omission or rearrangement is indicated by spaced dots. The editorial procedure is identical to that used for printing the Bodley Version, with the important exception that an attempt is made to restore the forms of the lost archetype of the Latin text.

In the critical apparatus below the text are printed contaminated readings of the manuscript which have been rejected after collation with the five other manuscripts of this version. The account of the Koran, corresponding to the passage beginning at 66/24 and ending at 70/26, which has been deleted

from the text, is not, however, printed in the apparatus because of its length. Unless otherwise stated, corrected readings are supplied from Hunterian Museum MS. T. 4. 1. A folio reference which immediately follows an omission, indicated by spaced dots, does not necessarily precede the first word of that folio in the manuscript.

To facilitate reference to other editions of *Mandeville's Travels*, a table of contents of the Bodley Version, based on the Editor's Analysis in Hamelius's edition (E.E.T.S., o.s. 153, pp. ix–xv), is added to the Contents on pp. ix–x.

The language of MS. e Musaeo 116]

A survey of the language of MS. e Musaeo 116, particularly in relation to its dialect and orthography, will appear elsewhere as part of a study which demonstrates that the scribe also wrote Cambridge University Library MS. Gg. iv. 27, Part I, and which suggests that this man may have been the first amanuensis of Margery Kempe; but the main points of linguistic interest may be briefly noted. The manuscript was written in East Anglia between 1400 and 1450, possibly at Lynn about 1430. The scribe copied his exemplar letter by letter, rather than word by word, without having perfectly understood his text. He emended those readings in his exemplar which he did not understand by substituting forms as close as possible to the rejected readings with little regard for the contextual sense. While these remarkable scribal practices lie behind all the unique contaminations of the manuscript, apart from copyist's errors, the many apparent idiosyncrasies of the orthography may be severally paralleled in other manuscripts of the same date and provenance.

MANDEVILLE'S TRAVELS

ITINERARIUM
IOHANNIS MAUNDEVILE
DE MIRABILIBUS
MUNDI

[f. 40ra] Quia plures desiderant audire de terra sancta, id est de terra promissionis, et eciam de aliis terris transmarinis in diuersis mundi partibus constitutis, ego Iohannes Maundeuill miles, licet indignus, natus et nutritus in Anglia de villa sancti Albani, qui transiui mare anno domini millesimo trecentesimo vicesimo secundo die sancti Michaelis; et deinceps fui vltra mare multo tempore, et vidi in circuitu diuersas prouincias, regiones, ac insulas, et transiui per terram Turchorum, per Armeniam maiorem et minorem, per terram Tartarorum, per terram Persarum, per Siriam, per Arabiam, per Egyptum inferiorem et superiorem, per Libiam, per Caldeam, per magnam partem Ethiopie, per terram Amazonum, per Indiam minorem, per vnam partem Indie maioris, et per multas diuersas insulas in circuitu Indie, in quibus morantur plures diuerse naciones diuersarum legum, sectarum, et linguarum; de quibus omnibus dicturus sum plenius postea in isto libello, prout deus donauerit.

Specialiter hoc opus aggredior pro eis qui desiderium habent visitandi sanctam ciuitatem Ierusalem et alia loca sancta que in circuitu sunt, ostendam enim eis euidenter quam viam recte tenere possint versus loca predicta, quia multociens ibi fui ac sepius per eadem loca transiui et equitaui cum comitatu bono, benedictus deus.

Nunc ergo in nomine domini, qui voluerit mare transire versus loca predicta potest diuersis itineribus ire per mare

HIC INCIPIT TRACTUS IOHANNIS MAUNDEUYLE MILITIS DE MIRABILIBUS MUNDI PER IPSUM VISIS ET AUDITIS IN DIUERSIS REGIONIBUS IN PEREGRINACIONE SUA

[f. 6ᵛᵃ] [F]orthy that manye men desyryn to heryn of dyuers londis and of the Holy Lond and of the Lond of Beheste and of othere dyuerse reumys beyonde the see in dyuerse partiis of the world, I Iohn Maundevile, knyght, thow I be vnworthi, born and norisched in the reume of Ingeland of the toun of Seynt Albonys passede the see vpon a day of Seynt Michel the Archaungel in the yer of oure lord Iesu Crist m.ccc. and xxii. I was beyonde the see long tyme, sau and passede thorw manye dyuerse regeonys, londis, and reumys, and ylis, that is for to seye the reume of Turkye, Hermonye bothe the Lasse and the More, Tartarye, Pers and Syrie, Arabye, Egipt, Libie, Calde, and thorw a gret partie of Ethiope, Amason, Inde the Lasse and the More, and thorw manye dyuers ylis withinne the serkele of [f. 6ᵛᵇ] Inde, in the which are wonande manye dyuers nacionys of dyuerse tongis and lawis; of the whiche I thynke to speke of and shewe yow pleynly aftyrward, yf God wele yeue me grace.

This werk pryncipally I began for hym that desyryth for to visityn the Holy Lond and the cete of Ierusalem and othere holye placys that ben withinne the cerkle beforesayd. I schal shew hym the weye redily, what weye they shal haldyn to the place beforesaid, for I haue ful ofte sythis [ben] there and passed bothe on horse and on fote in good compaynye, blyssed be God.

He that wele passyn the placys beforesaid, he may at his wil holdyn and passyn dyuerse woyes bothe by the lond and by the

6 Forthy] *MS.* orthy, *after blank space for initial*   desyryn] *R* desireth and coveytith   8 see] *R* see, that is to seye, be esten   14 regeonys ... ylis] *R* londes, rewmes, touns, and ilis   19-20 wonande ... lawis] *R* manye dyuers tongis and nacions dwellande and also lawes and customes vsid   21 and shewe ... grace] *R om.*   23 Lond and the] *R om.*   26 ben] *MS. om.*   27 blyssed be God] *R* And thus in proce I shal bigynne this werke, because that often in romaunce and ryme is defawt and nouȝt accordement founden to the matir, but be bestyghes sekande, as they wole come to mynde

simul et per terram secundum diuersitatem regionis sue. Primo enim qui vadit de partibus occidentis, sicut de Anglia, Hibernia, Wallia, Scocia, Northguegia, potest ire, si voluerit, per Alemanniam et per regnum Hungarie, quod coterminum est terre
5 Polonie, Panonie, et Swesie.

Et est rex istius Hungarie multum potens et multas terras fortiter tenet, habet enim Hungaria[m], Sclavonia[m], et magnam partem Comagnie, Bulgarie, et regni quod vocatur Roussie, quod extenditur vsque ad terram de Nislan et coniungitur terre
10 de Prussie.

Et transit homo per terram istius domini per ciuitatem de Chiproune et per quandam villam versus finem Hungarie. Ibi transire oportetur fluuium [f. 40rb] Danubii, qui est fluuius magnus valde et vadit in Alemanniam subter montes versus
15 Lombardiam, et recipit in se quadraginta fluuios alios, et currit per mediam Hungariam et per Greciam et prouinciam que vocatur Trachie, et intrat in mare versus orientem. Et in introitu suo ita fortiter impellit aquam maris quod aqua illius fluuii retinet dulcedinem suam xx. leucis infra mare absque mixtione
20 sui cum aqua maris.

Postea transitur ad Belgraue et intrat homo per terram que appellatur Bulgrorum, et ibi transit per pontem lapideum super fluuium de Marmore et transit per terram de Pinteras et sic venitur in Greciam, vbi est pulcra ecclesia in ciuitate que dicitur
25 Sternes, [et postea ad ciuitatem de Finepap], deinde ad ciuitatem de Andrenopoli et Constantinopoli, olim Bizancium nominatus, vbi moratur comuniter imperator Grecie. Ibi est ecclesia nobilissima sancte Sophie.

7 Hungariam] Hungaria   Sclavoniam] Sclavonia   25 et postea ad ciuitatem de Finepap] ad fines Epapye

see aftyr the dyuersete of reumys. Fyrst, ho so comyth from the west, as out of Yngeland, Irland, Walis, and Skotlande and Norwey, he may go yf he wele thorw Almaynne [f. 7ra] and by the reume of Hongery that lestyth to the lond of Poleyne and Panouns.

This eche kyng of Hongery is a ful myghty kyng and thorw his grete pouste haldyth thorw strenth manye londys ondyr his subieccioun, that is for to seye Hongry, Slauony, and a gret partye of the lond that is callid Comagyn [and Bu]lgary and of the reume that is callid Ros, that lastyth to the lond of Noscelawe and ioynes with the lond of Doros.

And as men goon thorw the reumys beforeseyd, they mowe passe thorw a cete that is callid Cypron an by a gret toun in the ende of Hongry. And there they moun passe by the reuyr of Danby that is a ful gret ryuer, and it rennyth thorw Almayn vndyr the monteynys thorw Lonbardye. And that eche reuer resceyuyth into him othere lx. reuerys, and it rennyth into the rem [f. 7rb] of Vngarye and thorw Grece and thorw al te prouynce that is callyd Charchie, and it entrith into the see and in the partiis of that eche prouynce toward the est. And at his entre in te see he comyth with so gret fors rennende his cours that it puttyth awey the cours of the watyr of the see and haldith his owene swettnesse xx. myle withinne the se withoutyn myngynge of the salte watyr of that ilke see.

And thanne men entre into a lond that is callyd *B*ugres, and ther they shal passe a ryuer that is callyd Marro ouer a brege of ston, and thanne thour the lond of Pyncemacert, and thanne shul come into Gres to the cete of Sti, and from then into the cete of Fynpap and to the cete of Andropolyn, and so forth into Costantyn the Noble where the Emperour of Gres is [f. 7va] comunly dwellynge. And there is a solempne dwellynge and a solempne kyrke in the honour of Seynt Sophie.

9 and Bulgary] *MS*. Algary 11 ioynes] *MS. and R* Iaynes 14 ende] *R* londe 15 rennyth] *R* renneth into the see 17 lx. reuerys] *R* xl. principal ryuers comynge out of dyuers londes and manye othir smale ryuers, the wiche liȝtely may noȝt be nombrid 18 al te] *MS*. alle 19–20 the partiis] *R* three parties 21 in te] *MS*. into 22 watyr of the see] *R* salte see 23 swettnesse] *MS*. swiftnesse myngynge] *R* noyinge or medlinge 25 Bugres] *MS*. Augres 32 a solempne dwellynge and] *R om*.

Et ante ecclesiam ymago Iustiniani imperatoris deaurata, seden[s] in equo, capite coronato. Et solebat tenere in vna manu pomum aureum quod significat rotunditatem mundi quia sperice figure, sed postea cecidit pomum de manu eius. Et dicebatur quod prefigurauit futuram amissionem dominii imperatoris, nam prius erat imperator Rome, Greci[e], Asie minoris, Syrie, terre Iuda, Egypti, Persie, et Arabie; nunc pene omnia amisit preter Greciam. Temptauerunt nonnulli sepius reponere pomum in manum dextram ymaginis, sed numquam voluit illud tenere. Aliam vero manum tenet ymago erectam contra orientem ad instar inferentis minas contra malefactores. Dicta vero ymago sistitur versus quoddam sedile marmoreum ibidem.

In hac ciuitate Constantinopoli est lignum crucis Cristi et spongia cum arundine vnde dominus fuit felle potatus. Est ibi eciam vnus de clauis ferreis quibus confixus erat. Quidam credunt medietatem crucis Cristi esse in Cypro in vna abbathia que vocatur Mons Sancte Crucis, sed non est ita; hec enim crux que habetur in Cypro est crux illius latronis beati qui vocabatur Dismas, sed hoc plures ignorant quod malefactum est. Crucem domini Iudei absconderunt in terra sub quadam rupe montis Caluarie, et ibi latebat plus quam ducentis annis donec inuenta fuerat ab Elena, matre Constantini imperatoris.

Vna pars corone spinee et vnus clauorum et ferrum lancee cum pluribus et aliis reliquiis sunt in Francia in capella regia, et iacet corona in vase cristallino pulcherimo; quidam enim rex [f. 40va] Francie omnes istas reliquias quondam emit de Ianuensibus, quibus propter certam summam pecunie imperator eas inpignorauit. Et licet dicatur corona spinea, fuit tamen de iuncis marinis albis que non minus pungunt quam spine. Vidi ego ipse, et partem corone que est Parisius et illam que est Constantinopolim, et adhuc habeo vnam de illis spinis albis

2 sedens] seden   6 Grecie] Greci

BODLEY VERSION 7

And byforn the kyrke is set an ymage of the Emperour endorid, sittynge vpon an hors with a ryche corone vpon his hed. That eche ymage was wone to holdyn an appil of gold in the ton hand, and aftyrward it fel out of his hand by the self, and that fallynge men seydyn shulde betokene gret los tha*t* was comende to the Emperour. And so it befel aftyrwar[d]; for ferst he was Emperour of Rome and of Grece, of Assie, of Sirrye, of Iuda, Egipt, Parthi, and of Araby, and now hath he lost al but Grece. Ful oftyn hath many man asayed to puttyn te appil ayen into the hond of that eche ymage, but it wolde not holdyn it stylle. That iche ymage holdyth [f. 7vb] his othyr hon euermore toward the est as it were in maner of manas to mysdoeris.

In that cete of Costantyn the Noble is a porcioun of the cros that God was don vpon and the sponge with the red that they yeue to Crist eysel and galle to drinke whan he was vpon the cros. And there is on of the naylys of yryn that Crist was nayled withal. Som men sen that the haluyndel of the cros that Crist was don vpon is in Cipre in an abbey that is callyd the Mont of that Holy Cros, but it is not so; for that cros that is in Cipre, ther the thef Dismas was don on in despit of Crist. The cros that Crist was don on, the Iewis heddyn it vndyr the erthe vndyr a roche of the Mount of Ca[l]uorye, and there it was more than cc. yer [f. 8ra] tyl tyme that it was founde be Elene, the modyr of Costantyn the noble emperour.

A parti of the coroun of thornys and on of the nayly[s] that God was nayled with and the spere hed that Crist was pyned withal, with manye othere relykys, ben in France in the kyngis chapel, and the coron lyth in a fayr vessel of cristal. And I mynself, Iohn Mandeuyle knyth, saw on porcioun of the coroun that is at Parys, and [that] that is at Costantyn the Nobel, and yit I haue on of the thornys that is whit, the whech was yeuyn

---

2 endorid] *R om.*   4 self] *R* seluen withouten mevynge of wynde or garynge of man   5 that] *MS.* thas   6 aftyrward] *MS.* aftyrwar   8–9 al but Grece] *R* alle thes rewmes al but Grece   12 manas to mysdoeris] *R* manasynge   13 *MS. has rubric* Nota de montibus super nubes   16 cros] *R* cros for our sake   22 Caluorye] *MS.* Cauorye   24 noble emperour] *R* emperoure, thoru3 myracle, the wiche fyndynge and Elyne we worshipe onys in the 3eer for Christis sake   25 naylys] *MS.* nayly   30 that] *deleted in MS.*   31 whit] *R* at Parys, with the wiche I presentid to our lord of Engelonde

que michi dabatur pro magna specialitate. Plures enim iacent fracte in vase illo cristallino propter siccitatem iuncci et frequentem ostensionem peregrinis et nobilibus personis. Haftam lancee habet imperator Alemannie, sed ferrum est Parisius.
5 Tamen imperator Constantinopolitanus dicit se habere ferrum lancee. Vtrumque ferrum vidi, et est illud Constantinopolis maius ferro alio.

Item, Constantinopolim iacet sancta Anna, mater domine nostre Marie, cuius corpus predicta Elena imperatrix illuc de-
10 portari fecit de Ierusalem. Item, iacet ibi corpus Iohannis Crisostomi archiepiscopi eiusdem vrbis. Item, corpus sancti Luce euangeliste, cuius ossa de Bithinia, vbi prius fuerant tumulata, ad hanc ciuitatem fuerant deportata et ibi recondita cum aliis reliquiis innumeris sanctorum. . . .
15 Ciuitas ista Constantinopolis valde pulcra est, nobilis, et amena bene in circuitu murata, et est forme triangularis. Est ibi vnum brachium maris, quod vocatur Ellespontum et a quibusdam dicitur Bucca Constantinopolis et ab aliis vocatur Brachium sancti Georgii. Istud brachium claudit duas partes
20 ciuitatis, et superius versus capud istius brachii maris, scilicet versus occeanum vel magnum mare, erat olim Troiana ciuitas super ripam aque in loco pulcherimo et plano. Sed nunc modicum ibi apparet quia diu est quod destructa fuerat ciuitas perlibata.
25 Circa Greciam sunt plures insule, videlicet Calistra, Colchos, Creritigia, Tresbria, Athos, Minex, Flaxonia, Melo, Caipateia, et Lempina. In ista est mons qui vocatur Caucasus qui transcendit nubes. Sunt preterea plures patrie diuerse et diuerse languagia. Omnes tamen obediunt imperatori.
30 Inter ceteras prouincias est ibi Macedonia vnde Alexander magnus oriundus fuit. Ibi natus fuit Aristotiles in ciuitate que vocatur Stragores iuxta prouinciam que appellatur

26 Melo, Caipateia] Melocaipateia

me for gret specyalte. And manye of the thornys lyn brokyn in the uessel of cristal for ouermeche dreynesse and for oftyn shewynge to pilgrymis and to othere grete lordys that thedyr comyn. The spere shaft hath the Emperour of Almayne, but the hed is at Parys. And the Emper[our] of Costantyn the Noble seith that he hat the hed [f. 8rb] of the spere. I haue sen hym bothyn, and the hed that is at Costantyn the Noble is more than the tothyr.

At Costantyn the Noble lyth Seynt Anne, the modyr of oure lady Seynte Marye, that fyrst was leyd at Rome. And Elyne the Empresse dede bryngyn it thene into Costantyn the Noble, and ther it is and shal ben for euere more. And in that cete lyth the body of Seynt Iohn that men callyth Crisostamus that was an erchebischop, and the body of Seynt Luk the euangelist that fyrst was grauyd in Betanye and thedyr brought and leyd among othere relykys in the nombre of halwyn.

The cete of Costantyn the Noble is a faye cete, noble and delitable and wel wallyd al aboute. Ther is an arm of the see that is callyd the Bras of Seynt George. It encloseth ii. partyis of the cete, and operemore toward the hed of this eche reuer and toward the west was [f. 8va] sumtyme the cete of Tray vpon a reuer in a fayr pleyne place. But now ther schewith but litil therof, for it is longe sythen that it was stroyed.

Abotyn Grece arn manye ylys, that is for to wetyn Calysta, Talcas, Turritigia, Tresbria, Mincafla, Soma, Meleta, Ypateia, and Lympyna. In these ylis is a gret hyl that is callyd Caucasis. That eche hil is aboue the *h*yght of the cloudys. Many dyuerse cunctres aryn aboutyn Grece and manye dyuers langagis, and manye are they obeysaunt to the Emperour of Grece.

Ther is a reume that is callyd Messodonye. In that reume was Alisandir the Conquerour born. And in that reume was Aristotil born, in a cete callyd Stageres. And in that cete is the cepulcre of Aristotyl. And aboue the graue of hym is mad an

2 dreynesse] *R* dryenes of hemselfen for so longe kepinge, as noo wonder is   5 Emperour] *MS.* emper   7 tothyr] *R* thothir, and thus they arn bothe in doute wiche it is. And I myself also am in doute, for the sothe can no man telle   10 into] *R* and buryed hir bones at   15 relykys in the nombre of] *R* holy   19 this eche] *R* the   20–21 vpon a reuer] *R* neer the ryuere stondande   22 stroyed] *R* distried, brent, and dungen adoun with enemyes   26 hyght of the cloudys] *MS. and R* cloudys of the lyght   29 that reume] *MS. adds* was Aristotil born and in that reume

[f. 40ᵛᵇ] Trachie. In ipsa ciuitate Stragores est sepulchrum Aristotilis, cui superpositum est altare, super quod tenere solent gentes patrie consilia sua maiora, putantes quod per inspiracionem diuinam ibi eis proueniet consilium sanum et vtile in agendis, Aristotilem enim ibi venerantur quasi sanctum.

In hac patria est mons magnus Olimpi excelsus valde, diuidens Macedoniam et prouinciam de Trachie, et est ibi eciam mons alius qui vocatur Athos tante altitudinis quod vmbra eius extendit usque ad Lempnam, que distat per lxxvii. miliaria. In sumitate istorum est aer ita subitilis et rarus quod nullum animal ibi viuere possit. Et ideo philosophi olim, quando volebant ascendere montes istos gracia contemplacionis, sumebant secum spongias plenas aqua ut possent ex eis attrahere aerem humidum et grossum; aliter deficeret eis alitus. Scribebant quoque super montes istos litteras quasdam digitis suis in puluere, quas post annum reuolutum sanas et integras inuenerunt, vnde aliquando apparet quod cacumina illorum moncium excedunt locum aeris in quo fiunt venti, pluuie, et alie tempestates.

Item, in ciuitate Constantinopolim est palacium imperatoris pulcrum satis et bene dispositum, iuxta quod est locus pulcherimus pro hastiludiis et aliis exercitiis armorum. Qui locus dispositus est gradibus quibusdam in circuitu ab ymo usque ad summum ita quod quilibet videre possit sine nocumento alterius, et sub gradibus istis sunt stabula pro equis imperatoris, bene voltata et columpnis marmoreis decorata.

Infra ecclesiam sancte Sophie quidam imperator se fecit quondam sepeliri et cum corpore suo laminam auream reponi fecit in sepulcro, in qua lamina, sicut postea repertum fuerat,

[f. 8ᵛᵇ] auter vpon the wheche the folk of the cete wer wone for to holde custumabely here conseyl whan ony gret thyng was for to do, supposende that thorw the inspiracioun of the Holy Gost Crist wolde sendyn hem helful and profitable conseil. And in that contre they dede worchep to Aristotil as to an holy man.

NOTA DE MONTIBUS SUPER NUBES

In that cuntre arn two mounteynys so mechil and so heye that the height of hem passith aboue the cloudys, and in the hyghte of tho hillys the eyr is so sotyl and so latsom that no beste may come thedyr. And forthi the filysofris of that contre somtyme woldyn gon on here [contem]pleyinge onto the heighte of tho hillis, and for ther was non moystoure of the eyr they tokyn with hem sponges with watyr that they myghtyn drawe watyr out of hem and moistere, and ellis shulde here [f. 9ʳᵃ] onde a fayled hem. And whan they comyn to the highte of tho hillis, they woldyn write letterys with here fyngeris in the erthe and in the drye sond. And whan they come thedyr ayen at the ende of the yer they myghte fynde alle the letteris as hol as they leftyn hem vnwemmyd. Thanne me thynkyth that it semeth wel that the heighte of tho hillis passyn the plase wher reyn and wynd and alle sweche tempestis comyn fro.

In the cete of Costantyn the Noble is the paleys of the Emperour, fayr and worschepfuly [arayed] in alle thynge. And ner besyde the paleys is a fayr pleyn place for iustyng and turnement wel ordeynyd and for alle othere dedis of armys. And al aboute the place are ordeyned greces wel arayed in swich maner that alle that comyn to se what reuel ther is mad may wel stonde [f. 9ʳᵇ] and se al that ther is don withoutyn ony lettynge. And vndyr the grecis arn ordeynyd stablis for the Emperouris hors wel wrough[t] with marbyl.

And withinne the cherche of Seynt Sophye an emperour dede sumtyme berien his body, and with his body dede leyn a table of gold in the sepulture, in the whech table, as aftyrward was

3–4 Holy Gost] *R* Holy Goost and cause of Aristotil   5 an holy man] *R* a seynt for profi3te that they of him hadde   11 contempleyinge] *MS. and R* pleyinge   14–15 fayled hem] *R* fayled hem and perauenture they shulde haue deyed   19 vnwemmyd] *R* the firste day   23 arayed] *MS. om.*   28 se al that ther is don] *R* may se it at his wille   30 wrought] *MS.* wrough

talis erat scriptura litteris hebraicis, grecis, et latinis exarata, 'Iesus Cristus nascetur ex virgine Maria et credo in eum.' Et scriptura ista testabatur quod corpus cum lamina sepultum fuerat ante incarnacionem Cristi ii.^{m} annis elapsis. Adhuc lamina
5 conseruatur in thesauria ecclesie.

Sciendum preterea quod quamuis Greci Cristiani sunt in pluribus, tamen discordare videntur a nobis in hiis que ad fidem pertinent; dicunt enim quod spiritus sanctus procedit non a Filio sed a Patre tantum. Non obediunt ecclesie romane nec
10 domino pape, sed dicunt quod tantam potestatem habent patriarche eorum in partibus illis sicut dominus papa hic.

Iohannes enim papa [f. 41ra] vicesimus secundus scripsit eis quod Cristianitas deberet esse vna sub vnius potestate qui esset vicarius Cristi et successor Petri, cui dominus contulit plenam
15 potestatem ligandi ac soluendi, vnde obedire deberent sibi tamquam vero successori beati Petri. Sed ipsi Greci rescripserunt in hunc modum: 'Potenciam tuam summam circa tuos subditos firmiter credimus. Superbiam tuam summam tollerare non possumus. Auariciam tuam summam saciare non intendimus.
20 Dominus tecum, quia Dominus nobiscum est.' Aliud responsum habere non potuit ab eis papa.

Conficiunt Greci sacramentum altaris de pane fermentato, et dicunt nos errare qui conficimus de pane non fermentato. In cena domini fermentant et in sole desiccant panem suum, et
25 seruant per totum annum. Inde communicant infirmos suos loco eukaristie. Vnam tamen immersionem faciunt in baptismo.

foundyn and prouyd how letterys were wretyn in Ebrew, Grew, and Latyn, and seidyn thus: 'Iesu Crist shal be born of the virgine Marye and I beleue in hym.' And that eche scripture beryth witnesse [that] that eche body was beryed before the incarnacyoun of Crist mm. yer. And yit that ech table is kept and holdyn in the tresorye of that eche cherche among othere relikys.

It is for to wetyn that thow it be so that the Grekis are Cristene men, yit [f. 9va] they varyen from vs in manye poyntys that fallyth to oure lawe; for they seyn that the Holy Gost comyth not from the Sone but only from the Fadyr, and they obeye not to the Court of Rome ne to the Pape, but they seyn and trowyn and affermyn that here patriark in here contre hath as meche power as oure pape here.

Iohan that was Pape of Rome th[e] xxii., he wrot his letteres and sente to hem and seyde that alle Cristen[te] shulde be as on and vndyr the power of hym that were Cristis vekyr and the successour of Peter, to whom that oure lord yaf the power to bynde and vnbynde; wherfore that hym thoug[h]te that they shulde obeyse to his ordenaunce of holy cherche as to the verry successour of Seynt Petyr. The Grekys wretyn ageyn to the Pape in this maner: 'Thyn souereyn [f. 9vb] powyr aboutyn [thyn] subiectis we trowe it stedefastly. Thyn souereyn pryde may we nat takyn away, ne thyn souereynte of aueryce wele we nat ben aboute to fulfille. God be with the, for he is with vs.' Othir answere than thus myghte the Pape nat getyn of hem.

NOTA DE SACRAMENTO GRECORUM

The Grekys make the sacrement of the auter of sour bred, and seyn that we erryn that makyn it of bred not sour. They dreyen here bred in the sonne and kepyn it thourw al the yer, and therwith they hoselyn here seke men. They sey also and trowe it wel that no soule shal ben in purgatorye aftyr the deth out

4 that] *MS. om.*   5 mm. yer] *R* two m. 3eer and odde daies   9 men] *R* men in partye folowande oure lawe   12 Pape] *R* Pope our holy fader   13 and affermyn] *R* verrely   15 the] *MS.* th   xxii.] *R* xii   16 Cristente] *MS.* cristen   17 on] *R* oon in vnytee and in pees   19 thoughte] *MS.* thougte   23 thyn] *MS. and R* vs   subiectis] *R* we subietteth and   26 hem] *R* hem, and sithenes that tyme wolde ther neuere pope chalaunge hem vnto his suggestis   32 purgatorye] *R* peyne of purgarye

Dicunt quoque non esse purgatorium post mortem nec euenire animabus exutis vel penam vel gloriam ante diem iudicii.

Fornicacionem non dicunt esse peccatum mortale sed naturale, quia res in se naturalis est. Secundas nupcias detestantur.
5 Sacerdotes eorum vtuntur matrimonio. Vsuriam mortale peccatum non dicunt esse. Venalia sunt ibi ecclesie beneficia. Dicunt eciam quod in quadragesima non debet missa cantari nisi dominicis diebus et sabbatis. Nullo tempore anni ieiunant die sabbati, et si esset vigilia natalis domini vel pasche, latinos celebrare
10 in suis altaribus non permittunt. Et si forte celebrauerint, lauant altaria ipsa aqua benedicta. Dicunt quoque in vno altari non est nisi vna missa celebranda in die. Dominum Iesum dicunt nunquam manducasse veraciter sed similitudine tantum.

Peccatum mortale nobis imponunt quod barbas radimus,
15 quia barba signum est virilitatis et donum dei, et qui radunt barbas ideo faciunt vt placeant mundo et vxoribus suis. Dicunt eciam nos peccare eo quod comedimus animalia prohibita in veteri testamento, scilicet porcas et lepores et cetera animalia que non ruminant. Item, pro peccato imputant nobis quod
20 carnes comedimus in septimana ante quadragesimam et in diebus mercurii, et quod lacticinia comedimus diebus veneris. Excommunicant eciam omnes qui a carnibus diebus sabbatorum se abstineant.

Item, imperator Constantinopolis ipse constituit patriarcham,
25 archiepiscopos, et episcopos. Ipse confert beneficia et dignitates ecclesiasticas. Ipse pro voluntate sua personas ecclesiasticas priuat beneficiis suis [f. 41rb] cum causa subest. Et ita est ipse dominus temporalitatis et spiritualitatis. . . .

De Constantinopoli qui voluerit ire per terram Turchorum
30 debet iter arripere versus ciuitatem que vocatur Nik, et sic per portum de Chieuetout et ad montem de Chieuetoun, qui est mons altus ad vnum miliare et dimidium. De ciuitate Nik per mare transit homo de Brachio sancti Georgii, et intrat in mare

of this world, ne that no soule shal haue neythir ioye ne peyne before the Day of Dome.

They seye that fornycacioun is no dedly synne. Here prestis are weddede men in that contre. They seyn [f. 10ra] also that semonye is no dedly synne. They seyn also that in Lente shulde no masse be do only but on the Sonedayes and on the Satyrdayes. Thour al the yer they faste neuere no Satirdayes. And yif that Yol Euyn falle on the Satyrday or Pask, they wele not suffere a maner of men that me calle Latynys syngyn vpon here auterys. And if it falle that cas that ony of hem do, they wele thanne wasche here auterys with holy watyr. Thei seyn that vpon an auter shulde ben don but on masse vpon the day.

The Grekys rettyn to vs for dedly synne whan we schauyn oure berdys, for oure berdis they sey it is a sygneof oure manhod and a specyal yifte of God, and ho so shaue his berd, he doth it for to plese the world and wemen. They seye also that we synnyn also whan we etyn of the bestys that are for[f. 10rb]bodyn in the Olde Lawe, that is for to seye swyn and haris and othere bestis that chewith nat the code. And they rettyn to vs for synne whan we ety[n] flesch in the wouke before Lente, and on the Wedenysday that we etyn mylk and on the Frydayes. And they cursen alle tho that forberyth to etyn flesch vpon the Satyrday.

The Emperour of Costantyn the Noble, he yeuyth her patriark his dygnete. He yeuyth benefisys to erchebeschopis of holy cherche, and in hym he fyndyth defaute and verry cause he depreuith hem of here benefyses. And so is he there lord temporal and spiritual.

And ho so wel gon by Turkye, he schal passe by a cete that is called Neuke and so by the port of Chiethus and thanne to the Mount of Chetheuettoun, that is a ful high hil and stondyth but a myle and an half from the cete of Neuke. And [f. 10va] by the se men may passe the Bras of Seynt Iorge and be rowynge entere into the place where Seynt Nicholas lyth and into manye

---

3 synne] *R* synne but a kyndely synne   5 semonye] *R* oker
8 Yol Euyn] *R* Cristemasse Daye   10 that] *MS.* thas   16 wemen] *R* women and doeth displesaunce vnto God, and his manhoode he forsaketh   19 chewith] MS. chowith   20 etyn] *MS.* ety   24 erchebeschopis] *R* erchebisshopes and bisshoppis and alle othir manere benefices   26 there] *R* bothe   31 And] *MS.* and and   33–17.1 and into manye othere holie placis] *R* that is to seye, to the cete of Bare

nauigando versus locum que dictur Pateram, vbi sanctus Nicholaus iacet, et versus multa alia loca. . . . Postea vadit homo per insulam de Pathmos, vbi sanctus Iohannes euangelista scripsit Apocalipsim. Deinde venitur in Ephesum que est ciuitas pulcra,
5 sita iuxta mare. Ibi obiit beatus Iohannes, et sepultus est retro altare in quadam tumba. . . .

De ciuitate Ephesi pergendum est per plures insulas maris vsque ad ciuitatem Pateran, vbi natus erat sanctus Nicholaus, deinde ad ciuitatem Mirreorum, vbi fuerat episcopus ordinatus.
10 Ibi crescunt optima vina et forcia valde. Inde transitur ad insulam Crete, quam imperator donauit olim Ianuensibus, inde ad insulam Choos et per insulam Langho, quarum insularum Ypocras quondam fuit dominus.

Et dicitur adhuc in insula de Langho est filia ipsius Ypocratis
15 in specie longissimi draconis, et appellatur domina patrie a gente insule ipsius, et iacet in quodam castello antiquo deserto. Bis vel ter in anno se ostendit, nullum malum alicui facit nisi aliquis ei malum intulerit.

Dicunt homines insule quod hanc filiam Ypocratis, cum esset
20 virgo speciosa, quedam dea nomine Diana transformauit in draconem, sed redditura est in formam priorem cum venerit miles aliquis audax et eam osculatus [f. 41va] fuerit, sed non viuet illa postmodum nisi breui tempore.

Referunt eciam ibidem quod miles quidam de Hospitali de

othere holie placis. And aftyr that men may gon to the yle that is called Patenos, where Seynt Iohan the euangelist [wrot] the Apocalips. And from then men may gon to the cete of Eiffrasim that is a fayr cete, and it is set besydyn the see. In that cete deyede Seynt Iohan and is grauyn behyndyn an auter in a fair toumbe.

Fro the cete of Effesym men may passe be manye ylis of the see er they come to the cete of Patran, where Seynt Nicholas was born, and from thene to the cete of Mirre, where he was ordeyned to ben bischop, and from thene to the [ile] of Grece, and from then to the [ile] of Choos and by the yle of Longo, of whiche yle Ypocras was sumtyme lord.

And it is seid in [f. 10vb] manye contreis that in the yle of Longo is yit the doughtyr of Ypocras in the liknesse of an orrible dragoun, and she is callid lady of that contre with the folk that wonede in that yle. And she dwelled in an eld castel in diserd, and eche yer twyes or thries she schewith here opynly, non harm doinge to no man but ony man do here skathe.

NOTA DE FILIA IPOCRATO

The folk that wonyn in that yle seyn that the doughtir of Ypocras, whan she was fayr, yong, and louely, that a goddesse that hight Dyane, for gret enuye that she hadde to here grete beute, shop here into the lyknesse of an oryble dragoun, and there to be tyl a knyght come that were so hardy of hymself that he durste come thedyr and kysse the dragoun; and thanne she shulde turnyn ayen into here owene liknesse and forme of beute in alle thynge as she was beforn. But thi [f. 11ra] seyn she shulde not leue longe tyme but short tyme aftyr.

And they seye that ther come sumtyme a knyght of the Rodis

---

2 wrot] *MS*. lytht *deleted*   4 and it is set besydyn the see] *R* edified beside the see richely   7 Fro] *MS*. for   8 er they come to the cete of Patran] *R* but noȝt entre into hem, the wiche were ouere longe to telle off, rowinge vnto the cite of Patran   10, 11 ile] *MS*. cete   14 Ypocras] *R* Ypocras that somtyme was a gret surgen and lorde of Longo   15 dragoun] *R* dragoun but somtyme she turneth, but noȝt fully, into a womanes liknes certayn tymes in the ȝeer twoo daies   17 schewith] *R* chaungeth and sheweth   opynly] *R* appertly and openly to the puple   21 that a goddesse] *R* she had a god   22–23 to here grete beute] *R om.*   24 to be] *R* to be and duelle foreuere   25 the dragoun] *R* hir whenne she were in the liknes of a dragoun   27 as she was beforn] *R om.*

Rodes, qui probus fuerat et animosus valde, venit ad osculandum draconem. Qui ascenso equo iter arripuit versus castellum draconis, et intrans cameram eius aspexit draconem capud leuare contra se. Quo viso, miles inhorruit et fugam meditari
5 cepit, ac illa militem insecuta in quamdam rupem super mare impulit et sic in mare proiecit.

Alio tempore iu[ue]nis quidam, qui nil audierat de dracone, exiens de naui perambulabat insulam, et tandem venit ad ipsum castellum. Intransque speluncam pergebat explorando donec
10 inuenit vnam cameram, in qua repperit domicellam pulcherimam sedentem et sese in speculo quodam aspicientem, et erat in circuitu puelle maxima copia thesauri. Cogitauit ille quod ipsa esset meretrix aliqua que ibi morabatur ad recipiendum superuenientes.

15 Cum vero illa percepisset vmbram hominis in speculo, conuertit se et dixit ei, 'Quid hic queris?' Ac homo respondit, 'Amasius vester esse cupio, si placet.' 'Es tu,' inquid, 'miles?' Ac ille ait, 'Non sum, domina.'

Cui illa tunc, 'Meus amasius esse non potes. Vade ad socios
20 tuos et fias miles. Et crastina die egrediar de loco isto, et tu, cum michi obuiaueris, osculum michi audacter prebe quia tibi nil nocebo. Et licet tibi horribilis apparuero, hoc factum est michi per incantationem, quia veraciter talis sum qualem nunc me vides. Et si me cras osculatus fueris, totum istum thesaurum
25 habebis et eris maritus meus et dominus insule istius.'

Hiis dictis, recessit ille ad socios suos in naui et se fecit militem fieri. Crastina die rediit ad castellum, et videns draconem exire

7 iuuenis] iunis

BODLEY VERSION 19

that was a hardy knyght and an amerous and wolde kysse the
dragon. He com and wente into the castel and entrid into here
chambre and saw wher sche lay, and [she] leftyd vp here hed
ageyns hym. And whan he say here so oryble, he was adrad and
turned the bak and fledde. And she ros and folwed faste aftyr 5
and ouyrtok hym at a roche, and sche tok hym and cast hym
into the see.

Anothyr tyme ther cam a fayr yong man that not ne woste of
the dragon ne neuere ne hadde herd speke of here. [He] went
out of a shep that rod vndyr that yle for to pleye hym awhyle 10
and disportyn him vpon the lond. He saw the castel and yede
thedyr in and yede aboute, and at the laste he com into a chambre
and say a fayr yong damesel syttynge alone and lok[yng] in an
[f. 11rb] merour, and aboutyn here lay gret tresor. He wende
sche hadde ben a woman that hadde leuyd by her bod[i] and 15
so hadde wonyn al that richesse.

The damesele saw at the laste the shadewe of a man in the
merour and loked aboute and saw hym and seyde, 'Thow man,
what dost thow here?' 'Sertis,' he syde, 'ladye, to ben thyn
leman yif it be thyn wille.' 'Art thow thanne a knyght?' sche 20
side. 'Nay, forsothe,' he seyde, 'I am non.'

'No,' sche seyde, 'go to thynne felas and do makyn the a
knyht, and come ayen to this castel tomorwe. And I shal
comyn out of this place, and where that euere thow metyst me
kys me boldely, be I neuere so oryble, for I may do the non 25
skathe, for I am thorw enchauntement mad in this lyknesse.
And yif thow come tomorwe and kysse me boldely, thow shat
han al this tresor and ben myn leman and myn hosband and
lord of al this place and [f. 11va] this yle.'

He wyndyth forth to hese felawis and tok the ordere of knyght, 30
and on the morwe rapyd hym ayen to the castel. He saw the

3 lay] *R* laye foule and horryble to se, and whenne she was ware of him   she] *MS. om.*   9 He] *MS. om.*   10 that rod vndyr that yle] *R* vpon a daye and wente vnder the ile side   10–11 awhyle and disportyn him] *R om.*   13 lokyng] *MS.* loked   14 aboutyn here lay] *R* he loked aboute and saw3   tresor] *R* riches and tresour   15 bodi] *MS.* bod   18 Thow man] *R om.*   22 No] *R om.*   go] *R* goo blive   25 be I neuere so oryble] *R* and be no3t afferde, be I neuere so horryble to thy si3t   27 And 3if... boldely] *R om.*   28 tresor] *MS.* trosor   29 al this place and] *R om.*

tam horribiliter quasi ad deuorandum eum, nimio terrore correptus omni celeritate qua potuit aufugit. Illa quoque insecuta est pene usque ad nauem, ac cum eum vidisset nauem ingressum et de reditu eius desperare, cepit horrendis vocibus
5 clamare et vlulare pro dolore, sicque clamans reuersa est ad locum suum. Non multum post miles ipse mortuus est.

Et ex tunc nullus miles draconem videre potuit nisi in breui moreretur. Creditur tamen quod adhuc veniet miles qui draconem osculabitur et mutabit in formam priorem.

10 De insula ista transitur ad insulam de Rodes, quam Hospitalarii tenent. . . . [f. 41vb] Ista insula distat a Constantinopoli per viii.$^{c.}$ leucas itinere maris. De ista insula transitur in Cyprum, vbi habetur vinum fortissimum quod primum rubeum est sed post annum mutatur in album, et quanto plus fuerit vetuscum
15 tanto plus redditur album, clarum, et odoriferum.

Et vadit homo iuxta Goulf de [Catha]lie, que patria olim fuerat perdita per stultitias iuuenis vnius qui habebat amasiam pulcram que subito mortua est et posita in quodam sarcofago marmoreo. Et ob amoris magnitudinem quam habebat iuuenis
20 ad pṽellam, perrexit noctanter ad tumbam ipsius et aperuit, intrauitque et iacuit cum illa, et post recessit.

Post autem tres menses venit ad eum vox dicens, 'Vade ad tumbam talis femine et aperiens eam respicias quod ex ea

16 Cathalie] lie, *after blank space*

BODLEY VERSION 21

dragoun come so orible ayen hym as she shulde a wordede hym.
Than he wex so adred that he ne wost what was best, but
turnede the bak and fledde awoy as faste as he myghte. And
whan sche say that, she folwid hym almost to the shep, and
whan sche say hym entryn into the ship and was dispaired of 5
his comynge ageyn, thanne sche criede with orible vois and
made a gret lamentacioun for sorwe that she hadde, and turned
ayen to here place. And the knyght deyede sone aftyr.

And neuere sithyn come knyght thedyr for to se the dragon
that he ne deyed within a short tyme. But yit they seyn and 10
trowyn wel that a knygh[t] sha*l* come thedyr and kysse the
dragon and bryngyn hym into his ferste forme, but they sey she
shal [f. 11ᵛᵇ] not leue longe aftyr.

Fro the yle of Longo men shal passe to the yle of the Roodis
that the Hospitaleris holdyn, and that yle is from Costantyn the 15
Noble by [see viii.ᶜ·] myle. And from Rodis [men shal passe]
to Sipre, where good wyn and strong is; fyrst it is red of colour,
and whan the yer is passid, it turnyth into whit colour, and ay
the eldere that it waxeth, the whiter is the colour and clerere
and [more] sauory. 20

And thanne ho so goth the ryghte woye may passe beside the
Gulfe of Cathaly, that is a cuntre that sumtyme was tynt thour
the folye of a yong man that hadde a fayr leman, the whiche
that he louede meche, and she deyed sodeynly from hym and
was leyd in a fayr tombe of marbyl. And for the grete loue and 25
longynge that he hadde to that woman, he yede vpon a nyght
to here tombe and opened it and lay by here, and sperid the
graue as it was before and wente his way.

And aftyr the tyme that [f. 12ʳᵃ] a yer was past, ther cam a
vois and seide to hym and bat hym gon to the graue of swich 30
a woman 'and opyn it and se what thow hast getyn on here. And

2 wex] *R* seynge hir so horrible waxe   3-4 And whan . . . shep] *R om.*
8 place] *R* wonynge place   9 knyʒt] *R* nothir sqwyer ne knyʒt   10
tyme] *R* tyme aftir but neuere the lees ʒit it were gret almesse to helpe hir
ʒif any durste take it on honde   11 knyʒt] *MS.* knygh   sha*l*] *MS.* shat
12 his ferste forme] hir owne shappe and fourme off woman ageyn   16 by
see viii.ᶜ·] *MS.* by viii   men shal passe] *MS. om.*   19 clerere] *R* miʒtier
20 more] *MS. om.*   sauory] *R* savory thenne our wyne is   26-27 vpon
a nyght to here tombe] *R* soone aftir whenne she was grauen vnto hir
toumbe

genuisti. Et si nolueris ire, scias grande tibi malum futurum.' Abiit ille ad tumbam et aperuit, volauitque de ea quasi capud vnum horribile et deforme quasi monstrum. Cum pervolasset ciuitatem et patriam, statim ciuitas absorta est in abissum. Et est
5 ibi transitus periculosus.

De insula Rodes vsque ad Cyprum sunt bene miliaria v.^{c.} Et scias quod homo posset transire ad Cyprum absque hoc quod intraret insulam de Rodes, dimittendo scilicet insulam de Rodes in vno latere. Ciprus insula est magna et pulcra, habens quattuor
10 ciuitates principales. Sunt ibi tres episcopi et vnus archiepiscopus. Apud ciuitatem de Famagoust est portus principalis tocius mundi. Ibi intrant Cristiani, Saraceni, et gentes omnium nacionum. Est et alius portus apud ciuitatem de Lymettes. In ista insula est Mons Sancte Crucis, vbi est abbathia nigrorum mona-
15 chorum vbi habetur crux boni latronis, vt superius dictum est. In Cypro iuxta ciuitatem de Famagoust natus fuit sanctus Barnabas apostolus. In hac insula venantur homines cum papionibus, que similes sunt leopardis, et capiunt feras velocius quam canes aliqui.

20 Item, in hac insula est consuetudo, tam nobilium quam aliorum, comedere super terram, faciunt enim fossas in terra usque ad genua et ibi sedent comedentes propter calorem patrie. In aduentu tamen extraneorum mensas ponunt sicut alibi.

De Cypro venitur ad mare versus Ierusalem et alia loca que
25 nunc Saraceni tenent. In spacio diei et noctis venitur ad portum Tyri et est in introitu Sirie; solebat enim Tyrus esse ciuitas valde pulcra, sed iam pro magna parte destructa est per

18 leopardis] leopardiis

yif thow wit not don so, wete thow wel that mechil ille and
tribulacioun for certeyn shal fallyn to the in short tyme.' He
wente to the tombe and opened it as the vois bad hym, and ther
fley out the graue as it wer the hed of a forschapyn beste, foul
and hedous. And whanne it hadde floun aboutyn the cete and 5
the contre, as tyd the cete sank doun and fordede al that was
therinne. And therby is passage perlious.

From the yle of Rodys onto Cipre are [v.$^{c.}$] myle. And I do yow
to wetyn that men may come to Cipre and not come in the yle of
the Rodys but letyn it on the ton hand. The yle of Cipre is a gret 10
yle, and therin ben iiii. pryncipal ceteis and iii. byschopis and an
[f. 12rb] erchebechop. At the cete of Famagost ther is port pryncipal of al this world, for thedyr repayryth Cristene men and Sarazynys and alle maner of nacionys vndyr Crist. And ther is anothir
port of the cete that is callid Limites. In that yle is the Mount of 15
the Holy Crois, and ther is an abbey of blake monkys, and at the
abbey is the cros that on of the theuys was don on whan Crist
deyed. In Cype beside the cete of Famagost was Seynt Bernabe
the Apostil born. And ther men huntyn with a maner of beste
that is callid papoynes, lik to an lebbard, and with hym men 20
takyn alle maner of bestis swiftere than with onye hondys.

In that yle is a custome, as wel among grete lordys as othere
comounys, for to etyn here mete vpon the erthe. And there they
shal ete, thei don make pittis in the [f. 12va] [erthe] and there
the pyttyn here feet vnto the kneis, and there they etyn for 25
the grete hete that is there in that cuntre. Not forthy, whanne
onye stronge men comyn among hem, they settyn vp [bordes]
as they don in othere placys.

Out of Cypre men behouyt to come be the see to Ierusalem
and to othere placys that now arn occupied with Sarasynys, and 30
that may men don withinne the space of a day and of a nyght.
The fyrst port that men behouyn to come to is clepid Tirus,
and it is in the entre of Cirry. And it was wont to ben a fayr cete
and a gret, but the moste partye is now stroyed thorw Sarazynys,

2 for certeyn] *R om.*   5 hedous] *MS.* hodous   6 fordede al] *R* al forferde
sodenly and alle thoo   7 perlious] *R* certayn ful euel   8 v.$^{c.}$] *MS.* v.
10 ton] *R* ri3t   12 At the cete of] *R* at oon of the citees that hi3te   Famagost] *MS.* Flamagost   17 don on] *R* doen vpon in the dispite of Crist
24 erthe] *MS. om.*   27 bordes] *MS.* ladderys   31 nyght] *R* ny3t if
the wynde wole hem serue

Saracenos, et nunc custodiunt portum multum curiose propter metum Cristianorum. In hac ciuitate Tyri dixit mulier euangelica, *Beatus venter qui te portauit et vbera que suxisti.*

Ante ciuitatem solebat [f. 42ra] esse lapis super quem dominus
5 sedebat predicans et docens de regno dei; super quam eciam petram fundata fuit ecclesia sancti saluatoris. . . .

Qui voluerit plus mare transire versus Ierusalem, vadat de Cypro ad portum Iapheth, qui est propinquior portus ciuitatis Ierusalem, non enim distat nisi per vnam dietam et dimidium.
10 Ista est ciuitas Ioppe, que appellatur Iapheth propter vnum de filiis Noe qui vocabatur Iaphet et hanc ciuitatem fundauit. Et dicitur esse antiquior ciuitas mundi eo quod fundata fuerat ante diluuium; adhuc enim apparet in rupe vbi defixe fuerant cathene ferree quibus vinctus fuerat Andremades gigas in carcere ante
15 diluuium, cuius gygantis costa lateris xl. pedes longitudinis habebat. . . .

[f. 42rb] Qui voluerit primo transire ad Babilonem, vbi soldanus moratur comuniter, ad impetrandum licenciam eundi securius in illis partibus uel *ad* transeund*um* ad montem Synay antequam
20 vadat Ierusalem, tunc iturus est de ciuitate Gaza ad castellum Daire. Et postea intrat homo desertum vbi sunt vie sabulose, et durat illud desertum bene per octo dietas. Semper tamen inueniuntur in illo itinere hostillarii certis locis qui vendunt itinerantibus ea que necessaria sunt corpori in victualibus.
25 Appellatur hoc desertum Alhelec. Post transitum istius deserti ingreditur homo in Egyptum, qui eciam vocatur Canopak et alia lingua appellatur Mersin. Ibi primo inuenitur vna villa bona vocabulo Balbeor, et inde itur ad Babilonem.

Ibi est ecclesia pulcherima beate Marie, vbi mansit septem
30 annis quando fugit cum puero Iesu de terra Iuda propter metum Herodis. Ibi iacet corpus sancte Barbare virginis. Ibi habitauit Ioseph cum venditus fuisset a fratribus. Ibi fuit Nabugodonozor

19 ad transeundum] in transeundi

and now they kepe the port streytly for Cristene men. In that cete of Tyry sayde the woman the wordys of the Gospel, *Beatus uenter qui te portavit, Christe, et cetera*, that is for to seyne, 'Blissed by the wombe that The [f. 12ᵛᵇ] bar and the pappis that The yaf souke.' Byforn that cete was wont for to stondyn a ston that Crist, whan He wente in erthe, sat vpon, prechende the peple of the kyngdam of heuene.

And who wel go more by the se way to Ierusalem, he mot go from Cype to port Iaph, and that is the nexte port to the cete of Ierusalem, for it is but a day iurne and an half. That eche cete was callyd Iaph for on of Adamis sonys that highte Iaph, he foundede that cete, and it is callyd the eldeste cete of al this world because that it was foundyd before deluuie. And yit it shewyth there in a gret roche of ston where the cheynys were festenyd [that] the ieaunt Adromedis was boundyn with, inne prisoun there that he lay before the flod; of which ieaunt ther is yit a rib of his side that is forty fet long.

And ho so wele gon to [f. 13ʳᵃ] Babylonye where the Soudon is most dwellynge for to purchasyn hym leue sekyrly for to passyn to Gaza and to the castel of Darry for to performe cer-tey[n] pilgrymages by the weye, he moun thanne passyn þoure desert where by *he*lful weyes. And that desert lestith viii. iurneis. Nouth forthi, in that weie schal men fyndyn ostelries at certeyn places where men may hauyn for here mone vytailis necessarie to beye. And that desert is callyd Alheylek, and whan men arn passid that desert thanne shal men comyn into Egipt.

At Babyloyne is a cherche foundit of oure lady Seynte Marye wher sche dwellid vii. yer whan she fledde with here sone Iesu out of the lond of Iuda for dred of Erodis the kyng. In that cherche lyth the body of Seynt Barbare the virgyne, and in that cherche wonede [f. 13ʳᵇ] Iosep whan his bretheryn

1 men] *R* enemyes   6 sat vpon prechende] *R* satte and perchid vpon techynge   13 deluuie] *R* Noes flode   14 gret] *R om.*   cheynys] *R* chemeneyes   15 that] *MS.* to   16 there that he lay] *R om.*   flod] *R* flode of Noee   20 performe] *R* purchase   certeyn] *MS.* certey   21 weye] *R* waye as nedeful is   22 helful] *MS.* lefful   viii.] *R* vii   23 that weie] *R* that iornayes and that wayes   24–25 men . . . beye] *R* they may gete and haue vetailles and other necessaryes that is nedeful vnto men for her money to bye with   28 At] *MS.* Ant   31 virgyne] *R* holy virgyne   32 cherche] *R* ilke Babilonye

rex quando tres pueros misit in fornacem, scilicet Ananiam, Azariam, et Misaelem.

Ibi est sedes regia soldani in quodam castello pulcherimo super vnam rupem posito. In quo castello, quando soldanus
5 presens est, sunt continue vi. milia hominum ad seruiendum soldano et ad custodiendum castellum, qui omnes totidie necessaria accipiunt de curia soldani.

Modum curie ipsius cognoscere potui quia diu cum soldano moratus fui et suis stipendiis militaui in guerris ipsius. Qui
10 eciam volebat me nobiliter maritasse cum filia cuiusdam principis si voluissem renunciasse fidei Cristiane, sed nolebam.

Soldanus iste est dominus quinque regnorum que per conquestum sibi appropriauit, habet enim regnum Egypti, regnum Ierosolomitanum, regnum Sirie cuius capu*d* est Damascus,
15 regnum Alappie, regnum Arabie. Plures eciam terras habet in dicione sua et preter hoc eciam est caliphes, quod nomen est magne excellensie [f. 42ᵛᵃ] et dignitatis et interpretatur rex. Fuerunt olim quinque soldani secundum numerum predictorum quinque regnorum, sed modo vnus soldanus est, scilicet ille de
20 Egypto qui dicitur soldanus Babilonie. . . .

Postea fuit soldanus Sahaladyn, in cuius tempore Richardus rex Anglie fuit in partibus illis cum exercitu Cristianorum. Post Sahaladin regnauit . . . Molothdaer. Tempore cuius Edwardus rex Anglie bonus ingressus est Siriam [et] multa
25 dampna fecit Saracenis. Iste soldanus intoxicatus fuerat apud Damascum. Post quem volebat filius suus regnare iure hereditario et fecit se appellari Malechfait. Sed alius qui vocabatur

14 capud] capus   21 Richardus] Richardus Richardus   24 et] *om.*

haddyn sold hym. And ther also Nabagodonosor the kyng putte
the iii. chylderyn into the ovene.

NOTA DE NOBILITATE SOLDAN

At the cete of Babilonye is the principal wonyng of the Soudon
in a fayr castel set vpon an hey hil on a roche. And whan th[e] 5
Soudon is ther hymself, thanne arn there comounly seruande
hym vi.^{m.} men alle ordeynyd to hese seruyse and for the
kepynge of the castel, and alle thei take eche day that is nedful
of the Soudon.

The maner of that contre I myghte knowe for I dwellede long 10
tyme with the Soudon and at hes wagis and in hise werris
trauayled. And he wolde a maried me rycheli with a gret pryncis
doughtyr if I wolde a forsake myn lawe, but I wolde not.

Thi[s] eche Soudon is lord of v. reumys, the which he hath
wonnyn and proprist to hym thour conquest, that [f. 13va] is for 15
to seyne the reume of Egipt, the reume of Ierusalem, of Syrri
and Alopi, and the reume of Araby. And manye other londys
reche and noble he hath and holdyth hem vndyr his subieccioun,
and yet for al that he is Calipes, that is a name of gret dignete
and as meche comprehendith as a kyngis stat. For there were 20
sumtyme v. soudonys as the noumbre of v. kyngdomis, but now
there is but on, he of Egipt, that we holdyn the Soudon of
Babylonye.

Aftyrward regned Saladyn as soudon. In his tyme ca*m* Kyng
R[i]chard of Yngclond into that contre with his ost of Cristene 25
men. And aftyr the Soudon Saladyn regned Melyk Darre, and
in his tyme cam Kyng Edward of Yngeland into the contre with
his ost of Cristene men and entrid his lond in his reume of Syrry
and mekyl harm [f. 13vb] dede with his ost. Sone aftyr this that
soudon deyede and endit at Damask, at the cete of Damask, and 30

2 ovene] *R* brennynge oven the wiche men callide Ananya, Azaria, and
Misael, the wiche that tyme thoru3 inspiracion of the Holy Goost made the
psalme *Benedicite domino omnia opera, et cetera*   5 castel] *R* castel and
a stronge   the] *MS*. th   6 comounly] *R om*.   7 vi.] *MS*. vii.
10 that] *R* his hous and of the   12 pryncis] *MS*. pryncesse   13 not] *R*
no3t for thenne muste me haue forsake my Cristendome but God it forbede
14 This] *MS*. Thi   15 that] *MS*. that that   17 and Alopi] *R om*.
18 reche and noble] *R om*.   24 cam] *MS*. can   25 Richard] *MS*.
rchard   26 men] *R* men that is to seye into the Holi Londe   Darre]
R the sawdon   27 of] *R* the noble king of   30 at Damask] *R om*.
30–29.1 and he hadde a sone] *R* and aftir this Mellet regned Darre his sone

Elphi exiuit cum pluribus et se fecit soldanum. Qui eciam postea accepit ciuitatem Tripolis et occidit multos Cristianos anno domini m.cc.lxxxix. Postmodum ... [f. 42vb] Mellethmandabron, et iste fuit soldanus quando ego de partibus illis recessi.

5 Soldanus educere potuit de Egipto plus quam xx. milia armatorum. De Suria vero et de terra Turchorum et de aliis prouinciis sibi subiectis potest habere plus quam quinquaginta milia armatorum, et omnes isti stipendia capiunt et necessaria sua de ipso soldano, et sunt continue cum eo. Reliquum vulgus
10 innumerabile est, et capit quilibet predictorum de soldano per annum quasi vi.$^{xx·}$ florenos, set cum hoc oportet quemlibet eorum tenere tres equos et vnum camelum.

Et per ciuitates et villas constituuntur certe persone que vocantur admirals, quorum alicui committitur regimen quatuor
15 armatorum, alteri quinque, alteri sex, et sic ulterius plus vel minus. Et ta*ntu*m capit admirallus pro se, quantum omnes alii qui sunt sub ipso. Et ideo quando vult soldanus aliquem probum militem et strenuum promouere, constituit eum admirallum. Quando caristia in patria illa est, tunc milites pauperes vendunt
20 equos suos et armaturam.

Soldanus quatuor habet vxores, quarum vna Cristiana est et tres relique Saracene. Et ista vna moratur apud Ierusalem, alia apud Damascum, et tercia apud Ascalonem. Sed quandoque transducit eas ad alias ciuitates cum placuerit ei, vadit eas visitare,
25 habet enim amasias quot voluerit. Facit [enim] venire coram se puellas nobiles et pulcriores patrie, et iubet eas custodiri et satis honorifice seruiri, et quando voluerit vnam habere, facit omnes venire in conspectu suo, et que placuerit oculis eius, ad ipsam mittit vel proicit anulum digiti sui. Et confestim vadit
30 illa balneari et lauari. Deinde nobiliter vestitur et post cenam introducitur in cameram eius. Et sic facit quociens placuerit.

16 tantum] tamen   24 ad alias] ad alias ad alias   25 enim] autem

he hadde a sone that thorw ryght of his fadyr wolde regne, and he was callid Melchisak. But sone cam anothir, that hight Elphi, with gret compaynye and entrid the lond and dede makyn hym soudon. He tok the cete of Tripolle and slow manye Cristene men therin in the yer of oure lord Iesu Crist m.cc.l[xx]xix. And aftyr that Soudon Elphi regnede Mellechi Madrabon, and he was soudon whan I partyd out of that land.

The Soudon may lede out of that lond, *id est* Egipt, mo than xx.^{m.} men of armys. And out of the reume of Surry and out of Turkye and othere rewmys that arn ondyr his subieccioun he may brynge mo than l.^{m.} men of armys, and alle they takyn grete wagis and al that hem nedith of the Soudon; that is [f. 14ra] for to wetene, eche of hem takyth by the yer vi. skore floreynys, but eche of hem mot algate holde iii. hors and a chamele.

And there is ordeynyd amongis [hem] serteyne personys that are called admirales. And eche amerel shal han vndyr hym iiii. or v. or vi. men of armys, and eche amerel shal take by the yer as meche for hymself as for alle tho that aryn vndyr hym. Forthi whanne the amerelis soudon lokyth for to auansyn ony men of goode that is with hym, he makyth hym an amerel. And yif ony derthe come into the contre, pore knyghtis and soudeouris selle here armour for myschef of mone.

The Soudon hath eueremore iiii. wiuys, of the whiche on shal ben a Cristene woman and iii. othere Saresynys. And on of hem shal dwellyn at Ierusalem, and on at Damask, and the thredde at Askalon; and ay whan hym liste, he goth for to vi[f. 14rb]siten hem and ledyth hem sumwhile aboutyn with hem. Not forthan he hath as many lemanys as hym likyth, for whan he comyth to ony gret cete or toun, he doth brynge before hym alle the nobeleste maydenys and the fayreste that ben therin, and tho that hym lykyth best he doth hem take and kepyn hem and clothyn honurably. And whanne he wil haue on of hem, he doth hem

5 m.cc.lxxxix] *MS*. m.cc.lxix   11 brynge] *R* vnto bataille brynge   14 algate holde] *R om.*   15 hem] *MS. om.*   16–17 iiii. or v.] *R* the ledynge and governyng of v   21–22 contre . . . armour] *R* cuntre of vetailles, more wagis shal they no3t haue, but ecche ilike mechil as wel in derthe as nou3t. Thenne othir pore kny3tis that may no3t live be her wagis and also othir sowdiours selleth often tyme her harneys and her armoure   23 iiii.] *R* three wedded   24 iii. othere Saresynys] *R* the tother twoo no3t   27 ledyth hem] *MS*. ledyth hem hem   29 toun] *R* toun 3if him like   30 therin] *R* there aboute, non dare him agaynsaye   30–31.1 and tho . . . beforn hym] *R om.*

Coram soldano nullus extraneus venit qui non vestiatur panno aureo vel de tartaro vel de camaca, quibus Saraceni vtuntur. Et primo aspectu quo videt eum, aliquis oportet quod genuflectet et osculetur terram, nam talis est modus faciendi
5 reuerenciam soldano cum aliquis voluerit loqui cum eo. Et quamdiu nuncii extranei sunt coram eo loquentes, gens ipsius circa ipsum stat prope cum nudis gladiis et brachiis in altum leuatis quasi ad feriendum si aliquis dixerit quod displiceat soldano. Nullus eciam venit extraneus coram eo ad aliquid petendum
10 quin concedit ei, si fuerit rationabilis peticio eius et non contra legem suam. Consimiliter faciunt alii principes partium illarum, dicunt enim quod nullus deberet coram principe venire nisi [f. 43ra] lecior recedat quam accessit.

Noueritis preterea quod ista Babilon, vnde iam loquor, vbi
15 soldanus prope moratur, non est Babilonia magna vbi facta fuit confusio linguarum quando incepta fuit turris illa famosa, cuius muri fuerunt altitudinis lxiiii. stadiorum, que est ad magna deserta Arabie in itinere quo pergitur versus regionem de Cal[d]e. Sed iam diu est quod nullus ausus fuit appropinquare
20 turri, est enim deserta et draconibus, serpentibus, et aliis bestiis venenosis plena in circuitu. Turris hec cum ciuitate habuit in circuitu xxv. miliaria, prout dicitur in illa patria. Et licet dica[t]ur turris Babilonie, tamen fuerunt ibi plura edificia spaciosa et pulcra ita quod circuitus ipsius loci per quadrum continebat

19 Calde] Cale   22 dicatur] dicaur

alle brynge beforn hym, and ho is lykyngest to his sight, to here
he sendyth or puttyth his ryng. Thanne she schal be takyn and
waschyn and baumyd and honurabli ben clad and aftyr soper
ben brought to his schambere. And thus he doth ay whan hym
lykyth.

Before the Soudon schal no strong man come that he ne
behouyth ben clad in cloth of gold or of taris or in samelet, that
is a maner of clothynge that Sarasynys werith. And whanne he
comyth in [f. 14ᵛᵃ] his cyte, hym behouyt to knelyn dou[n] and
kyssyn the erthe; swich is the maner there to don reuerence to
the Soudon. And whan ony strong man comyth that is a massanger to hym out of fer londys in massage, his men shuln
stondyn aboutyn hym with swerdys drawyn in here handys and
holdyn here swerdis alofte, that yif he speke outh that displesith
the Soudon for to st[r]ekyn hym doun. There comyth neuere non
strong for to askyn non thyng of the Soudon that it ne shal ben
grauntyd hym his askynge, if it be resonable and not ageyn his
lawe. And right so don alle othere pryncis and lordis of that
contre, for the seyn that no man shulde come before prynce
that he ne shulde passe gladdere awoyward than he come
thedyrward.

And wete ye wel that this Babylonye that I speke of [f. 14ᵛᵇ]
is now where the Soudon is dwellynge, nys not the grete Babilonye where that the confusioun of tongis [was made], the
whech that is in the grete desertys of Arabye. But now it is
long tyme sithe that ony man durste go for to visite that eche
wreched place, for it is so ful of nederis and of dragonys and
othere venym bestis that no man may come thedyr. The serkel
of that tour, with the compas of that cete that there was,
sumtyme contynuede xxv. myle aboute. And thow it be callid
a tour, yit ther were in the cerkele manye fayre edificis that
now arn distroyed and now is al wildyrnesse. That eche tour

2 sendyth] *R* sendeth some of his kny3tis   3 waschyn] *R* wasshen clene
9 to] *MS.* tho   doun] *MS.* dou   11–12 that is massanger to hym] *R om.*
15 doun] *R* doun as faste   15 strekyn] *MS.* stekyn   17 not
ageyn] *R* no3t ageyn the dignyte of the sawdon ne ageynes   19 prynce]
R lorde, king or prince   23 nys] *R* is a gret cite and fair enhabitid but
it is   24 confusioun] *R* confusioun and dyuersite   was made] *MS. om.*
25 grete] *R om.*   27 ful of] *R* ful of vermyne and   28 bestis] *R*
beestiz for the vengeaunce that God toke atte bigynnynge of þat tour
come] *MS.* cone

x. miliaria. Hanc turrim fundauit rex Nembroth qui regnauit in terra illa, qui, ut dicitur, fuit primus rex terrenus. . . .

Ciuitas sita fuit in quodam pulcherimo plano . . . et currebat fluuius Eufrates per medium ciuitatis tunc temporis. Sed postmodum Cyrus rex Persarum subtraxit fluuium et ciuitatem destruxit cum turre; diuisit enim fluuium in ccc.lx. partes, eo quod fecerat iuramentum quod fluuium ipsum ad talem statum perduceret quod mulier ibi transire posset genibus non undatis, et hoc ideo quia in illo flumine submersi sunt plures viri valentes et strenui diuersis temporibus.

De Babilonia illa, vbi soldanus moratur, transeundo versus istam Babiloniam magnam sunt quasi quadraginta diete per desertum nec est illa deserta in dominio soldani sed in dicione Persarum. Tenetur tamen de magno Chaan, qui est imperator maximus inter omnes reges parcium illarum, qui eciam est dominus insule de Catay et de pluribus aliis patriis ibidem et eciam de magna parte Indie. Est autem terra eius confinis et vicina terre Presbiteri Iohannis. Habet iste Chaan tam magnum dominium quod nescit pene fines suos, et est maior et potencior sine comparacione quam soldanus. De eius potencia et statu magno dicturus sum inferius loco suo. . . .

[f. 43va] Est autem Egiptus fortis patria quia sunt ibi portus periculosi propter magnas rupes. Versus orientem est Mare Rubrum quod protenditur usque ad ciuitatem de Costoun. . . . Egyptus habet in longum spacium quindecim dietarum, sed nisi trium dietarum in latum preter deserta. Inter Egyptum et Numidiam sunt duodecim diete in deserto. Isti Numidiani sunt Cristiani, sed valde nigri sunt coloris propter nimium solis ardorem. . . .

mechil and heuge foundede the kyng Nembrok that was kyng of
that lond, and he was the fyrste erthely kyng that euere was.

That eche cete of Babilonye was set in a fayr pleyne vpon
the reuer of Eufrates that ran thour the [f. 15ra] cete that tyme.
But aftyrward Syrus the king of Pers withdrow the watyr and 5
distroyede the cete and al that contre theraboute, for they
dep[art]edyn the grete reuer of Eufrates and dedyn it rennyn
ccc. xl. sundery weyes, for he hadde mad his grete oth and swor
his grete oth, and so greuously, that because that so manye noble
haddyn ben drenk therin, that he shulde bryngyn it to swich 10
a stat that women schulde wadyn therouyr and not wetyn here
kneis. And so he dede, and yit it standyth in that degre.

F*ro* Babylonye, where that the Soudon dwellyth, for to pase
to the grete Babylonye arn xl. iurneis thour desert, and it is not
vndyr the subieccioun of the Soudon but withinne the lordshepe 15
of the kyng of Pers, and it is holdyn of the Grete Cane of
Tartarye, the whiche is a gret yle of Cathan, and of manye
othere contreis and of a gret par[f. 15rb]tye of Inde. His lon is
nytheborgh and marchid with Preter Ionis lond, and he hath so
gret lordshep that he wot neuere wher his lordshepe endyth. 20
He is myghtiere withoutyn comparisoun than the Soudon, of
which gret stat and maieste I thynke to speken of aftyrward
whan I haue come therto.

NOTA DE TERRA EGIPTI

Egipt is a strong contre and manye perilous hauenys ben therin, 25
for there lith in eche heuene toun gret roches in the entre of
the hauene. Toward the est is the Rede Se that rennyth right
to the cete of Costantyn the Noble. The contre of Egipt is in
lenthe v. iorneis but not but iii. in brede for desertys that aryn
there. Betwyn Egip and the lond that is callyd Nundynea arn 30
xii. iourneis in desertis. The folk that wonyde in that contre arn

1 mechil and heuge] *R om.*   3 pleyne] *R* playn feelde   5 Syrus]
MS. Syrus and   *R* the heyres of   7 departedyn] *MS.* depedyn
8 ccc.] *R* a thowsende and   weyes] *R* placis and weyes   his grete oth and]
R om.   12 degre] *R* ilke degre and eueremore shalle   13 Fro] *MS.*
For   17 a gret yle] *R* a gret emperour and the moost riche lorde of al this
worlde erthely for he is lorde of the ile   18–19 his lon is nytheborgh and]
R om.   21 Soudon] *R* Sawdon or any other is   23 therto] *R* therto in
the laste partie of this boke   24 EGIPTI] *MS.* Egitti   26 eche heuene
toun] *R* that hauene tweyne   roches] *MS.* ryches   29 v.] *R* xv

[f. 43^(vb)] In deserto terre Egypti quidam sanctus heremita obuiauit cuidam monstro, quod fuit forme humane ab vmbilico et inferius autem simile capre videbatur. Frontem cornutam habuit, et ipsa cornua acuta erant. Interrogauit ergo sanctus
5 quisnam esset, et cornutus illi respondit, dicens quod erat creatura mortalis qualem fecerat deus, et in illis desertis morabatur pro sustentacione sua querenda. Et rogauit heremitam quatinus pro eo dominum deprecare vellet, qui pro saluando genus humanum de celo descendit et de virgine natus est, passionem quoque
10 sustinuit, per quem nos omnes viuimus et sumus. Et adhuc habetur ibidem apud Alexandriam capud monstri cum cornibus pro miraculo. . . .

Item, in Egypto sunt loca que sepcies in anno fructum ferunt. . . . Item, apud ciuitatem de Cair venduntur et emuntur homines
15 et mulieres alterius secte ita comuniter sicut hic in partibus istis venduntur animalia in foro.

Item, habetur ibidem in ciuitate vna domus comunis plena paruis foraminibus quasi nidis gallinarum. Illuc mulieres patrie portant oua [f. 44^(ra)] gallinarum suarum et aucarum uel anatum,
20 et ponuntur in foraminibus illis. Certe autem persone ex officio domum custodiunt et per calidum fimum equorum oua educant in pullos suos sine gallina uel alia aue. Et ad finem trium vel quatuor septimanarum redeunt mulieres et capiunt pullos suos,

22 sine] sine de

Cristene men, but thy aryn blake of colour for the ouergret hete that is there [f. 15ᵛᵃ] and brennynge of the sonne.

NOTA DE CAPITE MONSTRI CORNUTI

In the desert of that lond of Egip an holy ermyte mette onys with a beste forshapyn, for it hadde the shap of a man from the nouyl dou[n]ward and from thene vpward the shap of a got with sharpe hornys stondynge in the hed. The ermyte askyd hym in Godis name what he was, and the beste answerde and seyde, 'I am a creature that Crist made dedliche, and in this desert I dwelle and go for to gete myn sustenance.' The beste preiede hym that he wolde preye for hym to God, that for saluacioun cam from heuene to erthe and was born of a virgine and suffered pascioun, thour whom we alle beleuyn and arn alle at his ordenaunce. And yit is that hed of that eche beste with the hornis holdyn and kept at Alysander for a meruayle.

In Egip arn stedis and placis wher the erthe beryth freut vii. tymys in the yer. [f. 15ᵛᵇ] And atte sete of Chathre they bryngyn to the market men and women and childeryn that arn of othere contreis and sellyn hem as thei *d*on bestis in othere placis and contreis.

NOTA DE NIDIS GALINARUM

Ther is also in the cete of Chayre, that is in the lond of Egipt, a comoun hous ordeyned and mad ful of holys as it were nestis, and thedyr the wemen of the contre bryngyn eyren of hennys and of gees and of dokys and leyn hem in tho nestis. And certeyn personys arn ordeynyd for to kepe that eche hows, and, thour the grete hete of horse donge that ther is, the yre bryngyn forth

4 ermyte] *R* hermyte that hiȝte Paul   5 forshapyn] *R* footshapen
6 dounward] *MS.* douward   11 that he] *R* as he that was an holy man
14 ordenaunce] R ordenaunce. Therefore I praye the to praye for me that I may be sauyd. And whenne this hermyte herde this beeste thus speke, he was al in dispeyr of this beeste but there he conioured it and seide on this wise: in the name of God I commaunde the that thou telle me what thou art. And thenne this beeste seide, I am god of this wildernes and be an holy man commaunded hider to duelle and to tempte Cristen men walkynge in this desert. Thenne seide the hermyte, Caste awey thyne hornes fro thyne heede with the skalpe. And he dide so and vanysshed awey   19 don] *MS.* hon
partly erased   22 that is in the lond of Egipt] *R* a custom the wiche they vse of   26 eche hows] *R* hous and the nestis   27 the yre] *R* withouten henne, goos, or doke the eggis

et deinceps nutriunt sic quod tota patria plena est huiusmodi pullis. Et hoc faciunt tam in hieme quam in estate.

Item, in hac patria venduntur poma certo tempore anni que appellantur ibi poma paradisi, et sunt dulcia et boni saporis.
5 Ista poma, cum scinduntur per medium in plures partes, semper inuenitur in medio figura crucis Cristi. Sed quia hec poma infra octo dies putrescunt, ideo ea nullus portare potest ad partes remotas. Arbor istorum pomorum folia habet longitudinis vnius pedis et dimidii. . . .

10 [f. 44vb] Postea de Cipro transitur per mare usque ad Ierusalem et per totam patriam ex parte sinistra. Et transitur deinceps per mare usque ad Egyptum vbi applicandum est ad ciuitatem Damiete, que solebat esse fortis valde et sita est in introitu Egypti. Postea transitur ad ciuitatem Alexandrie, que similiter sita est
15 super mare. In hac ciuitate decollata fuit sancta Katerina, et ibi eciam sanctus Marccus martirio coronatus est et ibidem sepultus, sed imperator Leo postmodum ossa eius deportari fecit apud Veneciam. . . . Et ibi fluuius Nili mare intrat, sicut alibi dictum est. In quo eciam fluuio inueniuntur lapides preciosi multi et de
20 ligno aloes, quod de paradiso venit et est medicinale pro pluribus et venditur foro satis caro. . . .

Nunc dicam consequenter quo itinere pergitur a Babilonia vsque ad montem Synay, vbi iacet corpus sancte Katerine. Oportet transire per deserta Arabie, vbi Moyses transduxit
25 populum Israel. In illo itinere est fons de quo refecit eos Moyses quando murmurabant aduersus eum pro siti. . . .

BODLEY VERSION 37

schekenys withoutyn hennys or ony othyr foul. And at the ende
of iii. wokys or iiii. wokis the women comyn that broughtyn tho
eyren and beryn awoy the schekenys and bryngyn hem forth
as the maner of the contre askyth. And thous is al the contre
replenyshed of sweche manere of fou[f. 16ra]lys. And thus they 5
don as wel in wyntyr as in somer.

In that contre men sellyn applis in certeyne tymys of the yer
that are callyd there applis of paradys, and they arn swete and
delicious in the mouth. And whan men cottyn hem in diuers
partiis, euermore in the myddis of the appil is foundyn the figur 10
of the Holy Cros. They wele ben rotyn withinne viii. dayes and
therfor they mow not ben caried into fer contres. The tres that
beryn tho applis han leuys that growyn and arn of lenthe a fote
and an half.

From the reume of Sypre men may passe by the see to Ieru- 15
salem and into Egipt and from thene into the borw of Alysandyr
that stondyth vpon the see. In that cete was Seynt Katerynis
hed strekyn of. And Seynt Mark was in that cete martyred and
dolue but aftyrward the Emperour Leo dede takyn hese bonys
and caryen hem to Venyse, [f. 16rb] and there they are yet. And 20
[at] the cete of Alysandir the riuer of Nyli enterede into the se,
and in that ryuer ben fondyn many precious stonys, and of the
tre that men callid aloes that comyth out of paradys; a metisynable tre it is for manye seknessis, and it is seld in markettys
ful dere. 25

Now wele I seye what woye men shul holde from Babyloyne to
the Mont Synay where the body of Seynt Kateryne lyth. Men
behouyth to passe thour the desert of Arabye where Moyses
ladde the peple of Ysrael. In the weye is the welle that Moyses

1 schekenys] *R* her chekenes and the bryddes   hennys or] *R om.*   4 al]
R om.   8–9 and delicious] *R om.*   12 therfor] *R* the trees that
bere thes applis hath leefis a foot and an half longe, and for they wole
so soone be roten   15–16 to Ierusalem and] *R om.*   19–20 but
aftyrward . . . yet] *R* and manye othir good seyntis as the boke of seintis telleth
vs that hiȝte Martelege. And aftir that Seint Kateryne was born with the
aungelis of Heuene to the Mount of Synay that is xii. daies iournay fro
Alizaundre   21 at] *MS. om.*   se] *R* see the wiche is also oon of
the gretteste ryuers of al the worlde, and it renneth thoruȝ the cuntree of
Nundya and thoruȝ manye othir dyuers londes   23 aloes] *R* lignum
aloes   29 Ysrael] *R* Israel. And in that cuntre is a brid that is called
Fenys, of wiche is but oon in al this worlde, and there it bredeth. The
kynde of this brid, as the book tellith, is this, that whenne he is oolde,

Qui vero voluerit ire alio itinere de Babilonia, vadit per Mare Rubrum, quod est vnum brachium Maris Occeani, vbi transierunt filii Israel sicco vestigio, Pharaone insequente. Et habet ibi in latum vi. miliaria. Non est autem [f. 45ra] aqua ista rubea
5 plus quam alia aqua maris, sed habet in quibusdam locis arenam rubeam. Ideo vocatur Mare Rubrum. Et currit istud mare usque ad confinium Arabie et Palestine. . . .

Et scias quod per ista deserta nullus equs transire potest, non enim inuenitur pabulum equorum nec aqua ad bibendum.
10 Et ideo fit transitus cum camelis, qui semper possunt habere arbusta vnde pascantur et abstinere possunt a potu duas dietas uel tres, quod equi facere non possunt. . . . Sic et in aliis locis oportet illarum parcium eciam secum portare victualia per deserta predicta. Mons Synay appellatur desertum Syn vbi vidit
15 Moyses dominum in igne et in rubo.

Ad pedem montis est abbathia multorum monachorum que bene clauditur muris et portis ferreis propter metum ferarum crudelium que in desertis morantur. Monachi isti sunt Arabes vel Greci similes heremitis. Vinum non bibunt nisi forte in
20 precipuis festis. Sunt viri valde deuoti, pauperem vitam ducentes, abstinencie multum dediti ac penitencie.

Ibi est ecclesia sancte Katerine vbi habentur lampades plurime ardentes. Est enim ibi oleum oliue quo vtuntur tam in cibo quam in lumine lampadarum, et hoc quasi per miraculum; veniunt

13 parcium] parcium portet

ledde hem to to drynke whan they madyn murmuracioun toward hym for threst.

And ho so wil gon othyr way from Babiloyne to Ierusalem, hym behouyth to passyn the Rede See, that is an arm of the West See. And there forth wentyn the childeryn of Israel with [f. 16ᵛᵃ] dreye fot whan Pharao folwede hem. The se hat the brede of vi. myle. That se is no raddere than the water of othir see is elliswhere, but for ther is mochil red grauel by the cost of that see, forwhy men callyn it the Rede See. And it turnyth to the marche of Arabye and Palestyn.

And wete ye wel that thour this desert may non hors passe for ther is in the woye non stable ne non esement for hors ne watyr to drynke; forthy men makyn that pilgrimage with camelys, for they may ay fyndyn bowys of wode in that way that they may ete, and that fode loue they wel, and they may forbere drynk ii. dayes or iii. and so may not the hors do. Thour that desert men may brynge with hem here mete and drynk that they shal leue by.

NOTA DE MONTE SYNAY

At the fot of Mont [f. 16ᵛᵇ] Synay is foundit an abbey of monkis wel enclosed with heye wallis and gatis of yryn for dred of crewel bestis and felle that wonyn in the desertys. The monkys that wonyn in that abbey arn Arrabitis and Grekys. They drynke no wyn come[n]ly but in here festiual dayes. They arn pore men and denoute men of lyf, and leuyn in gret abstynence and penaunce.

Ther is the cherche of Seynt Kateryne with manye laumpis brennande. Th[e]r is o*yl*e of olyue that they vsyn as wel for metis as for brynnyng of lampis. That o*yl*e comyth to hem as

thenne he gooth to the hiȝest mount theraboute and gadreth manye drye stikes on an heepe, and thenne he fleeth vp into the eyr as hiȝe as he goodely may, and thenne he cometh doun aȝen with so gret fors and so mochel heete he bryngeth therwith that he fireth thoo stikes with fire and heete. And thenne setteth hee himself in the myddes of the fire and brenneth so vnto powder. And of that powder gendreth and cometh anothir fenyx at the ȝeeris ende be verray kynde. And thus ther is but oon fenyx in al the worlde   7 vi] *MS*. viii
12 for hors] *R om*.   14 bowys of wode] *R* bowes and croppes of trees
16 the hors] *R* non hors ne asse   17–18 that they shal leue by] *R* til they haue doen her pilgrimage bothe for goynge and comynge   24 comenly] *MS*. comely   festiual] *R* feestful   26 penance] *R* penaunce for her soule heele   28 Ther] *MS*. thr   28, 29 oyle] *MS*. olye

enim corui et coruicule et alie aues huiusmodi, volentes circa locum quolibet anno semel in magna multitudine ac si peregrinacionem facerent modo suo, et affert quelibet earum in rostro suo loco oblacionis ramum oliue et ibi relinqunt; vnde monachis
5 datur magna quantitas olei prouidencia diuina. Cum igitur aues que racione carent faciunt talem peregrinacionem ad hanc virginem gloriosam, bene deberent homines Cristiani ipsam visitare cum deuocione.

A retro altare huius ecclesie est locus vbi Moyses vidit dominum
10 in rubo ardentem. Vnde, quando monachi ibi ingrediuntur, discalceant se, quia Moysi dictum est, 'Solue calciamenta de pedibus tuis, locus in quo stas terra sancta est.' Hunc locum appellant monachi Deseleel, id est vmbra dei.

Et iuxta magnum altare sunt tres gradus ascendendi ad fere-
15 trum, quod est de alabastro, vbi iacet corpus virginis. Prelatus monachorum osten[f. 45rb]dit reliquias peregrinis cum quodam instrumento argenteo fricans ossa martiris, et exit modicum olei quasi sudor, sed nec est oleo simile nec balsamo quia plus nigrum esse videtur. De hoc modicum distribuit peregrinis, quia
20 modice quantitatis est. Deinde ostendit caput sancte Katerine et pannum quo fuerat obuoluta quando angeli corpus eius portabant ad montem Synay, et illuc sepelierunt cum eodem panno qui eciam adhuc cernitur sanguinolentus. Et monstratur quoque ibidem rubus incombustus quem viderat Moyses in eodem loco.
25 Plures eciam alie reliquie monstrantur peregrinis.

Quando prelatus abbathie moritur, dictum michi erat quod lampas eius per se extinguitur, et in electione alterius, si dignus sit, lampas eius per se illuminatur gracia diuina. Habet enim

by merakele, for there comyth rokys and crowis and othere foulys flyende eche yer aboutyn the place in gret multytude aboutyn togedere as they shulde makyn pilgrymage in here manere, and eche of hem bryngith in here billys in the ste[f. 17ʳᵃ]de of offerynge a braunche of olyue and leue it hem 5 there; and on that wyse is gret plente of oyle of olyue left to the sustenaunce of the hous. Than sythyn it is so that foulis that no reson ne can doth swich reuerence to the holye gloryouse virgine, wel owyn we that aryn Cristene men to visyte that holy place with gret deuocioun. 10

Besydyn that auter of that cherche is the place where that Moyses saw oure lord Iesu Crist in the brennynge brom. Whanne the monkys come to the place, they don of hosyn and shon, for that Moyses seyde, 'Tak of thyn shon of thynne fet for the place that thow stondist on, it is holy erthe.' That place 15 is callyd the Schadewe of God.

And besyde that heye auter arn iii. grecis for to comyn vp to the tombe that is of alabastyr wher the body of the vir- [f. 17ʳᵇ]gyne is. The prelat of the monkys shewith the relikys to pilgrymmys. That eche prelat steryth the bonys of the martyr 20 with an instrument of syluyr, and thanne comyth a lytil oyle as it were swet; but it is not lik neythir oyle ne baumme for it is more blak, and therof they yeuyn lytil quantite to pilgrymys. And aftyr that they shewyn the hed of Seynt Kateryne and that cloth that *it* was wondyn in whanne the angel[is] broughte the 25 body vp to the Mon[t] of Synay, and there they grauyd it with that eche cloth that yet is blody and eueremor shal be. And they shewyn also the brende brom that Moyses saw.

Ich a monk of that hous hath eueremore a lampe bren- nende, and whanne the abbot deyeth his lampe goth out by the 30 [f. 17ᵛᵃ] seluyn. And as men tellyn there, in the chesynge of anothir

1 and crowis] *R* gladis, rafenes, dowfis   5 olyue] *R* olive leevis   6 there] *R* there and thenne fleeth aweye into the place that they come froo, 8 holye] *R om.*   12 brom] *R* busshe of thorn   18 the body of the virgyne] *R* Seint Kateryne   20 pilgrymmys] *R* pilgrymes whenne any cometh thider   the martyr] *R* that holy virgyne Seint Kateryne   22 swet] *R* swet of smellynge   23 and 24 they] *R* he   25 it] *MS.* is   angelis] *MS.* angel 25–26 the body] *R* hir out of Alizaundre as biforn is seide   26 Mont] *MS.* mon   Synay] *R* Synay that is of passage xii. iournayes bitwene 28 saw] *R* saw₃ but some men seyn that it shulde be of thorn   29 bren- nende] *R* brennynge in the chirche

quilibet eorum lampadem suam et sciunt per lampades quando aliquis eorum moriturus est, tunc enim incipit lumen paulatim deficere.

Alii michi dixerunt quod post mortem prelati qui celebrat per
5 se missam solempnem reperit super altare nomen prelati futuri in scripturis. De hiis vero interrogaui monachos, sed ipsi nichil aliud dicere volebant nisi quod pluries ita contigit. Nec hoc eciam primo dixerunt quousque eis dixi quod ipsi non deberent tacere [et] sub silencio tenere graciam dei sed eam puplicare deberent
10 ad exitandum fidelium deuocionem. . . .

In ista abbathia non intrant musce nec pulices nec tale aliquid fedum miraculo dei et beate Marie virginis. Solebat enim antiquitus tanta ibi esse huiusmodi animalium multitudo quod monachi ab eis infestati locum deserere volebant et iam egressi
15 montem ascendebant fugiendo. Quibus beata virgo obuiauit dicens eis quod redirent, deinceps talem molestiam non sustinerent. Reuersique monachi numquam de cetero muscam vel tale aliquid ibi viderunt.

Item, ante portam est fons vbi Moyses percussit petram et
20 fluxerunt aque. . . . [f. 45va] Et adhuc paululum superius in monte est capella Moysi et rupes vbi fugit quando vidit dominum facie ad faciem. In qua eciam rupe inprimitur forma corporis sui, tam valide eum se impulit ad rupem fugiendo quod miraculo dei formam ibi corporis sui dereliquit. Ibi prope est locus vbi
25 dominus ei tradidit x. precepta legis. Et ibi cernitur camera sub

9 et] eciam

abbot his lampe lytith by the self, if he be worthy, by the grace of God. Eche of tho monkys hath a lampe and they wete by the laumpe whan he shal deye, for ageyn that tyme that ony of hem shal deye the lampe wele yeuyn lytil light.

It was told to me ther that whan a prelat was ded and shulde 5 ben grauyn, that he that song the hye masse for hym shulde fyndyn in a skrowe vpon the heye auter beforn hym the name of hym that shulde be chosyn to ben here prelat. And I askede the monkys if it were so, an they woldyn not ellis tellyn me but that sumtyme it fel so. An I seyde it fel not for hem to ho*l*de 10 conseyl Godis werkys and his marakelis and his grace but puppliche it in a pert for[f. 17ᵛᵇ]me for to exite men to more deuocioun.

In that eche abbey neyther flen ne flyen comyn ne non othir of swech maner of onclene corrupcyoun thour merakele of 15 God and of his modyr oure lady Seynte Marie and of the holy virgyne Seynt Kateryne. Sumtyme ther was so gret multytude of swich vermyn that the monkys of that abbey were so turmentyd with hem that they leftyn that abbey and wentyn awey, thene flende from hem vp onto the mont. And right so come 20 ther the blyssede virgyne Sente Kateryne and mette with hem and bad hem turnyn agen to here abbey and they shuldyn neuer more hauyn swiche greuaunce ne desese of hem. And they dedyn right so as she bad hem and turnedyn ayen, and neuere aftyr that day hadde man in that abbey fle [f. 18ʳᵃ] ne no maner 25 of swich corrupcioun to greuyn hem.

Beforn the gate of the abbey is the welle wher Moyses strok vpon the ston with his yerde, and ther ran out watyr and so it shal don eueremor. Vppere more into the mont is Moysesis chapel and the roche that he fledde into whan he saw oure lord 30 Iesu Crist; in the wheche roche is the prent of the forme of his body, so faste he putte his body therto fleende that thorw the merakel of Cryst the forme of his body leste eueremore there in that roche. And the[r] fasteby is that place where Crist yaf to

3 he] *R* any of hem   7 vpon the heye auter] *R* wreten   10 for hem] *R* to her ordre holde] *MS.* hyde   14 flyen] *R* flies ne loppis   15 maner of] *R om.* corrupcyoun] *R* wormes nor non othir vermyn   16 and of the] *R* and also thoru3 the preyer of   17 multytude] *MS.* multytude of peple   18 vermyn] *R* vnclene vermyn   23 ne desese] *R om.* hem] *R* that ilke vermyne   25 fle] *R* flee ne flie ne loppe   28 and so] *R* and 3it doeth and   34 ther] *MS.* the

rupe vbi Moyses morabatur quando ieiunauit xl. diebus et noctibus. Sed mortuus est in terra promissionis et nescitur locus sepulture eius. . . .

Iam post visitacionem locorum sanctorum reuertendum est ad Ierusalem, accepta primo licencia et valedicto ab hiis sanctis monachis et facta recomendacione su*a* eorum orationibus sanctis, qui eciam solent dare peregrinis partem victualium suorum pro desertis versus Syriam que durant per xiii. dietas.

In hiis desertis morantur multi Arabes, quos appellant Bedeyns et Aschopariz. Hec est gens repleta omni iniquitate et malicia. Domos non habent ad habitandum nisi tentoria que sibi faciunt de pellibus camelorum et aliarum ferarum quas manducant, bibentes aquam vbi inueniri potest, videlicet de Mari Rubro et aliis locis raris. Est enim in desertis illis magna penuria aquarum, et sepe contingit quod vbi inuenitur aqua vno tempore anni non inuenitur alio. Ideo isti non faciunt sibi habitaciones in certo loco, sed nunc hic nunc ibi prout aqua inueniri poterit.

Gens ista non laborat in cultura terre, non enim vescuntur pane nisi sunt aliqui qui habitant prope aliquam [f. 45vb] villam bonam ad quam ire possent et panem comedere ibidem. Assare enim solebant carnes et pisces suos super petras solis ardore calescentes. Fortes tamen sunt et bellicosi [et numerosi] valde. Nil aliud faciunt nisi quod feras insecuntur et perquirunt ad comedendum. Non curant de se ipsis nec appreciant vitam suam. Ideo nec timent soldanum nec alium principem mundi, quin pugnare vellent cum eo si eis aliquid grauamen inferret. Sepe

6 sua] sui   23 et numerosi] *om.*

Moyses the x. comaundementis of oure lawe. And also there it shewith in a chambre vndyr a roche where Moyses wonede whan he fastid xl. dayes, but he deyede in the Holy Lond and no man wot were he was grauyn.

[f. 18ʳᵇ] Thanne aftyr tyme that pilgrymys haddyn visityd this place holy and othere there aboutyn, they tokyn here leue of the holy monk[ys] and they yeue hem part of here vitaylys to here sustenaunce thour the desert toward Cyrrye, that lestyth xiii. iorneis ageyn to Ierusalem.

In t*e* desert toward Arrabye dwelled mechil peple but they aryn fulfyllid of alle maner of wekednesse and malyce. Housis han they none but logis that they make with skynnys of camyles and of wilde bestis that they ete. And [they] drynke watyr whan they may ony getyn, f*or* there in t*e* desert is a gret defaut of watir, for oftyn it fa*l*lyth there that where watir is foundyn a tyme of the yer, it is not there anothir tyme. And therfore they dar makyn hem none housys in certeyn placis, but now here and now there as they may [f. 18ᵛᵃ] [fynde] watyr.

This folk that I speke of trauaylyn [n]eueremor aboutyn tylynge of lond for they etyn kome[n]ly non bred, but it be ony that dwellyth nygh ony good toun that may gon *þ*edyr and gete bred to etyn. They roste here flesch and fysch vpon stonys thour hete of the sonne. Neuere the les yit are they stalworthy men and grete fyteris, and gret multitude is there of hem. They don [noght] but fo*l*wyn wilde bestis and takyn of hem to here mete. They rekkyn neuere of hemself ne they yeue right not of here lyuys, for they dredyn neythir God ne the Soudon ne no

---

3 but he deyede in the Holy Lond] *R* and fro that Moises passid into the Holy Lond and there he deide   7 monkys] *MS.* monk   hem] *R* hem part of her goode dedis and of her goodes and the monkes ʒiveth hem   8 thour] *R* and thenne they turne ageyn thoruʒ   9 xiii.] *MS.* xiiii   Ierusalem] *R* Ierusalem and that ilke desert of Arabye thoruʒ the wiche he come bifore, there men shal se manye ferlies and wondris, of the wiche I shal telle. Men byhoueth to turne ageyne thoruʒ the desert of Arabie towarde Ierusalem fro the mount of Synay th[r]ouʒ the wiche they come bifore, as it is iseide
10 In te] *MS.* into   Arrabye] *MS.* Cyrrye Arrabye   13 they] *MS. om.*
14 for] *MS.* fer   in te] *MS.* into   15 fallyth] *MS.* faylyth   18 fynde] *MS. om.*   watyr] *R* water to live bye   19 neueremor] *MS.* eueremor
20 komenly] *MS.* komely   21 *þ*edyr] *MS.* dedyr   23 stalworthy] *R* stronge men and staleworthe   25 noght] *MS.* right   folwyn] *MS.* forwyn
27 God] *R* God ne Seint Marie, why for they knowe hem nouʒt

pugnauerunt cum soldano precipue eo tempore quod steti cum eo. Arma eorum sunt tantummodo scutum et lancea. Alia arma non habent.

Post transitum huius deserti veniendo versus Ierusalem itur
5 Bersabee, que solebat esse pulcra villa et bona Cristianorum, et adhuc sunt ibi alique ecclesie. In hoc loco morabatur diu patriarcha Abraham. Hanc villam fundauit Bersabee vxor Vrie, vbi eciam rex Dauid ex ea genuit Salamonem qui regnauit xl. annis in Ierusalem.

10 Deinde transitur ad ciuitatem Ebron ii. miliariis, que alio nomine appellatur vallis Mambre, et aliter eciam dicitur vallis lacrimarum eo quod Adam fleuit centum annis in ipsa valle propter mortem filii sui Abel quem Cayn occidit. . . . In Ebron regnauit Dauid primo septem annis et dimidio, et in Ierusalem
15 regnauit xxxiii. annis et dimidio.

Ibi in Ebron sunt sepulcra Adam, Abraham, Ysaac, et Iacob patriarcharum et vxorum suarum in descensu montis. . . . Satis prope est vna camera in rupe vbi Adam et Eua habitabant cum eiecti essent de paradiso, et [f. 46ra] filios suos genuerunt. Ibi eciam
20 secundum aliquos, Adam creatus fuerat, et solebat locus vocari Ager Damascenus, et inde fuit Adam translatus in paradisum, ut dicitur, et illuc reductus fuerat postquam de paradiso erat emissus. Ibi incipit vallis Ebron et durat pene usque Ierusalem. Ibi eciam precepit angelus Ade quod habitaret ibidem cum vxore
25 sua, de qua genuit Seth, de cuius stirpe Iesus Cristus natus est. . . .

Ibi habetur quercus quam Saraceni appellant Drip et est de tempore Abrahe. Hec est arbor que vulgariter dicitur arbor

prynce ne no lord that leuyth in this world. But they wele gladli
fightyn with alle tho that comyn to hem. They foutyn oftyn
with the Sou[f.18ᵛᵇ]don whan I was with hym. Armour han they
non but only sheld and spere.

Aftyr that men are passed the desertys comende to Ierusalem 5
men goth by a cete that is callyd Bersabe, that was wone to ben
a fair cete and a good and was wel enabytid with Cristen men.
And sumtyme oure fadyr Abraham wonede therinne, and Bersabe, Vryes wif, foundede that cete and called it aftyr hereself.
And in that cete Dauyd the kyng gat on here Salomon that was 10
kyng of Ierusalem xl. yer.

NOTA DE UALLE EBRON

From thene men shal gon to the cete of Ebron and, sum men
seyn, to the cete of wepynge because that Adam oure forme
fadyr made his lamentacyoun therin an c. yer with *ofte grettynge* 15
for his sone [f. 19ʳᵃ] Abel that Caym slow. Dauyd regnede in
that cete vii. yer and an half; in Ierusalem [he regned xxxiii.
yere and a halfe].

In that cete of Ebron aryn the cepulturys of Adam, Abraham,
Isak, and Iacob, and alle here wyvys there. And ther ner besyde 20
is a chaumbir in a roche of ston wher Adam and Eue dwelledyn
whan they were put out of paradis. And in that stede they getyn
here chylderyn. And Adam, as some men seyn, was mad in that
place, and from thene was translatyd into paradys and thedyr
was brought ayen with Cristis aungel and comaundede him that 25
he shulde dwelle there with his wif, and ther he gat on here Set,
of whos kynde Crist com and was born.

Ner the uale of Ebron is the sepulture of Loth. And there is
an ok that the Sarazynys callyn Drippe and is of Abra-
[f. 19ʳᵇ]hamis tyme, drye and beryth no lef. The comoun word is 30

---

1 that leuyth in this world] *R* ne noon othir man of this worlde nothir the
deuel of helle; bettir fiȝters knowe I noon thenne they arn   4 spere]
R spere but neueretheles ȝit comonly they gete the bettir of her enemyes
in bataille   5 desertys] *R* desertis of Arabie   13 thene] *R* the cite of
Bersabe   15 ofte grettynge] *MS*. of the gretteste   16 his sone] *R* his
synne and his sone   17 vii.] *MS*. viii   17–18 he regned...halfe] *MS*.
om.; R he regned of the forseide ȝeeris xxx. ȝeer and an half   26 wif] *R*
wiff Eve   27 born] *R* born to safe al this worlde that was forlorn thoruȝ
mannes synne   30 lef] *MS*. lof

sicca. Fama est ibidem quod arbor ista fuit ab inicio mundi et semper extitit viridis usque ad tempus passionis Cristi, et ex tunc remansit sicca. Et sic fecerunt, ut dicitur, cetere arbores per totum mundum, scilicet vel deuenerunt aride vel liquor interius periit et facte sunt vacue quasi mortue, de quibus plurime adhuc extant diuersis locis. Dicunt eciam quedam prophecie quod vnus dominus princeps occidentis adquiret terram promissionis auxilio Cristianorum et faciet celebrare missam sub predicta arbore arida, et postea arbor ipsa reuirescet et flores cum fructu portabit. Propter quod miraculum plures tam Iudei quam Saraceni ad fidem Cristi conuertentur. Et ideo habetur arbor illa in magna reuerencia apud gentem illam et bene custodiunt eam. Quamuis autem dicatur sicca, nichilominus non paruam habet virtutem, nam quicumque super se portat aliquam eius partem, non vexabitur morbo caduco nec eciam equs eius infundi potest. Plures quoque virtutes alias dicitur habere, quare preciosa satis in illis partibus reputatur. . . .

[f. 46rb] Et ibi prope ad tres passus est presepe bouis et asini et puteus vbi prope iuxta monstratur vbi cecidit stella que magos adduxit, quorum sunt nomina Iaspar, et Melchior, et Balthasar. . . . Hi tres reges optulerunt domino aurum, thus, et mirram, et non illuc venerunt per dietas humanas sed diuino miraculo, quo tanta terrarum spacia tam breui tempore transire potuerunt.

Item, iuxta illam ecclesiam in dextro latere ascendendo per gradus xviii. est locus vbi reponuntur ossa innocencium. Et ante locum natiuitatis Cristi est tumba sancti Ieronimi, quidem qui fuit presbiter cardinalis, qui eciam Bibliam transtulit de hebreo in latinum. Eciam ext[r]a monasterium est cathedra ipsius in qua

28 extra] exta

there that it hath ben there syn the fyrste begynnyng of the world and ay was grene and bar leuys til that Crist deyede, but thanne it wex dreye and so, seyn men, manye treis dede thour al this world, of whiche ther ben manye yet stondynge in manye stedis. In dyuerse prophesies it is seyd that a lord and a prynce of the west shal conquere the Holy Lond with helpe of othere Cristene, and he shal do synge a masse vndyr that drie ok, and aftyr that it shal waxen grene ayen and bere leuys and freut. And thour vertu of that ilke merakele ther shal manye, as wel Iewes as Sarasynys, ben conuertyd and turne to the [f. 19va] Cristene lawe. And forsothe that tre is holdyn in gret prys there, and gret reuerence the folk of that contre *d*oth therto and kepyn it wel. And thow it be callid the dreye tre, neuertheles ther is gret vertue therin; who so bere ony porcioun therof on hym, he shal neuere ben trauayled with the fallynge euyl, ne his hors shal neuere ben foundered whil he hath it on hym. And manye othere vertues hath that dreie tre.

NOTA DE CIUITATE BETHLEM

And ther besyde is the cete of Bethelem wher Crist was born. And ther is the stabil of the oxe and the asse, and there is the pit that the sterre fil in, that ledde the iii. kyngis to oure lord, whos namis ben Iasper, Melchior, [f. 19vb] and Baltasar. These iii. offeredyn to oure lord Iesu Crist gold, rechellis, and myrre. Thedyr come they neuere thour ymaginacioun of manys wit but only thorw the merakele of Crist, that comyn from so fer in so short tyme.

And ther in a cherche is a place where the bonis of [the] Ynnocentis lyn and were leid before the berthe of Crist. And there is the sepulture of Seynt Ierom the doctour that was a cardenale, and he translatid the Byble out of Ebrew into Latyn.

1 begynnyng *MS*.] bogynnyng   2 deyede] *R* deide for mannes synne
3 manye treis dede] *MS*. manye dede treis   4 stedis] *R* placis and forestis
5 prophesies] *R* prophetis   12 doth] *MS*. goth   17 hath that dreie tre] *R* it hath more thenne any man can telle or know   19 besyde] *R* besides the citee of Ebron   22 Iasper, Melchior, and Baltasar] *R* Iasper the ooldest, Melcheor the mydleste, and Balthasar the ȝongeste   23 rechellis and myrre] *R* mirre and encens, and alle three they ligge at Coleyn be the watir of the Reene   27 ther in a cherche is a place] *R* in the cite of Betheleem is a chirche   the] *MS*. om.   28 lyn and were leid] *R* buriede and leide that deide for Cristis sake   30 cardenale] *R* cardenal of Rome

sedens Bibliam transtulit. Non longe ab ista ecclesia est alia sancti Nicholai, vbi beata virgo quiescebat post puerperium suum quia lacte habundabat in mamillis ita quod ei nocebat, et iecit partem inde super lapides rubei marmoris qui ibi erant. Et adhuc
5 cernuntur albe gutte super predictas petras.

Noueris autem quod pene omnes qui habitant in Bethleem sunt Cristiani. Sunt ibi vites pulcre in circuitu ciuitatis et magna copia vini habetur ibidem operacione Cristianorum. Nam Saraceni vineas non colunt nec vinum bibunt propter prohibicionem
10 legis sue, quam dedit eis Machometus in libro quam vocant Alchoranum; alio nomine appellatur Meshaaf; a quibusdam vero dicitur Arme. In hoc libro Machometus maledicit omnibus qui vinum vendunt, eo quod preterito tempore imponebant sibi quod ipse in ebrietate vini interfecit quemdam heremitam
15 [f. 46va] sibi familiarem et amicum, et ideo maledixit vinum et omnes vinum bibentes. Sed maledictio sua in capud suum reuertatur, sicut dicit Dauid, *Et in verticem ipsius iniquitas eius descendet* et cetera. . . .

De ciuitate Bethleem oriundus erat Dauid rex qui habuit lx.
20 vxores, quarum prima vocabatur Michol. Habuit quoque trecentas concubinas. . . .

[f. 46vb] Preterea noueris quod quando peregrini apud Ierusalem sunt primitus transeunt ad ecclesiam sancti sepulcri, que est extra ciuitatem versus partem borealem, sed tamen muro clauditur
25 cum ciuitate . . . . Infra istam ecclesiam habetur vnum tabernaculum in loco medio quasi esset domus parua, et habet formam semicirculi, et artificiose ornatur auro et argento et azario

BODLEY VERSION 51

And withoutyn the menstre is yet there the chayer that he sat in whan he translatid the Bible. Not fier from this cherche is anothir cherche of Seynt Nicholas, where oure lady Seynt Marie, blis[f. 20ra]sed mote she ben, restid here aftyr the berthe. And the mylk aboundede in here pappis, and it greuede here right 5 sore. And there she sat here doun and mylkede here pappis vpon stonis of red marbil that were there, and yit the spottys ben sene of the mylk vpon the stonys.

Almost [alle] tho that dwellyn in Bedlem aryn Cristene men. And there ben gret plente of vynys and of wyn of the ordenaunce 10 of Cristen men. The Sarazynis drynke non wyn ne delytyn with no vynys, for it is defendid in here lawe that Macomede yaf hem, as it is rehersed in his bok that is callid Alcorane. In that bok Macomede cursede alle tho that dronkyn wyn. And that was for he was onys dronkyn of wyn, and in his dronkennesse 15 [f. 20rb] he slow an ermyte that was his seruant, and therfore he cursede the wyn and alle tho that it dronkyn. But his cursynge lighte vpon his owene hed as Dauid seyth, *Et in uerticem ipsius iniquitas descendet*.

In the cete of Bethlem was Dauyd born, that was kyng of 20 Ierusalem. He hadde *lx*. wyuys, of whiche the ferste highte Mechel, and he hadde also ccc. concubynys.

NOTA DE PEREGRINACIONE IERUSALEM

Whanne the pilgrymys arn comyn to Ierusalem, they gon to the cherche were that the holy sepulcre is in, that is withoute 25 the cherche to the north syde ward, but it is enclosed with a wal to the sete. Withinne that chirche ther is a tabernakele craftyly wrought [f. 20va] with gold and syluyr and aseur and with othere frosche coloures; withinne the wheche tabernakele toward the

4 blissed mote she be] *R om.*   7 red] *R om.*   8 stonys] *R* same ston and eueremore shal be   9 alle] *MS. om.*   11 Sarazynis] *R* Sarazayns that dwellen in Betheleem   delytyn] *R* deyle   14 wyn] *R* wyne but the cursynge falleth vpon his owne heede   17 his cursynge] *R* as I seide bifore the cursynge   21 lx.] *MS.* xl. *R* l.   22 concybynys] *R* concubynes to thoo wifis. And whenne men hath doen at Betheleem they shal thenne come vnto Ierusalem, of the wiche I thynk to speke off in the secunde partie of this book. Now wole I telle of the pilgrymage of Ierusalem   27-28 craftyly wrought] *R* craftely and coryously iwrouȝt and is igarnysshed

aliisque coloribus multimodis. In huius tabernaculi parte dextra est sepulcrum domini. Est autem longitudo tabernaculi octo pedum et latitudo vero quinque pedum et altitudo vndecim pedum.

5   Et non est diu ex quo sepulcrum fuit discoopertum ita quod quilibet eum tangere potest et osculari. Sed quia peregrini et alii auferre nitebantur semper de lapide vel de puluere, ideo soldanus fecit muro circumcingi sepulcrum ita quod tangi non posset. Sed in parte sinistra muri illius tabernaculi, in altitudine
10 corporis hominis, est vna petra de grossitudine capitis humani que fuit de sancto sepulcro, et hanc petram osculantur peregrini.

In hoc tabernaculo non sunt fenestre sed la[m]p*a*dibus illuminatur. E[s]t eciam lampas dependens ante sepulcrum semper ardens, que in parasceue extinguitur per se et die resurreccionis iterum per se illuminatur eadem hora qua Cristus surrexit a
15 mortuis.

Item, infra ecclesiam in parte dextra prope capud ipsius ecclesie est mons Caluarie vbi dominus crucifixus est. . . . In illa quoque fissura inuentum fuit capud Ade post diluuium, et hoc in signum quod peccatum Ade redimendum esset in eodem loco. Super hanc
20 rupem fecit Abraham sacrificium deo. Et est ibi altare ante quod [f. 47ra] iacent sepulti Godefridus de Bullioun et Baldewynus et alii qui fuerunt ibidem reges Cristiani in Ierusalem.

Prope vbi dominus crucifixus est sic scribitur in greco, *Otheos basileoun ymon proseonas ergasa sotheos emesotisgis*, quod est in
25 latinis, *Hic deus rex ante secula operatus est iusticiam in medio terre*. Item, super rupem vbi crux defixa fuerat sculpitur in rupe sic, *Oios nist ys basis tou pisteos thoy thesmosi*; hoc est dicere, *Quod vides est fundamentum tocius fidei mundi huius*. Et notum esse tibi volo quando Cristus crucifixus est fuit ipse de etate
30 triginta trium annorum et trium mensium. . . .

12 lampadibus] lapidibus   13 Est] et

BODLEY VERSION 53

sepulture is the holye sepulcre of oure lord Iesu Crist. The lenthe of that tabernakele is viii. feet, and the brede therof is [v. fet, and the heighte is] xi. fet.

It is not long tyme sithyn that pilgrymys myghte com to the sepulcre and opynly sen it and touchyn it and kyssyn it. But 5 *be*cause that some pilgrimys that comyn thedyr tokyn sum porcioun therof by stalthe and boryn it awey with hem for to kepyn it as for a relyke, therfore the Soudon hath don it enclosyd with an wal al aboutyn that no man may neghen it. But in the left syde of the wal in that [f. 20vb] eche tabernakele, the 10 heyte of a man, is a ston of the sepulcre set and it is no more than a fote, and that ston pilgrymys kyssyn.

And [in] that tabernakele aryn lampis brennende [in] wyndowis, but ther is alwoy a lampe brennende byfore the sepulcre, the which eueremore vpon the Goode Fryday goth out by the 15 self alone, and vpon the Pask Day it lighti[th] ayen alone at the same tyme that Crist ros from deth to lyue ayen.

And withinne the cherche is the Mont of Caluerye where oure lord Iesu Crist was crucified. And therby in a roche, as men seith, was the hed of Adam oure forme fadyr foundyn aftyr 20 the delyuie in tokenyng that Adam[f. 21ra]is synne shulde ben bought ageyn in that ech place. And vpon that ech roche made Abraham his sacrifise to God. And ther is an autir beforn the which Godfrey de Boloyne and Baudewen of Surry and othere that were kyngis of Ierusalem lyn grauyd. 25

Ner besyde ther oure lord Iesu Crist was crucifyed is wretyn of old tyme these wordys, 'Here oure lord God wroughte helle in myddis the world.' And right vpon the roche where the cros was foundyn, that oure lord was don vpon, arn grauyn in the roche these wordis, *Hoc quod uidis est fundamentum* 30 *tocius fidei mundi huius*. And I do yow to wetyn whan oure lord Iesu Crist was crucified [he was] of [age] xxx. and iii. yer and iii. monethis.

3 v. fet and the heighte is] *MS. om.*   6 because] *MS.* the cause   10 in] *R* and in   11 and it] *R* and that stoon of the sepulcre and it   12 than] *R* thenne the gretnesse of   13 And in] *MS.* and   in] *MS.* and   14 alwoy] *R om.*   16 lightith] *MS.* lighti   23 God] *R* God of his sone Isaak, and there the aungel come fro hevene and hilde the swerde of Abraham with the wiche he wolde haue slayn Isaak his sone thoru3 the biddynge of God   28 wroughte helle] *R* bifore that he this worlde wrou3te hire   32 he was of age] *MS.* of

Item, prope montem Caluarie ad desertum est altare vbi iacet columpna ad quam ligabatur in flagellacione sua. Et ibi iuxta sunt tres columpne de petra que semper distillant aquam, et dicunt aliqui quod deplorant mortem Cristi.

5 Et iuxta predictum altare, in loco subterraneo de profunditate quadraginta et duorum graduum, inuenta fuit crux Cristi ab Helena vbi Iudei eam absconderant sub rupe. Inuente fuerant ibidem tres cruces, vna Cristi et due duorum latronum. Helena vero, dubitans que illarum fuit crux Cristi, applicauit vnam post
10 aliam cuidam mortuo ibidem, qui contactu crucis Cristi mox surrexit.

Est et ibi locus vbi quatuor claui absconditi fuerant, quorum duo erant in manibus et duo in pedibus. De vno eorum fecit imperator Constantinus frenum equi sui, quo vsus est in bellis
15 cuius virtute hostes suos vincebat, conquerendo totam Asiam minorem, Siriam, Ierosolomitanam, Arabiam, Persidam, Mesopothamiam, regnum de Halappe, Egyptum superiorem et inferiorem, [f. 47rb] cum pluribus terris aliis vsque Ethiopiam et Indiam minorem. Quequidem terre et regiones ex tunc inhabi-
20 tabantur Cristianis pro magna parte. . . . Nunc vero omnes terre predicte sunt in manibus Saracenorum et paganorum. . . .

In medio ecclesie predicte, id est in medio chori, circulus est infra quem Ioseph de Arimathia posuit corpus domini quando deposuit eum de cruce. In eodem loco lauit plagas eius.
25 Hunc circulum dicunt quidam esse verum medium locum

20 pro magna] pro magna pro magna

Besyde the Mont of Calue[f. 21ʳᵇ]rie at the right side of the auter ther is the peler that oure lord Iesu Crist was bondyn to in his flagellacioun. And there ner arn iii. pelerys of ston that eueremor droppyn of watyr.

NOTA DE INUENCIONE SANCTI CRUCIS

I do yow to wetyn that in an hole that there is, vndyr the erthe the depnesse of xlii. grecis, Seynt Elyne fond the cros that oure lord Iesu Crist was don vpon, wher the Iewis haddyn hid it vndyr the erthe vndyr a roche. And ther weryn fondyn also ii. crossis that the ii. theuys were don vpon. An Elyne wiste not witterly whiche was the cros that oure lord Iesu Crist was don vpon, and therfore she tok eche on aftyr othir and leyd hem to a ded man. [f. 21ᵛᵃ] And whan the cros that oure lord Iesu Crist was don vpon touched the cors, it ros from deth to lyue.

Ther is also the place wher [i]iii. naylis were foundyn that oure lord Iesu Crist hadde thour fet and handis. And on of the naylis the Emperour that hight Costantyn the Noble let makyn an bit to his brydyl, the which brydyl he vsede eueremore whan he yede to batayle. And thour the vertew of that brydil he conquered hese enemyis in manye dyuerse reumys, that is for to seyne, Asye the Lesse, Turkye, Hermonye the Lasse and the More, Syrrye, Ierusalem, Arabye, Perside, Mesopotanye, the reume of Alape, Egipt the More and the Lesse, and manye other londis, the which were than [f. 21ᵛᵇ] for the more partye holdyn and enabitid with Cristen men, and now for the more partie it is in Sarasynys handys.

In myd of that iche cherche, in myd the [quere], ther is the cerkele in the whiche Iosep of Aremathie leyde the body of oure lord Iesu Crist whan he tok hym dou[n] of the cros. And in that place he wesch hese woundis. Tha[t] eche serkele the

---

3 iii. pelerys of ston] *R* the pilers   4 watyr] *R* clene watir   6 I do yow to wetyn that] *R* and   7–10 cros that ... were don vpon] *R* crossis alle three, both that Iesu Crist was doen vpon and thoo that thefis were doen vpon, in the erthe vnder a roche   10 witterly] *R* vttirly   15 iiii.] *MS.* iii.   16 hadde thour fet and handis] *R* was naylid with vpon the cros thoruȝ hondes and foote for our saluacion   17 that hight] *R om.*   20 conquered] *R* ouercome and conquered   22 the More, Syrrye] *R* Surry the More   27 quere] *MS.* flor   28 Aremathie] *MS.* Baremathie   leyde] *MS.* leyde to   29 doun] *MS.* dou   30 That] *MS.* tha

mundi. . . . Et ibi primo apparuit Marie Magdalene post resurreccionem. . . .

Et ibi prope est Porta Aurea que aperiri non potest. Per eam intrauit dominus ciuitatem die palmarum super asinam sedens, 5 et porte ante eum ultro aperte sunt quando perrexit ad Templum. Et adhuc apparent vestigia asine in tribus locis graduum qui de duris petris construuntur. . . .

[f. 47va] De ecclesia sancti sepulcri ad spacium viii.$^{xx.}$ passuum versus orientem est Templum Domini, locus pulcherimus et 10 spaciosus. . . . Saraceni vero non permittunt Iudeos intrare neque Cristianos, quia dicunt quod gens tam feda et reproba tam sanctum locum intrare non debent. Sed ego ibidem intraui et eciam alibi vbi volebam virtute litterarum soldani; in quibus specialiter preceptum fuit omnibus subditis suis quod me 15 permitterent omnia loca videre et michi ostenderent tam res quam loca prout michi placeret, et quod me eciam deducerent de ciuitate in ciuitatem si necesse esset et benigne me reciperent et socios meos, fauendo peticionibus meis racionabilibus si non essent contra regalem dignitatem soldani vel legis sue. Aliis 20 autem qui petunt ab ipso soldano graciam transeundi per loca illa non solet dare nisi signetum suum, quod peregrini [coram] se gestant per patriam illam in vna lancea; cui magnum honorem exhibent homines patrie illius. Michi autem, quia [in eius seruicio steti], specialiorem graciam fecit.

25 Predicto autem signeto talem impendunt reuerenciam quod quando illud vident coram se transire, genuflectent sicut nos facimus transeunte presbitero cum sacramento altaris. Litteris vero suis maiorem reuerenciam faciunt, nam cum fuerint presentate alicui magnati, primitus ante recepcionem inclinat,

21 coram] Saraceni   23–24 in eius seruicio steti] cum meis steti cum illo

sey that it is in the myddis of the world. And in that place fyrst Iesu Crist aperede to Marie Maudelyn aftyr his resoreccioun.

And there besydyn is the gate that is callyd Porta Aur*e*a that may neuere ben openyd til the day of dome. In at [that] yat cam Crist rydende vpon the Palme Soneday vpon an [f. 22ra] asse, and that gate openyd ayens hym whan he come to the Temple. And yit arn the steppis sene of the assis fet in certeyn placys that arn mad of harde stonys and euermor shul ben.

From the cherche wher the holy sepulcre is in, the space of [viii.^{c.}] paas toward the est, is the place that is callyd *Templum Domini*, a fayr place and a delitable. The Sarasynys wil suffere neythir Cristen ne Iewis comyn therin, for they sey that so foule men ne so reprouable as they arn shuldyn not entryn into so holy a place. But I Iohn Maundeuyle come in there, and ellisswhere there me lyked, be vertu of the Soudonis letteris that I hadde; in which letteris he comaunded streytly [f. 22rb] to alle hese subiectis that they shulde lete me see alle the placis where I come and schewe me as wel the relykys as the place at myn wil, and ledde me from cete to othir yif myster were. They resseyued me fayre and wel and alle myne felawis, obesiound to myn askyng in alle thynge that was resonable, but it were ayen the real dignete of the Soudon or ellis ageyn here lawe. To othere that askyn leue of the Soudon and grace to pace by the placys aforseid, he yeuyth neuere but his sygnet, the which that pilgrymis beryn befor hem thour the contre on a yerde; to which signet the folk of the contre and of the lond don gret [f. 22va] reuerence. But to me, for I was longe in his seruyse, he dede special grace.

To his forseyde synet swich reuerence thei do that whan they sen it passe besydyn hem, they knelyn dou[n] therto, righ[t] as we don whan we se the prest passyn besyde vs with the sacrement of God. To hese letterys they don gret reuerence, for whan they come befoɹn hem, that is for to say, befron ony lord

3 Aurea] *MS.* Auria   4 til the day of dome] *R om.*   that] *MS. om.*   10 viii.^{c.}] *MS. and R* viii.   15 ellisswhere] *R* ȝede aboute   18 where I come...place] *R* and reliquys that they had   schewe] *MS.* schewede   19 ledde] *MS.* they ledde   19–21 They resseyued...resonable] *R* And also they bad me that I sholde aske what thing that I wolde, and they wolde graunte me   25 yerde] *R* ȝerde that is cloven aboven   27 reuerence] *R* reuerence whenne they seene itt   30 doun] *MS.* dou   therto] *R* vnto his lettres   right] *MS.* righ

deinde eas recipit et super capud suum ponit, et postea eas osculatur, et tandem legit genuflectendo cum maxima reuerencia. Offertque se paratum ad faciendum ipsis portitoribus secundum earum tenorem. . . .

5   Titus enim, Vaspasiani filius, [f. 47vb] imperator romanus obsedit Ierusalem eo quod Cristum crucifixerunt sine voluntate imperatoris et, ciuitate victa et capta, combussit templum et destruxit. Iudeos omnes cepit et plures ex ipsis interfecit, scilicet xl. milia. Reliquos incarcerauit et in seruitutem vendidit vili
10 precio, videlicet triginta pro vno denario, eo quod audierat Cristum fuisse venditum pro triginta denariis.

Posteriore autem tempore, cum esset Iulianus Apostata in imperio sublimatus, dedit Iudeis licenciam ad reedificandum templum quia odio habuit Cristianos, licet ipse Cristianus primo
15 fuerit et postea a fide apostauit. Templo vero reedificato, dei nutu venit terre motus et iterum subuertit templum.

Tempore tandem Adriani imperatoris a gente eiusdem imperatoris reparata est ciuitas Ierusalem et templum restitutum in forma qua constructum fuerat a Salamone. Sed non permisit
20 tamen imperator Iudeos ibidem habitare sed tantum Cristianos, quamuis enim Cristianus non esset, tamen Cristianos plus amauit ceteris nacionibus post gentem secte sue. . . .

Saraceni vero faciunt huic templo reuerenciam magnam et dicunt locum sanctum esse. Et quando ingrediuntur illuc dis-
25 calciant se, sepius flectentes genua. Quod socii mei et ego videntes discalciauimus nos, quia arbitra[ba]mur quod nos multo forcius hoc facere deberemus ob diuinam reuerenciam quam infideles. . . .

26 nos quia arbitrabamur] et nos quia arbitramur

or be ony othir man, as sone as they sen it, thei bowyn doun therto reuerently and resseyuyn hem and leyn hem on here hed and thanne kyssyn hem and redyn hem on here knein and ordeynyn in alle thynge to don reuerence to the bryngere of the lettere aftir the te[f. 22ᵛᵇ]nour of hym.

NARRACIO TITUS

Tytus, that was the sone of Vaspasianus the Emperour of Rome, segit Ierusalem for they dede Crist to the deth withoutyn the assent of the Emperour. He tok the cete and brend it and the Temple, distroyed it and alle the Iewys, that is for to say xi.ᶜ· thousand. And al the remenant of hem he tok hem and put hem in pryson, and seld xxx. for a peny for he herde seyn that they selde Crist for xxx. penys.

Yit aftir this, long tyme, the Emperour Iulianus that was Apostata hade forsake the Cristen lawe. He yaf hym leue to reparayle the Temple ayen for he hatyd Cristen men, al thow he hadde ben Cristene hymself before. And whanne it was reparailed ayen honurabely, ther cam ay thour the sonde of God an [f. 23ʳᵃ] erthedene that fylde doun ayen al the Temple and clene fordede it.

And yet in the tyme of Adrian, that was Emperour of Rome, hese men reparayledyn the cete of Ierusalem and restoreden the Temple and madyn it newe ageyn in maner it was fyrst, rial and noble. But the Emperour wolde neuere letyn Iewis dwelle therin but only the Cristene men, al thow he were [neuere] Cristen hymself.

The Sarasynis don gret reuerence to the Temple and callyn [it] her stede. And whan they comyn into that Temple, they knelyn oftyn sythis and puttyn of here shon for gret reuerence. And whan myn felawys and I sewyn hem so don, we dedyn of oure, and [me thouȝte] that it was more skil that we Cristen men dedyn so reuerence than [f. 23ʳᵇ] the Sarasynys.

1 othir man] *R* manere of state   4–5 of the lettere] *R om.*   8 Crist] *MS.* cristen   9 assent] *R* assent or leefe   10 distroyed it and] *R* also and distroied   13 penys] *R* pens and he dide in the same manere of hem   14 Yit aftir this, long tyme] *R* long tyme aftir this Titus come   20 clene] *R* al tocleef it and   23 rial and] *R* more realle and more   25 neuere] *MS. om.*   27–28 callyn it] *MS.* callynd   29 shon] *R* hosen and her shoon   31 oure] *R* our harneys but oonly our shoon   me thouȝte] *MS. om.*

Ex altera parte templi rupis que solebat vocari Moriak, postea vocabatur Botell, vbi archa dei cum aliis reliquiis Iudeorum seruabatur. Archam istam cum reliquiis Tytus abduxit et Romam portari fecit post destructionem ciuitatis. In archa vero erant
5 tabule Moysi et virga Aaron et [f. 48ra] virga Moysi qua Rubrum Mare diuisit in transitu filiorum Israel. Cum ipsa quoque virga percussit petram et fluxerunt aque. Fecit et alia plura mirabilia in conspectu eorum. Erat autem in archa dei manna vna cum ornamentis Aaron pontificis et vna cum lamina aurea quadrata
10 cum duodecim lapidibus preciosis et pixis. Vna eciam ibi erat de viridi iaspide, continens septem figuras nominum dei, et plures alie reliquie et res preciose que ad diuinum cultum pertinebant. . . .

[f. 49va] Istud Mare Mortuum diuidit terram Iudee et Arabiam,
15 et protenditur hoc mare a Zoara vsque ad Arabiam. Aqua huius maris valde amara est et salsa, et si terra humectetur hac aqua non portabit fructum. Hec aqua variat sepius suum colorem. . . . Et vocatur ideo Mare Mortuum quia non currit, nec homo nec animal viuens mori potest in illo. . . . Hoc vero sepius fuerat ex-
20 pertum, fuerunt enim qui morti erant addicti ibidem proiecti frequenter et viuebant iii. vel iiii. diebus in mari illo nec mori poterant, eo quod aqua ista nichil viuum in se recipit. De ipsa quoque aqua nullus bibere potest. Et si ferrum proiceretur in ipso mari cicius supra nataret. Pluma vero proiecta mergeretur
25 in profundum, quod videtur contra naturam. Sic et pro peccato quod contra naturam erat, scilicet propter sodomiam, submerse sunt et delete ciuitates olim ibi existentes, videlicet Sodoma et Gomorra cum aliis vicinis.

11 viridi] viride

NOTA DE ARCHA DEI

On that othir syde of the Temple is a roche that was wone to ben callid Mariak, where Cristis *archa* with othere relikis where kept. This eche ark with the relikis Titus tok awey and dede bryngyn hem to Rome aftir distroccioun of the cete of Ierusalem. 5
In that ark were the tablys of Moises and Aronys yerde and the yerde of Moyses, wherwith he departede the Rede Se whan the childeryn of Israel enteredyn thedyr whan the kyng Pharoo folwede hem. And with that eche yerde Moyses strok on the dreye roche whan the watir com out rennande gret foysoun to 10 hem. And in that eche ark was manna, that men callyn aungellis mete, with manye ornamentis of Aaron the bischop [f. 23va] and a table of gold and manye other relykis and preciouse thyngis that parteynyn to Godis werkis.

NOTA DE MARE MORTUO 15

In that contre is a watyr that is callyd the Dede Se, the whiche that departyth the lond of Iuda and the lond of Arabye. The watir of that see is ful bittyr and salt, and if that watir be cast vpon the erthe, it sha*l* bere no freut. The watyr chongith ofte colour. And it is callid the Dede See for it stondyth ay stylle and 20 neythir ebbith ne flowith. And neythir men ne beste that is cast therinne may deyen, for that hath ben prouyd oftyn tyme with queke men and bestis that han ben cast therin iii. or iiii. dayes and nyghtys and yet myghte neuere deyc. Of that watyr may [f. 23vb] no man dry[n]ke. And if that yryn be cast therin, it 25 wele fletyn aboue; and if that a fedyr be cast therin, it wele synke to the grond. And that semyth ayen kynde. Right so [was] the synne ayen kynde that was vsed in the cetes of Sodom and Gomore that were sonkyn in that plase, there they stodyn, for vengeaunce of the synne. 30

4 This] *MS.* ther is   5 cete of Ierusalem] *R* temple and of the citee, and there a man may hem se in Lente ȝif he be there   9 hem] *R* hem and therinne he was drowned   10 roche] *R* ston bifore the Mount Synay   12 mete] *R* mete or aungellis foode   16 In that contre] *R* nere biside withoute the cite of Ierusalem   19 shal] *MS.* shan   20 it is callid the Dede See] for *R om.*   24 may] *MS.* may may   25 drynke] *MS.* dryke   26 aboue] *R* aboue the watir   27 was] *MS. om.*   29–30 that were sonkyn ... synne] *R* the wiche citees sonken and were drowned for her synne, the wiche synne is ȝit called *Sodomiticum Peccatum* aftir the citee of Sodom

Iuxta litus maris illius crescunt arbores poma portantes colore et aspectu pulcherima, quibus tamen incisis [nichil] reperitur nisi puluis et cinis in signum ire dei qui ciuitates et terram loci illius combussit igne infernali. Quidam vocant
5 hoc mare Lachdalfend, alii vero flumen putridum quia aqua illius fetida est. Erant olim in hoc, vt dixi, pulcherrime ciuitates inter quas precipue erant quinque, scilicet Sodoma, Gomorra, Aldamia, Sobayn, et Segor. Que ad preces Loth saluata fuit pro magna parte, que sita fuerat in monte, et adhuc cernitur vestigium
10 eius in aqua claro tempore, videlicet pars murorum eius. . . .

[f. 50ra] Et paulo superius est villa nomine Sabach. In locis illis habitant plures Cristiani sub tributo. Inde transitur ad Nazareth vnde dominus cognomen habuit, et de Ierusalem vsque illuc iter est trium dierum. . . .

15 [f. 50vb] Scias autem quod beata virgo dominum peperit anno quintodecimo etatis sue, et cum eo conuersata est triginta tribus annis et tribus mensibus. Et post eius passionem superuixit illa viginti quatuor annis. . . .

Est tamen ibi locus quem appellant scolam dei vbi dominus
20 discipulos docebat secreta celestia. Ad pedem montis Melchisedech qui fuit rex Salem, que nunc est Ierusalem, qui eciam fuit sacerdos dei altissimi, obuiauit Abrahe in descensum montis post cedem Amalech. In hoc monte dominus transfiguratus est coram Petro, Iohanne, et Iacobo vbi viderunt Moysen et
25 Helyam cum ipso loquentes.

    2 nichil] *om.*   22 obuiauit] et obuiauit

Ner besyde that watir growyn treis that beryn appillis that aryn fayre to the syght. And whan men cuttyn hem, thanne shul they fynde withinne hem not but poudyr and aschis in tokenynge of wrethe of Crist, that he brente the ceteis and the lond of that place with the fer of helle. In that stede, as I seyde before, were 5 fayre ceteis amongis hem, [f. 24ra] of whiche there were v. pryncipal, that is for to say, Sodom and Gomor, Aldama, Soboym, and Segor. But the moste party of Segor was sauid at the preyer of Loth, for it stod vpon an hey hil, and men may in cler wedyr and fair sen a party of the wallis of the cete. Forsothe 10 I say hem with mynne eyen.

Vperemore into the contre is a toun that is called Soboak where manye Cristene men dweldyn sumtyme and wonedyn vndyr tribut. From thene men shal passyn to Nazareth wher Crist hadde his surname, and from Ierusalem thedyr is but 15 iii. iurneis to gon in iii. dayes.

NOTA DE ETATE BEATE MARIE VIRGINYS

Wete ye wel that oure lady Sente Marie whan sche bar Crist was [xv.] yer of eld, and with hym sche was in erthe [f. 24rb] xxx. and iii. yerr and iii. monethis. And aftyr hys passioun sche 20 leuede in erthe [x]xiiii. yer. And so sche leuede in erthe lx[x]. yer and [to] and iii. monethis.

And there is a place that men callyn the Skole of God where Crist techede hese apostolis the priuite of heuene. And at that mountis fot Melchisadek, that was kyng of Ierusalem and Cristis 25 prest, mette Abraham in the comynge doun from the mount. And in that lond oure lord transfigurede hymself byfore Petir and Iamys and Ion whan they seye hym spekyn with Moyses and Elye.

1 treis] *R* fair trees   appillis] *R* frute as applis   2 hem] *R* hem on sundre
4 brente] *R* drowned   4–5 the lond . . . helle] *R* brent hem with the fire of helle for vengeauce of that synne   6–7 amongis hem . . . pryncipal] *R* amonge alle other v. the principal citees were distroied
10 cler] *R* fair   and fair] *R om.*   14 tribut] *R* trybute of Pharoo
19 xv.] *MS.* fortene   21 xxiiii.] *MS.* xiiii   21–22 lxx. yer and to] *MS.* lx. yer and on   24–26 And at . . . prest] *R* neer ther biside is the mount of Melchisedek, called aftir the king of Ierusalem and aftir Goddis prest, the wiche   28 Ion] *R* Iohn as the gospelle of Seint Mathewe bereth witnesse

In monte ipso et loco in die iudicii tubas canent quatuor angeli, quorum sonitu mortui suscitabuntur et venient coram iudice in vallem Iosephath die sancto pasche hora resureccionis Cristi. Et incipiet iudicium hora qua descendit [f. 51ra] ad inferos
5 et spoliauit infernum, nam simili modo spoliabit mundum, amicos suos perducens ad gloriam et reprobos ad perpetuam penam. . . .

Super hoc mare dominus ambulauit quando Petro dixit, *Modice fidei, quare* et cetera. Et post resureccionem suam
10 apparuit discipulis in hoc mari piscantibus, et impleuit rethe eorum magnis piscibus quando optulerunt ei partem piscis assi et fauum mellis. In hoc mari piscatores erant Petrus et Andreas, Iacobus et Iohannes quando vocauit eos, ac illi relictis rethibus suis continuo secuti sunt eum. Iuxta ciuitatem Tyberiadis est
15 mons vbi dominus saciauit quinque milia hominum de quinque panibus et duobus piscibus. . . .

[f. 51rb] In hac regione Syrie sunt hec regna contenta, videlicet Iudea prouincia, Palestine, Galilee, Sem, Sicilie, et alie plures prouincie. In hac patria et pluribus aliis consuetudo talis ibidem
20 habetur quod quando duo prouincie guerram habent adinuicem et altera pars obsidet ciuitatem uel castellum, loco nunciorum ad deferendum litteras inter partes vtuntur ministerio columbarum; ligant enim litteras in collo vnius columbe et permittunt eam volare. Et ipsa frequenti vsu assuefacta litteras defert ad locum
25 destinatum et iterum reuertitur ad eos apud quos nutrita fuerat.

Inter Saracenos quoque multi Cristiani habitant in diuersis locis, quiquidem Cristiani diuersis ritibus et consuetudinibus

NOTA DE IUDICIO

In that eche mount and in that eche stede vpon the day of dome the iiii. angelis schul blewe here trompis, and at the sound of hem alle [f. 24va] tho that arn dede shuln risyn and come beforn the Iuge in that vale of Iosephath vpon the Pask Day in the tyme of the resurexioun of Crist. And the iugement shal be youyn that tyme that he yede to helle and spolyede it, and in that eche maner he shal [spoyle] this world and takyn hese frendys and ledyn hem to ioye withoutyn ende, and iuge the wekede men withoutyn ende.

Oure lord yede vpon the se that is clepid Tiber[i]adis whan he seyde to Petyr, *Modico fidei, quare dubitasti?*, that is to seyne Man of litel feyth, whi dredist the? And aftyr his resorexioun he aperid to hese disciplis fyschende in that se and fillyde here net with grete fisch whan they proferedyn hym part of an rostid fysch and an hony comb. In that tyme were fis[f. 24vb]chende Petyr, Andrew, Iamys, and Ion. Whan Crist callede hem, they leftyn here netys and folwede hym. Besyde the cete of Tiberiadis is the hil there Crist fedde v.$^{m.}$ men with v. lovis of barly bred and ii. fischis.

In the rew[m]e of Cirie are these reumys contynued, that is for to seye, Iuda prouyncie, Palestine, Galile, Cecile, and othere manye prouyncis. Among these contreis and manye other there aboutyn is swich a custom that whan that to remys arn wrothe togedere and eythir syde bescge castel or toun, that in the stede of massangeris to gon betwen partyis they ordeyne dowis for to beryn letterys; and byndyn hem in the dowys nekke and letyn the dowe fleen forth. And the dowe [f. 25ra] thorw comoun custome and vsage fleit to the tothere partye. And whan the letteris ben takyn from her, [sche] flye ageyn where sche was norished.

Among the Saresenys dwellyn manye Cristen men in dyuerse placis, the wheche that vsyn dyuerse lawis and costomys aftir

5 come] *MS*. cone   Pask] *MS*. palk   8 shal spoyle] *MS*. spoliede shal
10 withoutyn ende] *R* vnto perpetuel peyne   11 Tiberiadis] *MS*. Tiberadis   20 ii.] *R* foure   21 rewme] *MS*. rewe   22 Galile] *MS. and R* Galice   24 wrothe] *R* at werre   25 castel] *R* castel or cite   30 her] *MS*. hem   sche] *MS*. they   where sche was norished] *R* fro whennes she come froo vnto hir place thoru3 custom and vsage   31 Among] *R* Now wole I telle of the bileeue of Sarazeyns that arn Cristen in partie, for among

vtuntur secundum tradiciones maiorum suorum. Omnes tamen sunt baptizati et credunt in deum, patrem et filium et spiritum sanctum. Errant tamen comuniter in aliquo articulo fidei nostre.

Quidam enim vocantur Iacobite quos apostolus Iacobus
5 conuertit et Iohannes euangelista baptizauit. Hii afferunt quod confessio soli deo facienda est, quia dicit scriptura, *Confitebor tibi, domine, in toto corde meo* et cetera, et alibi, *Delictum meum cognitum tibi feci* et cetera. Vnde quando isti confiteri volunt, ponunt iuxta se focum et mittunt in eum incensum et fumo
10 ascendente confitentur deo, veniam petentes.

Sunt alii qui vocantur Suriani. Isti fidem tenent medio modo inter nos et Grecos. Barbas nutriunt ut Greci, et conficiunt sacramentum de pane fermentato et litteris grecis vtuntur. Confessionem faciunt vt Iacobite.

15 Alii vero sunt qui Georgii dicuntur quos sanctus Georgius ad fidem conuertit, quem et ipsi [f. 51va] venerantur et colunt pre ceteris sanctis. Isti vtuntur coronis rasis in capitibus, clerici quidem rotundis, laici vero quadratis. Fidem autem tenent vt Greci. . . . Alii Indici qui sunt de terra Presbiteri
20 Iohannis. Vniuersi autem Cristiani vocantur et plures articulos nostre fidei obseruant. In quibusdam vero discrepant a nobis. Omnes autem differencias eorum longum esset enarrare. . . .

* *From Hunterian Museum MS. T. 4. 1, ff. 294^v–5*

Nunc de secta et lege Saracenorum aliquid dicere volo, scilicet
25 de eorum credulitate et fide, prout habetur in libro legis eorum qui dicitur Alkoranus, quem librum Machometa eis tradidit.

* See Introduction, p. xix.

the constitucionys and the ordenaunce of the reumys ther they dwelle. Neuertheless all are they baptised and trowyn in God, Fadyr and Sone and Holy Gost, and alle ere they in sum artikele of the feith.

NOTA DE IACOBITES

There ben Cristene men that aryn callede Iacobites, the which that Seyn Iamys the apostel conuertede, and Seynt Ion the ewangelist baptisede hem. They afermyn that confessioun shulde be mad only to Crist for that the Holy Scripture seyth, *Confitebor tibi,* [f. 25rb] *domine, in toto corde meo, et alibi, Delictum meum tibi cognitum feci, et cetera.* And therfore whan the Iacobites welyn ben shreuyn, they takyn fer and rechelis, and whan the smoke goth vpward, they sey, 'I schryue me to God and aske foryeuenesse of myn synne.'

Othere Cristene men that men calle Surrany, they holdyn oure lawe in mene betwen vs and the Grekis. And the Barbaryes holdyn the lawe that the Grekys don.

GEORGICY

Yit ther ben othere Cristen men that Seynt George conuertid, and hym they honour to don deuocioun to beforn alle othere halwyn, and they aryn callede Gorgicy. And eche man of hem hath his croun shauyn, the clerkys rounde and the lewede men foure cornerede. They holdyn the Grekys lawe. [f. 25va] They are of Pretir Ionys lond, and aryn Cristen men and manye of oure artikelys holdyn and vsyn. But natheles in manye poyntis they varien from vs awey. Al here differens wer long to telle.

NOTA DE OBSERUANCIA ET SECTA LEGIS SARAZINORUM

Now of the lawe and of the obseruaunce that the Sarasynys holdyn sumwhat wele I tellyn yow and shewyn yow, as it is recordit and wretyn in the bok of here lawe that is callid Alkarane,

---

3 ere] *MS.* are   4 the feith] *R* our feyth but nou3t alle troweth stedefastly   9 Crist] *R* God and nou3t vnto prest   10 *tibi*] *MS.* tibor tibi   14 myn synne] *R* alle my synnes and thus they doo contynuelly   17 don] *R* doen in al manere customs and vsagis   19 men] *R* men that arn callid Georgicis   23 Grekys lawe] same lawe that the Grekes doen in al manere thing   23–26 They are . . . telle] *R om.*

In ipso libro inter alia continetur quod boni post mortem ibunt in paradisum, mali vero in infernum. Et hoc credunt omnes Saraceni. Et si quis quesierit ab eis de quo paradiso loquitur, respondent quod de illo paradiso qui est locus deliciarum vbi
5 reponuntur omnia genera fructuum omni tempore anni, et sunt ibi fluuii emanantes lacte et melle, vino et aqua. Sunt ibi palacia pulcherima que dabunt cuilibet iuxta meritum suum. Et habebit quilibet nonaginta vxores et puellas formosas, cum quibus si voluerit cubabit et semper eas inueniet
10 virgines.

Item, Saraceni credunt incarnacionem et libenter loquitur de beata virgine, dicentes quod fuit ipsa edocta per angelum, et quod Gabriel angelus dixit ei quod fuit preelecta a deo ante constitucionem mundi ad concipiendum et pariendum Iesum
15 Cristum quem et peperit, et virgo mansit. Hoc bene testatur predictus liber Alkorani. Dicunt eciam quod Iesus locutus fuit quam cito natus fuit, et quod erat sanctus propheta et verus in factis et dictis, benignus et [f. 295] pius, iustus et innocens ab omni labe peccati.

20 Affirmant quoque quod angelo annunciante incarnacionem puella turbata est in sermone eius maxime propter metum cuiusdam malefici qui vocabatur Takina, qui tunc temporis circuibat per diuersa patrie loca circumueniens et infestans iuuenculas et illudens eis eius incantacionibus. Et ideo Maria
25 adiurauit angelum vt diceret si ipse esset Takina vel non.

Item, dicit Alkoranus quod cum Maria peperisset sub arbore

the whiche bok of here lawe Makamede, that made here lawe, yaf hem.

In that bok among alle othere thyngis is continu[e]d, aftir here deth goode men shuln gon to paradys and wikkede men to the peyne of helle. This trowyn stedestly Sarazenys. And if ony [f. 25ᵛᵇ] man aske hem whiche paradis is, they answeryn and seyn that paradis is a place of delyces wher alle maner of kynde of freut is foundyn al the tyme of the yer, and wher mylk, hony, wyn, and watyr is aboundaunt eueremore, and where fayre placis arn to yeuyn to euery man aftyr that he hath deserued. And euery man shal haue iiii.ˣˣ· wyuis and maydenys, and with hem he shal ly whan he wele and eueremore he shal fyndyn hem virgynes. This trowe they alle that thei shul hauyn in paradys, and this is ayen oure lawe.

The Sarazynys trowyn in the carnacioun, and gladly wele they speke of the virgyne Marie and seyn that she was lerid by the angel, and that the angel Gabriel seyde to here that she was chose of God before the world [f. 26ʳᵃ] was mad for to conseyue Iesu Crist and for to bere hym whom that she bar, and she maydyn and virgyne as beforn. This witnessith the bok of Alkorane. Thei seyn also Crist spak as sone as he was born, and that he was and is an holy prophete and a very in wordis and in dedys, blissed and happi, rightwis and innocent of alle maner of fallyng in synne.

They affermyn also that whan the angel grette oure lady that the virgyne was aschamyd and abasched of hese wordys. And they seye it was because of a mysdoere that was that tyme in that contre there aboute, that thour his chauntement he begilede yonge wemen [ofte sythes], that men callyn Tagyna. And therfore Mary coniourrede hym that he shulde sey here yif he were [f. 26ʳᵇ] Tagyna or not.

Here bok of Alkarane seith that whan Marye hadde child

1 that made here lawe] *R* made that was a gret clerk of her lawe, but he was a fals prophete. And in this book of Alcoroun he made and   3 continued] *MS.* continud   4 paradys] *R* heuene out of this worlde   5 of helle] *R* euerelastynge   7-8 of kynde] *R om.*   9-10 fayre placis] *R* paleis redy made   10 deserued] *R* diserued in this worlde hire   12 ly] *MS.* ly by   10-15 carnacioun] *R* birthe of Crist and his carnacioun   20 as] *R* aftir the birthe as she was   20-21 This ... Alkorane] *R om.*   23 alle] *R* any   25 oure] *MS.* oure oure   29 ofte sythes] *MS.* of the cetes   30 Mary] *MS.* Mars

palmarum, satis verecundabatur et plorabat dicens se velle mori. Et confestim infans locutus est et consolabatur eam, dicens ne timeat quia in ea deus recondidit sacramentum suum ad salutem mundi. Et eciam in aliis pluribus locis testatur Alkoranus quod Iesus locutus est statim cum esset natus. Dicit quoque liber ipse quod Iesus fuit a deo missus vt esset in speculum et exemplum omnibus hominibus.

Loquitur et predictus liber de die iudicii, quomodo venturus est deus ad iudicandum omnes gentes; bonos quidem trahet ad partem suum et glorificabit, malos vero dampnabit ad penas inferni.

Item, inter omnes prophetas Iesum dicunt excellenciorem et propinquiorem deo; et quod ipse fecit euangelia, in quibus est salutaris doctrina et veritas; et quod Iesus extitit plus quam propheta, et vixit sine peccato, illuminans cecos, mundans leprosos, suscitans mortuos; et quod totus ascendit in celum. Et librum euangeliorum, cum attingere possint, maxime vbi scribitur euangelium *Missus est angelus*, cum magna deuocione venerantur et osculantur.

Ieiunant quolibet anno mense integro et tunc non comedunt nisi de nocte, et abstinent a mulieribus; infirmi autem non coguntur ieiunare.

Loquitur insuper liber Alkorani de Iudeis quos detestatur eo quod credere noluerint Iesum a deo fuisse missum. Dicunt eciam quod male menciuntur Iudei de Maria et de filio eius Iesu, dicentes quod eum crucifixerunt; *non enim crucifixerunt ipsum Iesum quia hunc ascendere fecit deus ad se sine morte, sed transfigurauit Iesus vultum suum et formam corporis sui in Iudam Scarioth, et hunc Iudei crucifixerunt putantes quod Iesum crucifixissent.

Iesus vero receptus est in celum viuus et ita iterum descendet

* At this point the text of MS. Royal 13 E. IX is resumed.

vndyr a palme tre, that sche was wondirly ashamyd and gradde and seyde that sche wolde be ded. And as faste the child spak and conforted here and seyde to here, 'Be not aferd, for in the Crist hath had his sacrement for the helpe of this world.' The bok of Alkarane seyth [Crist] was sent for to ben merour and ensample to alle men.

That ech bok seyth and spekyth of the day of dome, how that God shal come and iuge alle folk that are goode and drawe to his parti and gloriefye hym in ioye withoutyn ende. And the wekkede men he schal dampnen to pyne of helle withoutyn ende.

Among alle the prophetis they holdyn Ion te ewangelist the [f. 26ᵛᵃ] moste excellent man and the moste nest to God, and that he made the gospel *Missus est angelus Gabriel*, and with gret deuocioun they kisse the gospel and worshepyn it gretly and honurably.

They fastyn euery yer a monyth al holly and etyn no mete neueremore tyl euyn, and forberyn wemen that tyme; but seke men ben not compellede therto for to fastyn.

The bok of A[l]karane seith th[a]t Iesu Crist made the euangelye, in the whiche is helful thing and sothfastnesse, and that Iesu Crist was more and grettere than anothir prophete and leuede withoutyn synne, and that he yaf to blynde men here syght; he helede hem that were in meselrye and reysede dede men from deth to lyue, and that he yede al holy to heuen.

[f. 26ᵛᵇ] The bok of Alkorane spekyth of the Iewis that wele not leuyn that Iesu Crist was sent from God. That bok seith that the Iewis lyen falsely of Marye and of here sone Iesu, that seith that they dedyn hym to the deth on the cros; for they crucifiedyn not Iesu Crist, but God tok hym vp to hym al hol withoutyn deth and transfygured the forme and the likne*s*se of his body into Iudas Skariot, and hym that was Iudas the Iewis crucifiedyn a[n]d trowyn that it was Iesu.

They seyn tha[t] Iesu Crist was takyn into heuene quik, and

4 sacrement] *R* priuetee and his sacrement   5 Crist] *MS. om.*   13 moste excellent man] *R* worthiest and moost excellent bothe be west and be est   18 wemen] *R* wyne   19 fastyn] *R* faste ageyns her wille but if they wel may doo it   20 Alkarane] *MS.* akarane   that] *MS.* tht   25 lyue] *MS.* hyue   31 transfygured] *MS.* transfyguredyn   liknesse] *MS.* liklesse   33 and] *MS.* ad   34 that] *MS.* tha

iudicare mundum. Sed dicunt Saraceni quod istud ignorant Cristiani, credentes insipienter quod Iesus ipse fuerat crucifixus. Hec omnia in predicto Alcorano continentur. Dicunt quoque Saraceni quod si Iesus crucifixus fuisset, deus contra suam iusticiam fecisset permittendo [f. 53va] scilicet talem innocentem mori sine culpa. Et in hoc dicunt nos errare quia non patitur dei iusticia ut innocens tali morte condempnetur.

Confitentur quidem omnia opera Cristi ac dicta fuisse bona et vera et miracula eius preclara; beatam quoque virginem sanctam fuisse et bonam immaculatam post partum sicut ante.

Vnde quia tam prope accedunt fidei in hiis et in aliis multis, ideo solent facilius conuerti per predicacionem Cristianorum. Bene sciunt per prophecias quod lex Machometi deficiet et lex Cristianorum durabit usque in finem.

Si quis vero eos interrogauerit de fide eorum, scilicet quomodo credunt, sic respondent, 'Nos vero credimus deum creatorem celi et terre, qui omnia fecit et sine quo nichil est factum. Et credimus diem iudicii quando recipiet vnusquisque mercedem secundum opera sua. Credimus et vera esse omnia que deus per orationem sanctorum prophetarum locutus est hominibus.'

Preterea Machometus precepit in libro Alcorani quod quilibet haberet tres uel quatuor vxores, sed nunc plures accipiunt scilicet vsque ad nouem. De concubinis vero tot habeat vnusquisque quot sustentare poterit. Si vxor alicuius adulterata fuerit, potest eam abicere et aliam ducere. Oportet tamen quod det ei porcionem de bonis suis.

21 quod] quod quod

yit he shal comyn into erthe and iuge the world, but this wot not the Cristen men but trowyn onhappily that they crucifiedyn Iesu Crist. Alle these poyntys arn [f. 27ra] conprehendede in the bok of Alkarane. The Sarasynys seyn that if Iesu Crist hadde ben crucified, that God hadde don thanne ayens rightfulnesse 5 for to suffere swich an innocent deyen withoutyn gilt. And they sey that we erryn, for Goddis rightfulnesse wolde not suffere that swich an innocent shulde ben dampned to swich a deth.

They arn wel beknowyn that alle the [werkes] of Crist and hese wordys wern and arn soth and hese merakellis verray and 10 clere, and the blyssede virgine Godis modyr Seynt Marye holy and good and vnwemmed aftyr here byrthe as byfore.

Therfore me thynkyth sithe that they gon so ner oure feith in this and in othere, meche sonere they shuldyn ben conuertid by oure lawe [f. 27rb] yif they haddyn good prechyng and tech- 15 yng of Cristene men. They wetyn wel and seyn that and fyndyn by here prophete that Makamedis lawe shal faylyn hem and that the Cristene lawe shal lastyn eueremore.

NOTA DE CREDENCIA SARAZYNORUM

If that ony man aske hem of here belewe and how they trowyn, 20 they answeren and sey, 'We trowyn in God that made heuen and erthe and al that is, withoutyn whom nothing ne is mad. And we trowyn the day of dome shal come wer euery man shal han his mede aftyr his desert. We trowyn also verrayly that al the werk that God made and alle the wordis that God spak to the 25 peple arn sothe by the prophetys whan they wen[f. 27va]tyn here in erthe.'

Makamede comaundede in the bok of Alkarane that euery man shulde han iii. or iiii. wyuys and, at the fertheste, to the nombre of ix. and no mo. But of concubynys euery man may 30 taken as manye as he may gouerne; fo[r] if that ony manys wyf let ony othir man ly by here, thanne it were lefful to here hosbonde to puttyn here awey from hym and takyn hym anothir

8 deth] *R* spitous deeth 9 werkes] *MS. om.* 11 the blyssede virgine] *R om.* 14 this] *R* thes poyntis othere] *R* manye othir 16–17 and fyndyn by here prophete that] *R om.* 18 lastyn eueremore] *R* hem holde 24 desert] *R* dede 28 Makamede] *R* but Makomede that is our prophete and made our lawe 31 for] *MS.* fo 33 from hym] *R* ȝif the soth be affermed

De trinitate vero liber Alcorani nichil loquitur; dicunt enim quod deus verbum habet, aliter esset mutus; confitentur quod spiritum habet, aliter esset sine vita. Item, quando loquitur ali[quis] eis de incarnacione, quomodo per verbum angeli misit deus sapienciam suam in terris, que eciam beate virgini obumbrauit, et quomodo per verbum dei mortui suscitabuntur et resurgent, respondent et dicunt omnia ista vera esse et quod magnam virtutem habet verbum dei, et qui ignorat verbum dei ignorat deum . . . .

Dicunt quod Abraham fuit amicus dei et Moyses fuit prolocutor dei; Iesus Cristus fuit verbum et spiritum dei; Machometa fuit nuncius dei; et horum quatuor Iesus Cristus fuit dignior et excellencior.

Et sic patet quod isti Saraceni habent plures articulos nostre fidei, licet imperfecte, et ideo sunt de facili conuertibiles ad fidem nostram, precipue illi qui habent noticiam scripturarum. Habent enim euangelia et totam bibliam scriptam in lingua sara[f. 53vb]cenica, sed non intelligunt sacram scripturam spiritualiter sed ad litteram tantum sicut Iudei. Item, dicunt Saraceni quod Iudei maligni sunt quia legem sibi diuinitus datam per Moysen violauerunt. Similiter Cristianos dicunt peruersos quia non custodiunt precepta euangelica que dedit eis Iesus Cristus.

    4 aliquis] ali   6 suscitabuntur] suscitabantur

in here stede. And yit behouyth hym to yeuyn here a porcioun of his good.

The bok of Alkarane spekyth [no3t] of the Trinyte and seyth that God hath word and ellis he wer doum, and that he hath the Holy Gost and ellis hym behouyth to ben withoutyn lyf. And 5 whan ony man spekyth to him of the incarnacioun [f. 27vb] of Crist, how thour the wordys of the angel Crist sente wit and wysdam into erthe and v*m*belappid the virgine Marye, and how that thour Godis word alle tho that arn dede shuln rysen ageyn, thanne they seye that al this they trowe wel that it is soth, and 10 that Gody[s] word hath ful gret vertu, and he that knowith [not] Godys word knowith not God.

They seye also that Abraham was Godys frend and Moyses was Godys foregoere and his spekere and Iesu Crist was Godis sone and Godys word, and Makamede was the verray mas- 15 sanger of Crist, and that of alle these foure Iesu Crist was the worthieste and the most excilent.

Thus it shewith that the Sarazinys han manye artikelis of oure trouthe, al thow it be not parfit, and therfor it were ligh[t]ere to bryngen hem to oure feith [f. 28ra] and namely tho that ar lettered 20 men and han konyng and knowynge of her scripture. They han among hem alle the ewangeilis and the prophetis and al the Byble wretyn in Sarasynys langage, but they vndyrstonde not holy scripture spiritually. The Sarasynys seyn that Iewis arn ille and cursede for they han broke here lawe that Moyses yaf hem, 25 and the Cristen men arn not goode for they holde not the comaundement of the euangelye that Crist bad hem.

Trowith this wel, for this haue I bothe herd and sen with mynne eyne and mynne eryn and myne felawys that were with me that weryn of dyuers regionys, for wete ye wel that al be it 30 wondyr to youre heryng, I am not set to lye yow lesyngis. Trowith yif ye welyn.

3 no3t] *MS om.*   5 lyf] *R* liff and thus trowe they alle fully   6 incarnacioun] *MS.* incrarnacioun   8 v*m*belappid] *MS.* vnbelappid   9 word] *MS.* world   ageyn] *R* ageyne to liff   11 Godys] *MS.* gody   not] *MS. om.*   14 foregoere and His spekere] *R* forespeker   14–15 Godis sone and] *R om.*   18 that] *MS.* that that   19 lightere] *MS.* lighere   21 and knowynge] *R om.*   22 alle the ewangeilis] *R* the foure euangelistis   24–25 ille and] *R om.*   25 yaf] *R* toke hem and 3af   27 bad hem] *R* bad to be doen in dede   28–32 Trowith this ... ye welyn] *R om.*

Et nunc dicam quid michi fecit soldanus quadam die in camera sua, omnibus nobilibus suis absentibus et nullis presentibus ibidem preter me, eo quod voluit habere mecum colloquium secretum. Interrogauit itaque me quomodo Cristianitas se 5 habebat in partibus nostris, et ego respondi quod bene, per graciam dei.

Ad quod ille inquit, 'Non est ita, nam flamines vestri non curant seruire deo in bonis operibus sicut deberent; ipsi preber[e deb]ent laicis exemplum bene viuendi, et econtra magis dant 10 eis exemplum tocius iniquitatis. Ideo diebus festiuis, quando *deb*eret populus [ire] ad templum ad seruiendum deo suo, tunc vadant ad tabernas et occupant totum diem et noctem in potacionibus et comesacionibus, sicut essent bestie que nesciunt quando satis est, et postea prorumpunt in verba contumeliosa, 15 in rixas et pugnas alterutrum usque ad mutuam interfectionem frequenter.

'Nituntur [eciam] Cristiani inuicem fraudare, inuicem iniuriari. Et cum hoc sunt ita superbi, vana gloria inflati, quod nesciunt qualiter volunt se vestire, nunc curtis, nunc longis, nunc 20 largis vtuntur vestibus, cum pocius deberent esse [simplices ac] humiles sicut Cristus fuit. Sed longe aliter est, sunt enim ad omne malum proni, superbi, inuidi, gulosi, et luxuriosi, et in tantum auari et cupidi, quod propter modicam pecuniam vendunt filias suas et sorores; proprias eciam vxores aliquando prostituunt 25 et exponunt luxurie. Et vnusquisque vxorem proximi sui violare presumit, nec fidem tenent inuicem, sic quod totam legem quam Cristus eis dedit nequiter transgrediuntur.

'Et certe propter peccata sua totam istam terram sanctam, quam nos nunc tenemus, amiserunt; nam deus tradidit eos in manus 30 nostras propter iniquitates eorum, non propter fortitudinem

---

8–9 prebere debent] preberent   11 deberet populus ire] populus accederet   17 eciam] autem   20 simplices ac] *om.*

NOTA QUALITER SALDANUS LOCUTUS FUIT IOHANNI MAUNDEUILE IN SECRETIS

Now wele I seye wat [f. 28rb] the Soudon dede to me vpon a day in his chambre. He dede alle the lordis and alle the othere men gon out that wer therinne, for that he wolde spekyn with me alone in priuite betwyn vs to. Whan alle men were awey, thanne he askede me how that Cristene men ferdyn in oure contres, and I seyde, 'Wel, thour the grace of God.'

Therto he answerde and seyde, 'Certis, nay not so. For youre clerkis seruyn not youre God in goode werkis as they shulde, for they shuld yeue lewede men exaumple of good leuynge and they yeve hem examplis of alle wikkednesse. For in festyual dayes, whan the peple shulde gon to cherche for to seruyn God, thanne they gon to the tauerne and ocupien al the day, perschauns and al the nyght [f. 28va] aftyr, in dronkenesse and glotenye, as they were bestis out of resoun that wot nat whan they han anow; and aftyr that perchaunce fallynge in fytynge thour dronkenesse with wordys perschaunce tyl euery man sle othir.

'And the Cristen men vsyn euery man to begilyn othir and for to swere othis falsely. And therwith they are so proude and brent with envie and veyn glorie that ye wetyn not werin ye mowe clothyn yow, but now with streyte and now with wyde, now with longe and now with shorte. Ye arn grete glotouns and luxuriouse and so auerous and coueytous that for lytyl mone ye wil selle youre doughteryn and youre systeryn and puttyn hem to foly ayens here wil and ayens youre lawe. And also eche of yow wil takyn otheris wyf, so that the lawe that Crist hath youe yow, ille and falsely [f. 28vb] and wikkidly ye brekyn it.

'And certeynly for youre synne al this Holy Lond ye haue tynt, the which that we han and holdyn. God hath youe it vs into oure hond for youre synnys and not for oure strenthe. And

---

3 the Soudon] *R* this ilke grete king and Sawdon of Babilonye   4–5 alle the lordis ... therinne] *R* doo calle lordes and othir men that in his chaumbre were and bad hem alle that they 'shulde goen out   10 for] *MS*. foy   16 out of resoun] *R* that cowde noo resoun, that knoweth nouȝt good from euel   17 fytynge] *R* fiȝtynge and stryvynge   18 with wordys] *R om*.   20 othis] *R* grete othis   21 brent with envie and veyn glorie] *R* so envious   24 auerous] *R* auerous and coveitous   for lytyl mone] *R om*.   27 yow] *MS*. your   otheris] *R* neyghbores   28 ille and] *R om*.

uel potenciam nostram. Et bene scimus quod cum recte seruirent deo suo et ei placuerint, nullus poterit contra eos stare. Scimus eciam per prophecias quod vos Cristiani recuperaturi estis terram istam in futurum, sed quamdiu taliter viuitis sicut nunc,
5 pro certo non habemus de vobis timorem.'

Tunc quesiui ab illo soldano qualiter ipse ad hanc noticiam status Cristianitatis [f. 54ra] deuenit. Qui fecit reuocare ad cameram suam proceres et nobiles suos, quos prius emiserat, ex quibus quatuor michi designauit magnos dominos, qui ita
10 manifeste et plene retulerunt omnem modum patrie mee et descripserunt alias patrias et terras Cristianitatis, ac si fuissent in ipsis patriis assidue commorantes. Loquebantur eciam, tam ipsi quam soldanus, lingua gallica multum bene, vnde satis mirabar. Intellexique quod soldanus mittit de suis in vniuersas
15 terras in specie mercatorum habentium copiam lapidum preciosorum et aliorum iocalium, qui explorantur modum cuiuslibet regionis. . . .

[f. 54va] Ciuitas Tropazande solebat esse de dominio imperatoris Constantinopolitani, sed quidam potens et diues, quem impera-
20 tor misit ad custodiendum patriam contra Turcos, vsurpauit sibi dominium terre et se appellauit imperatorem ibidem. De ciuitate Trapazande eundum est per Armeniam minorem, si placet.

In hac patria est quoddam castellum antiquum super rupem situm, quod vocatur Castrum Nisi, anglice *sperhauke*, et est
25 contra ciuitatem de Layais et iuxta villam [de] Persipie, que est domini Cruk, multum diuitis et boni Cristiani. Inuenitur in

25 de] *om.*

wel we wete that yif ȝe serwedyn God and youre Lord in due maner and verry lovynge to hym, ther myght no man don ayen yow ne in no maner greue yow ne stondyn ayen yow. Wel we wete by oure prophete that Cristen men shuln recure this lond al hol in tyme comynge, but as longe as they leue so as they don, we ne haue no dred of hem.'

When I Ion Maundeuyle herde the Soudon thus speke, I hadde meche mervayle, and askede hym with gret reuerence how [f. 29ra] he cam to haue so mech knowelechyng of the stat of Cr[i]sten men. Thanne he dede callyn in ageyn alle the lordys and alle othere men that weryn put out beforn. And of hem he assignede iiii. grete lordis for to speke with hym and with me, the which that rekenede to me al the maner of myn contre and discriede to me alle maner of othere contres, as wel and as verayly as they haddyn dwellyd euere therinne. And also the Soudon and they spokyn to me in Frensch langage wel and verayly, so that I vndyrstod wel and verayly at the laste that the Soudon sente his sondis into dyuerse contreis in gyse of marchaundyse with precious stonys and clothis of gold and othere iewelis. And so in swiche maner they wiste in dyuerse reumys to knowe the maner of other [f. 29rb] doingis.

NOTA DE CASTRO NISI

Now wele I tellyn forth of the meruayle of that contre and of Prestir Ionys lond in a contre that is callyd Trapasedye, that was wont sumtyme for to ben of the lordshep of the Emperour of Costantyn the Nobel.

Ther is an old castel stondynge and set vpon a roche that is callyd *Castrum Nisi*, that is for to seye, the Castel of the Sparhauk. It is besyde the cete of Layays and the toun of Cruke, a

---

1 ȝe] *MS.* we, *corrected in margin*   and youre Lord] *R om.*   2 and verry lovynge] *R* that hit were likynge   3 ne in no ... ayen yow] *R om.*
4 prophete] *R* prophecies   10 Cristen] *MS.* Crsten   Cristen men] *R* Cristendome and neuere had ben there   12 with hym and] *R om.*
16-17 to me in Frensch langage wel and verayly] *R* good Frenshe and Latyn
17-18 vndyrstod ... sondis] *R* myȝte wel vnderstonde worde by worde openly inowȝ. Thenne they tolde me how that they sente men   20-21 in dyuerse ... doingis] *R* the manere and the customme of vs. Also the Sawdon hath men with him dwellynge of al manere of speche that Cristen men vsen, three or foure of ilke a speche   23-24 forth ... lond] *R* more of wondris and ferlies and of many dyuers londes, ilis, customs, and rewmes that arn be esten
27 and set] *R om.*   29 Cruke] *R* the cros

castello nisus vnus sedens in pertica, iuxta quem est vna domina pulcherima et decora nimis custodiens nisum. Si quis voluerit hunc nisum custodire vigilando continue septem diebus et septem noctibus [vel, vt alii dicunt, tribus diebus et tribus
5 noctibus] solus sine societate, ad finem dierum veniet ipsa domina et dabit quicquid primo petierit de rebus terrenis. Et hoc sepius expertum est in partibus illis.

Quidam rex Armenie, valens et potens, vigilauit iuxta nisum vsque ad finem dierum. Venit domina et iussit petere quod
10 vellet. Dixit rex se esse satis potentem in omnibus, ideo nichil petere vellet nisi corpus ipsius domine ad voluntatem suam implendam.

Respondit domina, 'Satis insipienter petistis quia corpus meum habere non potes, ego enim non sum [f. 54vb] terrena sed
15 spiritualis.'

Dixit autem rex, 'Certe, scias quod nichil aliud petam.' Et domina inquit, 'Quia de stulticia tua non possum te retrahere, dabo tibi sine peticione quod dignum est. Tu ergo et omnes qui de te descendent guerram habe[b]*i*tis sine forma pacis et
20 eritis semper in subiectione inimicorum vestrorum usque ad nonum gradum, et habebitis penuriam omnium bonorum.'

Et ita factum est, rex enim terre illius numquam habeb*a*t pacem, nec est copia necessariorum ibidem sed viu*u*[n]t sub tributo Saracenorum.

25 Item, filius vnius pauperis venit vigilare nisum, qui petiit vt posset esse fortunatus in arte mercatoria ad lucrandum diuicias, et concessit domina. Postea factus est ditissimus mercator terre illius.

Miles et de Templariis vigilauit nisum ibidem, qui petiit
30 bursam semper plenam auro. Et concessit domina, sed dixit

4–5 vel . . . noctibus] *om.*   5 dierum] septem dierum   19 habebitis] habeatis   22 habebat] habebit   23 viuunt] viuit

riche toun and enabytid with Criste[n] men. Ther is in that
castel a sparhauk sy*t*tande vpon a perke and a fayr lady syttande
besyde the sparhauk, kepande it. And yif ony man wele come
and kepe that sparhauk wakynge contynually vii. nyght and vii.
dayis and as some seyn iii. dayes and iii. nyght, withoutyn felau- 5
shepe hym[f. 29ᵛᵃ]self alone, at the ende of iii. dayis the lady
shal come, and she shal yeue hym what that he wele aske of here
of ony erthely thing. And this hath ofte ben prouyd in tho
partyis.

There was onys a kyng of Ermonye, a myghti kyng and a 10
worthi. He cam and wok the sperhauk til the ende of tho dayis.
The lady cam and bad hym aske what he wolde as he that wel
hadde don. The kyng answerede ayen, 'I am a kyng, riche inow,
and therfor I wele nothing ellis askyn but thyn body at myn wil.'

The lady answerd therto and seyde, 'Vnhappily hast thow 15
askyd, for myn body myghtist thow not haue because that I am
not erthely but spiritual.'

'Certis,' seyth the kyng, 'non othir thing wele I haue.' And
the lady seyde, 'From thyn folye may I not drawyn [f. 29ᵛᵇ] the,
but I shal ȝeuyn the vnaskyd that is rightful. For thow and alle 20
tho that of the shal come shal haue werre withoutyn ferme pes,
and ye shal eueremore ben vndyr subieccioun of youre ennemys
til the ix. gre. And ye schul haue defaute of alle maner of good.'

And right so now it is betyd, for the kyng of Ermonye hadde
neuere pes syn that tyme, and he and alle hese ben euere pore 25
and nedy and leuyn vndyr the tribut of here enemyis.

A symple manis sone come onys and wok the hauk and
askede the lady that he myghte ben happy in marchaundye for
to wynne wordely good, and she grauntede hym, and he wex
the rycheste marchaunt of al his contre. 30

Thanne cam sone aftyr a knyght of the Temple and wok wel
this hauk. [f. 30ʳᵃ] And he asked for to haue alwoy ful his pors

---

1 Cristen] *MS.* Criste   2 syttande] *MS.* sydtande   4–5 vii.
nyght . . . seyn] *R om.*   6 hymself alone] *R om.*   10–11 and a worthi] *R
om.*   11 tho] *R* thes three   13 don] *R* doen and it shulde be grauntid
him   20 vnaskyd that is rightful] *R* vnasked thing and that is riȝtwis I
ȝive the   21 ferme pes] *R* reste or pees   23 good] *R* good and riȝt
27 hauk] *R* sparhawk to the ende of the three daies, and thenne the lady come
to him and bad him aske what thyng that he wolde and hit shulde be grauntid
him

quod petierat destructionem ordinis sui, quod foret propter confidenciam burse istius. Et ita postmodum euenit.

Sed caueat sibi qui vigilare voluerit ibidem, quia si dormierit incurrit perdicionem nec vmquam postea reuertetur ad homines. . . .

[f. 55rb] Postea vero prope terram Caldee est terra Amazonum; hec est terra feminarum. Ibi non permittunt mulieres quod habeant viri dominium terre illius. Erat enim quondam rex terre istius, nomine Colopheus, qui quodam tempore bellum habuit cum gente Scithie. Accidit autem ut moreretur rex in bello, cum quo et omnes nobiles terre pariter occisi sunt. Quod videns, regina cum aliis dominabus terre que fuerant viduate viriliter se armauerunt et coniurauerunt ut interficerent omnes viros terre qui relicti fuerant, ita quod alie mulieres vidue essent sicut ipse, quod et factum est.

Deinceps noluerunt vmquam permittere virum aliquem morari secum vltra septem dies, nec aliquem puerum masculum inter eas nutriri. Sed quando volunt habere consorcium virorum, trahunt se versus confinia aliarum patriarum vbi habent amasios suos, quos visitant et morantur cum eis octo vel decem diebus, et postea reuertuntur. Si autem grauide fuerint et peperint masculum, uel transmittunt eum ad patrem cum ceperit ire et solus comedere uel eum occidunt. Et si genuerint feminam, abscidunt ei vnam mamillam; in nobilibus quidem et generosis mamillam sinistram, vt melius possint scutum portare; in aliis vero inferioris sanguinis abscidunt mamillam dextram, ne impediat vsum sagittandi, nam multum bene sciunt artum sagittandi.

Est in terra ista regina [vna] cui incumbit regimen patrie, et sunt omnes ei obedientes. Semper hec regina constituitur per

18 eas] eos   28 vna] *om.*   incumbit] incumbebit

of mone of gold. And the lady grauntede hym his askynge, but sche seyde that he askede distruccioun of his ordere. And so befel it aftyrward.

But let hym bewar that wakyth there, for yif he slepe he shal ben lost and neuere ben foundyn aftyr that tyme ne come ther that men arn.

NOTA DE MAIDELOND

Besyde that reume of Caldes is the reume of Amazon that we calle Maydelond. In that lond the women of that lond wele not suffere men for to haue the gouernaunce of the reume. For ther was onys a kyng of the lond, his name was Cholophenus, the which hadde werre with a kyng besydyn hym. And so it befel that he wente onys to a batyle [f. 30rb] with that eche kyng his aduersarie, and was slayn in that batyle and alle the grete of his reume with hym. And whan the queen of that lond herde and knew how it was, thanne with [on] assent the ladyis of that lond that were wedewis armedyn hem stalworthyly and tokyn with hem gret company of women and, by assent, slowyn doun alle the men that were left amongis hem.

And syn that tyme hedyrward they woldyn neuere letyn men dwellyn with hem in that contre ouer seuene dayes, ne neuere soffere knaue child to ben norished amongis hem. But whan they wele haue felaushepe of men, they drawyn hem into the syde of the lond where here lemannys wone, and there they dwellen with hem ix. or x. dayes. [f. 30va] And yif they ben with childe and han a sone, thy kepyn it til it can gon and speke and ete, and thanne sendyn it to the fadyr or slen it. And yif it be a maydyn chyld, they shere awey the ton pappe; of a woman of greet stat the left pappe, for sche shal the betere bern here [s]child, and of othere menere women thi shere awey the right pappe, for it shal not lette hem for to shete, for they conne ryght wel the craft of shetynge.

Ther is eueremore a quen in that lond that hath the gouernayle of the lond, and to here they paye here obedyaunce. And euere-

---

5–6 ben foundyn . . . arn] *R* aftir be seen more in this worlde   7 MAI-
DELOND] *MS*. monte lond   15–16 and knew how it was] *R* seye that hir lorde was deed   16 on assent] *MS*. assent of   26–27 and ete] *R om.*
28 the ton pappe] *R om.*   30 schild] *MS. and R* child

eleccionem, [f. 55ᵛᵃ] eligunt enim valenciorem in armis. Et sunt iste femine fortes bellatrices et prudentes, ita quod frequenter reges vicini assumunt ex eis auxilium suum pro stipendiis suis ad pugnandum contra hostes eorum.

5 Est autem ista terra Amazonum insula vndique aquis conclusa, exceptis duobus locis vbi duo sunt introitus, et ultra istas aquas demorantur predicti amasii earum vbi vadunt solaciandi gratia cum voluerint. . . .

In [ista Mauritania] est fons vnus cuius aqua de die quidem est 10 ita frigida quod nullus potest inde bibere; de nocte vero ita calida quod nullus potest imponere manum suam. Vltra locum istum est grandis patria, sed non est habitabilis propter nimium calorem solis. In Ethiopia omnes aque turbide sunt et aliqualiter salse propter vehemenciam caloris. Gens terre istius faciliter in-15 ebriatur. Non magnum habent appetitum commedendi. Habent comuniter fluxum ventris, et non longo tempore viuunt.

In Ethiopia sunt gentes diuersarum formarum. Est ibi gens vnius tantum pedis, et currunt ita leuiter cum illo vno pede quod mirum est. Pes ipse tam largus est quod vmbra eius 20 cooperit totum corpus contra solem. . . .

De Ethiopia transitur in Indiam . . . in terciam partem que est versus septemtrionem, et est patria frigidissima ita quod propter frigus nimium et continuum gelu aqua congelatur in cristallum. Et super rupes cristalli boni adamantes crescunt qui 25 sunt de colore cristalli turbidi et subnigri . . . [f. 55ᵛᵇ] et sunt de ipsis quadrati et punctuati sine manu hominis. Et simul crescunt masculus et femella et nutriuntur rore celi. Et generant et concipiunt quasi paruos filios iuxta se, sicque multiplicantur et crescunt omnibus annis.

9 ista Mauritania] qua

more the quen is chosyn by eleccioun; here that is doutyest in armys, hyre they chese. And forthy kyngis of othere reumys besydyn takyn hem to helpyn hem in here wer[f. 30ᵛᵇ]ris ayen here enemys and yeuyn hem riche feis.

The reume of Amazon, wher the women wonyn in, is but an yle closid al aboutyn with watir, outakyn too sydys wher men may come therto, and there dwellyn here lemanys to whom they may gon to whan they lestyn to haue bodily lykynge of hem.

NOTA DE TERRA ETHIOPE

In the lond of Ethiop there is a welle that in the day it is so cold that no man may drynke therof, and in the nyght it is so hot that no man may suffer his hand therin. And in that eche lond of Ethiope alle the waters are so salte and drewy for ouergret hete of the sonne that no man may ne dar dele with hem. And the folk of that lond wele lyghtely ben dronkyn that they ne han gret talent to here mete, [f. 31ʳᵃ] and comounly they haue the flix. And they arn folk that leuyn [nought] long tyme.

In that lond are folk of dyuerse shappis. There are folk that han but on fot, and they wele renne so faste on that on fot that it is wondyr to sen. And that foot is so mechil that it is wondyr to se; it wele keuere al his body ayen the hete of the sonne.

NOTA DE ADDAMANDES

In that lond of Inde is a contre toward the west where the eyr is so cold that thour the grete cold there is a contynuel frost that the watir freseth, so that it turnyth into cristal. And vpon the rochis of cristal growyn goode adamas, *id est* adamaundes, that arn of the colour of cristal, but they are more blake than cristal and foure corneled of here owene growynge withoutyn schap of manys hand. And there growith togedere the male and the female and arn norysched of [f. 31ʳᵇ] the dew of heuene. And they gendere and conseyue as it were othere litel children in here kynde, and so they multyplye and growyn fully and swerly.

4 feis] *R* fees and goode wages   5 The reume of] *R* this ilke rewme
8 hem] *R* hem betymes   15 lyghtely ben] *R* ben but litil   17 nought]
MS. om.   19 fot and] *R* foote and that is three or foure foot brode
20 sen] *R* telle   20–21 it is wondyr to se] *R om.*   22 ADDAMANDES]
MS. Attamandes   24 there] *MS.* that there   there is a] *R* and
32 and swerly] *R om.*

Ego ipse vidi et probaui quod si accipiantur cum aliqua parte rupis vbi crescunt, ita quod non euellantur a radicibus, si humectentur sepius rore mensis Maii, bene crescunt visibiliter ita quod parui deueniunt grandiores. Item, in ista insula sunt
5 multe diuerse patrie. Vocatur autem India propter vnum fluuium currentem per terram illam cui nomen est Indus. In isto flumine reperiuntur anguille longitudinis triginta pedum. . . .

Et postea inuenitur insula que appellatur Grines, vbi mercatores de Venecia et Ianua et de aliis locis sepius veniunt mercan-
10 dizandi gratia. Sed in ista insula tantus est calor aeris quod testiculi hominum egrediuntur solitas metas longitudinis et pendent usque ad tibias propter calorem dissoluentem. Sed gens patrie istius et qui sciunt naturam patrie vtuntur vnguento restrictiuo et refrigerato pro remedio talis incomodi. In ista
15 patria et in Ethiopia et in quibusdam aliis locis vadunt homines nudi ad flumina et mulieres similiter, et ibi iacent nudi a diei hora tercia usque ad nonam, ita quod nichil apparet extra aquam nisi solum caput propter nimium calorem. . . .

[f. 56ra] Et sunt ratones ibidem de magnitudine canum nostro-
20 rum, et capiuntur cum magnis canibus quia murelegi eos capere non possunt. . . .

Item, versus caput istius foreste est ciuitas Palumbe, et iuxta ciuitatem est mons magnus qui vocatur eodem nomine, et habuit ciuitas nomen a monte. Ad pedem montis istius habetur fons
25 pulcherimus optimi odoris et saporis quasi essent in eo diuersa genera specierum. Et omni hora diei mutatur odor fontis et sapor diuersimode. Et qui biberit ter ieiunus de aqua fontis curatur de quocumque morbo tenetur. Et qui ibi habitant et sepius inde bibunt numquam [in]currunt infirmitatem et
30 apparent semper iuuenes.

29 incurrunt] currunt

And I mynself, Ion Maundeuyle, saw and provede that yif they be takyn awey from the roche where they growyn, withoutyn ony party of the roche, so that they ben not reuyn awey by the rotys from the roche, yif they ben oftyn wet with the dewis of the monyth of May, they growyn wel and visi[b]li so that the littille growyn and waxen grete. In a reuer in Ynde ther are elys xxx. fote longe.

In the lond of Ethiope is an yle that is callyd Trinor. Thedyr comyn merchaundis of Venyse and of Gene and of manye othere contreis with here marchaundyse to sellyn and to bey [f. 31va] othere marchaundye ayenward. That eche yle is so hot that thour the grete hete of the eyr that manys priuite hangith doun to here kneis that dwellyn ther. But the men of that contre that knowe the kynde of here lond vsyn colde medecynys and onymentis, that restreyneth it thour remedye for swich myschef and for gret vnese that fallyth among hem. In Ethiope men and wemen in tyme of somyr gon comounly to wateris and lyn therinne from vnderyn til it be noon of the day, al nakyd, for the gret hete of the sonne.

In an yle of that lond of Ethiope there are ratonys as meche as houndis arn here. They moun not ben [f. 31vb] takyn with none cattis but with meche houndis of that lond.

NOTA DE FONTE VIUO

In the cete of Polyne is a welle nobil and fair, and the watir therof is as swete and as sauory as dyuerse maneres of spices were therin. And manye tyme of the day the watir chaungith dyuersly. And ho that drynkyth thryes of that watyr fastynge, he is hol of ony seknesse or maladye that euere he haue. And forthi tho that wone nygh that welle drynkyn oftyn therof, and therfore they han neuere more non seknesse, and ay they seme yonge.

5 visibli] MS. wiseli   6 growyn and] R om.   grete] R grete. The kynde of hem is this, that ȝif the toon ende be putte to iren it draweth the iren to it; and ȝif the tother ende be putte to iren, thenne the iren draweth aweye. And thus seith the Maistir of Propirtees   13 that dwellyn ther] R thoruȝ the violens of the gret heete   14 of] MS. of of   14–16 medecynys ... among hem] R oynementis for such dissesis   19 sonne] R sonne and therfore they arn al blake of skyn   22 of that lond] R for they wole werye alle the litil doggis that they may come by, therfore they brynge vpp grete teyȝ doggis to slee hem with   24 In the cete of Polyne] R ther is a cite in Ethiope that is callid Pollane and in that cite   26 were] R were cast

Et ego vero inde bibi tribus vicibus, et adhuc me sencio meliorem et saniorem. A quibusdam appellatur Fons Iuuentutis et venit de paradiso, ut creditur propter virtutes eius. Per totam terram istam crescit optimum zinziberum, et veniunt mercatores illuc pro speciebus querendis.

In hac patria adorant bouem pro deo suo propter simplicitatem illius animalis et benignitatem et eciam propter vtilitatem que prouenit ex eo. Et dicunt bouem esse sanctissimum animal in terra, quia videtur eis quod habet virtutes plurimas in se. Sex annis uel septem faciunt bouem laborare, et postea comedunt eum.

Rex quoque patrie illius semper habet secum bouem talem quasi deum. Et ille qui custodit bouem recolligit fimum [f. 56rb] eius in vase vno aureo et vrinam in alio, et postea presentat vtrumque maximo prelato, quem appellant *Archioprothopaten*. Et iste portat vtrumque coram rege et facit desuper plures benedictiones. Deinde intingit rex manus suas in vrina bouis, quam ipsi appellant *gaul*, et humectat inde frontem suum et pectus. Postea se fricat cum fimo bouis cum magna reuerencia ea intencione quod impleatur virtutibus bouis supradictis et quod sanctificetur per virtutem huius rei sacre. Et post regem hoc idem faciunt omnes magnates et nobiles, et post eos ministri et alii inferiores quamdiu aliquid remanet de fimo et vrina predictis.

12 ille] illi

And I, Iohan Maundeuyle, knyght and pilgrym, drank of that welle watyr thryes and al myn compaynye, and euere sythe that tyme I felte me the bet and the heylere tyl the ty[f. 32ra]me that God wolde resseyue me vntyl His grace. Some men callyn it *Fons Iuuentutis*, that is for to seye, the Welle of Youthe. It comyth from paradis, as men trowith for the vertue that is foundyn therin.

NOTA DE BOUE QUASI DEUS EORUM

In that ich contre of Ethiope they honoure the oxe in stede of here god for the symplenes of hym and the goodnesse and for the profit that he doth and comyth of hym. For they seye that the oxe is the holyeste beste of al this world and manye vertues hath in hymself; for vi. or vii. yer the oxe wele drawe in the plow and helpyn to manys sustenance, and aftyr that men may etyn hym.

The kyng of the lond hath eueremor [f. 32rb] an oxe with hym whersoeuere he go and honoureth it as it were his god. And he that kepyth that oxe gaderyth that ech mok of hym in a vessel of gold and the vryne in anothir, and al that he gaderid al the nyght on the morwe he presentet it to the moste souereyn prelat of the contre, [an] erchebiscop or bischop, [and he] berith it to the kyng and makyth therof manye blyssyngis. And than the kyng put his hand into the donge and takith therof, and robith his theth, his brest, his forhed, and his visage; thanne with gret reuerence takyth [more] of the mok, and robbyth hym so that he shulde ben fulfyld of that holy oxe, and that he shal ben blyssid thour vertu of that holy thing. And aftyr the kyng [f. 32va] othere lordis and pryncis shuln don on the same maner, and aftyr hem seruauntys and othere menere men as longe as ony thing lastyth therof.

1 knyght and pilgrym] *R om.* 2 and al myn compaynye] *R om.* 5 *Fons* ... seye] *R om.* 6 vertue] *R* grete heele and vertue 7 therin] *R* therinne and ful wel it may bee 9 In that ich contre of Ethiope] *R* men of Ethiope in dyuers placis hath a custome that 9–11 in stede ... comyth of hym] *R* as for a prophete and goodnes that cometh of him 21 of the contre] *R* that is an] *MS. om.* bischop] *R* bisshoppe in the forseide vesselle of golde and he] *MS. om.* 22 blyssyngis] *R* blesyngis and seie orysouns 23 donge] *R* donge and vrayne therof] *R* of it a porcioun 24 theth ... visage] *R* fronte and his eyen 25 more] *MS. om.* 26 hym] *R* his brest al aboute therwith 27 thing] *R* donge and vrayn 29 menere] *MS.* manere

In ista patria faciunt ydola ... et coram istis ydolis occidunt sepius infantes suos et de eorum sanguine aspergunt ydola ipsa, et ita faciunt sacrificium suum. Et quando aliquis moritur in patria, comburunt corpus ipsius loco penitencie ne scilicet
5 sustineat penam in sepulcro per comestionem vermium.

Et si vxor eius non habuerit infantem, comburitur ipsa cum viro; dicunt enim rationem esse quod illa socia sit in alio seculo sicut fuit in isto. Si vero infantem habuerit, permittunt eam viuere cum infante ad nutriendum infantem, si tamen ipsa
10 voluerit. Si illa pocius elegerit viuere cum infante quam mori cum marito, ex tunc reputabitur infidelis et ingrata et numquam commendabitur nec confidet quisquam in ea. Et si mulier moriatur ante maritum, non comburetur maritus inuite, sed potest iterum matrimonium contrahere cum alia.

15 In ista patria crescunt forcia vina, et mulieres vinum bibunt et non viri. Similiter mulieres barbas radunt et non viri. De ista patria transitur per plura loca versus vnam patriam nomine Mabaron, que distat per [decem] dietas et est regio magna et spaciosa, habens plures ciuitates et villas bonas.

20 In ista terra iacet sanctus Thomas apostolus integer corpore in vna tumba pulcherima in ciuitate que vocatur Calame, nam ibi fuit martirizatus et sepultus. Sed Assirii postmodum transtulerunt corpus eius in Mesopotamiam in ciuitatem Edisse. Postmodum reportatum fuit corpus eius, et [adhuc] brachium
25 cum manu quod misit in latus saluatoris post resureccionem suam iacet exterius in quodam vase.

6 comburitur] comburetur   18 decem] *om.*   24 adhuc] hunc

NOTA DE [IN]FANTIBUS

In the contre of Ethyop they slen here childeryn byforn here goddys in stede of sacrifise, and takyn the blod and spryngyn it on here mamettis. And whan ony man deyeth in that lond, they takyn his body and brennyn it, that he schal soffere no peyne whan he is grauyn thour etynge of wermys.

And yif his wif haue no yong sone or yong child, sche shal be brent with hym that is here hosbonde, for they seyn that it is resoun that she be his felawe in that othyr world as she was in this. But and sche haue a yong child, sche shal leue and bryngyn [f. 32vb] forth here child yif she wele. And yif it be so that sche chese rathere to leue with here child than for to deye with here hosbonde, thanne shal she ben rettid for ontrowe and vnkynde, and sche shal neuere ben preysed, ne no man shal aftir that tyme trostyn to here. And yif they deye beforn here hosbonde, he shal not ben brent with here ageyns his wil but schal take anothir wif whan hym luste.

In that contre growyn *v*inys and good wyn. And there shal the wemyn drynke the wyn and not the men, and the wemen shul shaue the menys berdis and not the men. Wete ye wel this, that these meruaylis ben sothe. Trowe it yif ye welyn.

NOTA DE MANU SANCTI THOME APOSTOLI

In the lond of Mabron lyth Seynt Thomays the [f. 33ra] Apostyl, the body of hym al hol, in a fayr toumbe in the cete of Calomy, for ther he was martyryd and grauyd. But aftyr that the folk of Aserye tok his body and born it into the cete of Mesopotanye, and yit his arm, with the hond that he put in the syde of oure lord Iesu Crist aftyr his resureccioun, lyth withoutyn in a vessel.

1 INFANTIBUS] *MS.* fantibus   4 takyn his body and brennyn it] *R* brenne his body   9–10 and bryngyn . . . wele] *R om.*   13 preysed] *R* preysed off man nor of woman fro that tyme forth   17 vinys] *MS.* winys   19–20 Wete ye . . . welyn] *R om.*   22 In the lond] *R* from that ilke ile of Trynor men shal passe be manye dyuers placis or they come to a cuntre that is callid Mabron, that is x. iourneyes from thennes. And it is a gret rewme and a large, and manye fair citees and touns therinne. And in that londe   23 hol] *R* hool and nou3t roten   27–28 withoutyn in a vessel] *R* in a ful fair vessel withoute the toumbe

Per istam ma[num] faciunt homines patrie iudicia sua; nam quando oritur dissencio inter duas partes et vtraque pars contendit se ius habere in causa, tunc faciunt scribi causam [f. 56ᵛᵃ] vtriusque et ponunt scripta in manu sancti Thome. Et confestim manus ipsa proicit a se scriptum quod continet causam falsam et aliud scriptum sibi retinet, et ita apparet quis iustam causam habuerit in patria illa. Veniunt eciam de longinquis partibus pro iudiciis habendis in causis dubitabilibus.

Ecclesia sane vbi sanctus Thomas iacet satis est grandis et pulcra, et est plena similacris magne stature quorum minimum excedit magnitudinem duorum hominum. Et inter alia similacra est vnum magis ceteris coopertum auro et lapidibus preciosis [per totum], et eciam sedet in quadam cathedra nobiliter ornata. Et habet circa collum largas cincturas quasi zonas de auro purissimo et lapidibus preciosis. Et est ista ecclesia multum nobiliter aptata et ornata et per totum interius deaurata.

Ad predictum ydolum veniunt peregrini de longinquis ita comuniter sicut faciunt Cristiani ad sanctum Iacobum in Galacia, et hoc cum magna deuocione; plures enim qui peregre veniunt de longinquis versus ydolum ipsum, propter deuocionem quam habent semper ad terram respiciunt itinerando, nolentes respicere in circuitu nec oculos leuare ne forte aliquid videa[n]t quod posset impedire suam deuocionem. Quidam et peregrini portant in manibus cultellos acutos et se ipsos perc[ut]iunt et vulnerant in brachiis, tibiis, et aliis partibus corporis, effundentes sanguinem proprium pro amore illius ydoli. Et dicunt quod beatus est qui moritur pro deo suo. Nonnulli eciam adducunt secum infantes suos ad occidendum et sacrificandum coram ipso ydolo, aspergentes ipsum ydolum sanguine infancium predictorum. Alii vero a tempore quo recedunt a domibus propriis ad quoslibet tres passus genuflectent toto itinere quousque venerint ad predictum ydolum. Afferuntque secum incensum et alia odorifera ad thurificandum

1 manum] ma   13 per totum] *om.*   22 videant] videat
24 percutiunt] perciunt

And by that hand the men of that lond yeuyn here iugement; for whan ony discord or strif is betwyn hem and eythir party seyth and affermyth that he hath right in his cause, thanne they don wrytyn in twey skrowys the right of eythir partye and put hem into the hand of Seynt Thomays. And as faste the hand cast awey the skrowe that contynewith the false cause, and the tothir it holdyth stille. Men comyth out of fer contre thedyr for to declare ryghtwise causis be[f. 33rb]twen partye and partye.

The cherche where that Seynt Thomays lyth is mechil and fayr and ful of ymagerye of here maumetterye. The ymagis arn euerychon of the stature of two men. But ther is on that passyth alle othere of stature, and that is richely arayed with clothis of gold and precious stonys al aboutyn and set in a chayer nobli arayed. And he hath aboute his nekke grete gyrdelis of silk, harneysid with gold and precious stonys.

To that ymage, that is here pryncipal mamet, comyn pilgrymys out of fer contreis as comounly as Cr[i]stene men come to Seynt Iamys, and that with gret deuocioun and eueremore lokende doun to the erthe, not willynge to lo[f. 33va]ke aboute hem for thei shulde don nothing that shulde lette here deuocioun. Some pilgrymys bryngyn in here hondys sharpe knyuys and woundyn hemself in the armys and in the leggis and in othere partyes of her body, that the blod rennyth out right gret plente. And al that penaunce they don thour loue of here maumet, and seyn that he is blyssid and happy that may deye for his god. And they bryngyn with hem here childeryn and slen hem beforn here god, and makyn here sacrifise to hym, and takyn the blod of here childeryn and castyn it vpon here maumet. And some pilgrymys knelyn doun for deuocioun at euery thredde pas vpon the erthe from the tyme that they gon out of here houses til they come byforn the mau[f. 33vb]met that they holdyn for here god. And they bryngyn with hem ensens and othere goode smellyng thyngis for to yeuyn ensens

5 cast] *MS.* cast hem 7 stille] *R* stille til they take it out of his honde hemself, and therfore men seyn in that cuntre that it is an holy honde 15-16 grete . . . gold] *R* a iuel of gold 17 that is here pryncipal mamet] *R om.* 18 Cristene] *MS.* Crstene come] *MS.* cone 20-22 not willynge . . . deuocioun] *R* and they wole no3t loke bycause of her deuocioun 25-26 And al . . . maumet] *R om.* 30-33 And some . . . here god] *R om.*

ydolum ac si esset corpus domini. Est autem coram ipso ydolo quasi viuarium aut locus aliquis repletus aqua. Et in isto lacu proiciunt peregrini aurum et argentum et lapides preciosos absque numero loco oblationis. Et ideo quando ministri illius
5 ydoli indigent peccunia pro reparacione illius ecclesie uel alterius rei pertinentis ad ipsum ydolum, mox pergunt ad predictum locum et inde accipiunt quantum necesse fuerit. . . .

[f. 56vb] Post quas veniunt peregrini qui sunt de longinquis partibus qui ob deuociones ydoli illuc venerunt; horum quidam
10 feruore deuocionis cadunt sub rotis illius currus ut [v]el moriantur vel mutilentur amore dei sui, hoc pensantes quod quanto plus paciuntur penam vel tribulacionem causa dei sui, tanto erunt ei propinquiores et maiorem gloriam optinebunt in alio seculo. Et, ut breuiter dicam, tot et tantas penas ac martiria
15 diuersa suis corporibus inferunt amore illius ydoli quod vix aliquis Cristianus sustineret medietatem vel decimam partem pro amore Iesu Cristi. . . . Et tunc ob honorem ydoli et diei festi diuerse persone se occidunt, cc. uel ccc. numero, cum acutissimis cultellis ad hoc preparatis, quorum corpora ponuntur coram
20 ydolo et computantur in numero sanctorum. . . .

[f. 57ra] De ista patria transitur . . . ad vnam terram que satis spaciosa est et larga, cuius nomen est Lamoroy. In hac patria habundat calor, et est consuetudo quod omnes, tam viri quam femine, sunt nudi et derident alios quos vident vestitos. Dicunt
25 enim quod Adam et Eua facti sunt nudi, et nullus [debet] erubescere talem se ostendere qualis a deo factus est, nichil enim in natura fedum est. Dicunt eciam quod illi qui vestibus vtuntur homines sunt alterius seculi uel non credunt in deum qui creauit mundum, Adam et Euam, cum aliis vniuersis.

8 qui] si qui   10 vel] el   17 festi] festi et   25-26 debet erubescere] erubesceret

to here maumet. [Before that ymage is] as it were a *veuer* or a
pond ful of watyr. Thedyr castyn pilgrymys here gold and here
siluyr and precious stonys withoutyn noumbre in stede of here
offrynge. And forthy the maysteris that kepe that maumet, whan
they han myster of ony monee for reparacioun of here cherche 5
or for ony othir thing that fallyth to that eche maumet, as faste
they gon to that eche pond and takyn out of that eche tresor as
meche as they han myster of.

There comyn manye pilgrymys out of fer contreis thedyr for
deuocioun of that eche maumet that is here god. [And manye] 10
fallyn doun vndyr whelis of [f. 34ra] waynys and of cartis whan
they are charged in entent for to deye there, or to be sauyd
thorw the myrakele of that maumet that is here god, for they
seye that the more penaunce that they suffere for the loue of
here maumet, that is here god, in this world, the more ioye shal 15
they haue in the tothir world. But trewely, for to sey the sothe,
they suffere so meche penaunce and dyuers martyrdomys vpon
her bodyis for the loue of that maumet, here god, that vnnethes
wele ony Cristen man suffere half or the tende part for the loue
of Crist. For there are manye that with sharpe knyuys slen hem- 20
self, to or thre hundered vpon a day, for the loue of that maumet,
and of tho they take the bodyis and bryngyn byfore the maumet
and acountyn in the noumbre of halwis.

In that eche lond of Ethyope is a con[f. 34rb]tre, meche and
large and ful of folk, that is callyd Lamore. In that contre the 25
hete is so gret and so brennynge of the sonne that the custom is
there swich that euery man and woman ben nakyd and skornyn
hem that ben clothid. For they seyn Adam was nakyd and Eue
also, and that they weryn mad nakyd, and therfore no man
shulde thynkyn shame to shewe swich as God made hym. And 30
they seye also that folk that vsyn clothis arn men of anothir
world, or ellis they trowe not in God that made the world.

1 Before that ymage is] *MS. om.*   veuer] *MS.* reuer   4 the maysteris that kepe that maumet] *R om.*   8 meche] *MS.* moche   9–10 for
deuocioun ... god] *R* in her deuocions   10 And manye] *MS. om.*
11 whelis of] *R om.*   14 suffere] *R* haue and suffre   19 or the tende]
R om.   24 In that eche lond of Ethyope] *R* ther   25 Lamore] *R* La-
mor and it is in the londe of Mabron   26 of the sonne] *R* bothe in
wyntir and in somer   29 mad] *R* bothe   30 to shewe swich as God
made hym] *R* of suche gere as God hath 3oven him

Isti vxores non habent specialiter eis coniunctas, femine enim ibidem sunt omnibus comunes et virum nullum recipiunt sed omnes indifferenter admittunt. Dicunt enim quod grauiter peccaret aliter faciendo, eo quod deus precepit dicens, *Crescite et multiplicamini et replete terram* et cetera. Ideo nullus dicit in patria illa, 'Hec est vxor mea', nec dicit mulier, 'Hic est vir meus.' Et quando pariunt mulieres, tradunt infantes alicui eorum qui concubuerunt cum eis. Et sic [eciam] comunis est terra ibidem, tenetur enim ab vno per vnum annum et ab alio per annum alterum, et capit quilibet quodque nunc hic nunc illic quia omnia sunt comunia, ut dixi, et ita diues est vnus sicut alius.

Sed inter hec habent morem pessimum quod libencius comedunt carnem humanam quam aliquam aliam. Est autem patria habundans satis et fertilis de bladis, carnibus, et piscibus, de auro quoque et argento ac de bonis aliis plurimis. Ibi a mercatoribus venduntur pueri quos emunt gens patrie. Et si pingues sint statim comedunt eos. Si vero sint macilenti, faciunt eos ad tempus impinguari ut postea comedantur. Et dicunt quod hec est optima caro et dulcissima. . . .

[f. 66vb] Ab ista terra transitur versus regionem Bacthariorum vbi est gens pessima et crudelis. In hac terra sunt arbores portantes lanam ac si esset lana ouium, vnde faciunt ibi vestes. Sunt et ibi bestie que vocantur ypotami morantes tam in terra quam in aqua, aliquando in vna, aliquando in alia, et est [vna] medietas forme humane et alia forme equine, sicut alias dictum est. Comedunt vero homines quociens eos apprehendere possunt. Ibi sunt aque amarissime multo plus quam aqua maris.

In hac patria sunt griffones plurime, que magis habundant in hac terra quam alibi. Dicunt aliqui quod habent formam aquilinam a parte ante et bouinam a parte post. Certe verum dicunt quod vnus griffo forcior est et maior octo leonibus de

8 eciam] namque   23 ibi] sibi   25 est vna] est

Wete ye wel that in that contre is non mariage mad betwene man and woman, but alle the wemen of that contre aryn comoun to euery man. And the seye yf they dedyn othyrewyse, they synnyd greuously sithyn that God bad and seide, [*Crescite et multiplicamini*] [f. 34ᵛᵃ] that is for to say, Growith and multy- 5 plyeth and reple[ni]shit the erthe. And therfore no man seyth, 'There is myn wif,' ne non woman seyth, 'This is myn hosbonde.' And whan ony woman hath a child, sche yeuyth it to hym that fyrst lay by here. And the goodis of that contre aryn comoun to euery man of that contre, and non richere shal on 10 man ben than anothir, ne non desyrith for to be.

The folk that I speke of han a wekkede custome amongys hem, for they wele gladly etyn manys flesch more than ony othir flesch. Neueretheles the lond is replenyshid with flesch and fisch and gold and syluer and othir good inow. Thedyr 15 marchauntys bryngyn childeryn to selle, and the men of that contre beyen hem. And yif they ben fatte, they etyn hem [f. 34ᵛᵇ] *a*non; and if they ben lene, they fedyn hem tyl they ben fatte and etyn hem thanne.

There is anothir reume that is callid Baldasdor, that is vndyr 20 the lordshepe of the Grete Cane. In that ilke lond aryn wekkede men and crewel. In that lond arn tren that bern wolle as shep don in othere place, and the folk makyn hem clothis therof for to were. In that reume arn a maner of bestys that aryn callid [y]*potami* that wonyn as wel in the watir as on the lond, the 25 which bestys the on half of hem hath the shap of a man and that othir half of an hors. They etyn men whan euere they may getyn hem, nothing leuere of no manere mete.

In that contre aryn grefonys manye, that han the forme of the egele byfore and the forme of the lyoun byhynde. But a greffoun 30 [f. 35ʳᵃ] there is more and strengere than viii. lyonys of this contre and strengere than an hondered egellys here, for a grefoun hymself alone wele bere to his nest an hors with a man

---

4–5 *Crescite et multiplicamini*] MS. om. *leaving blank space*   6 replenishit] MS. repleshit   6–8 And therfore . . . hosbonde] R om. 14–19 Neueretheles . . . etyn hem thanne] R om.   18 anon] MS. among 21–22 In that . . . crewel] R om.   22–23 as shep don in othere place] R but it is gret and royde   25 ypotami] MS. rotanii   R irotamus   27–28 whan euere . . . mete] R rather thenne any othir thing ellis   31 viii.] R vii. 31–32 of this . . . here] R om.   33 hymself alone] R om.

partibus istis. Sic eciam est maior et forcior c. aquilis, solent
enim equm cum homine ad nidum suum portare in[si]dente uel
duos boues simul iugatos. Habet enim vngulas pedum sicut
cornua bouina sed multo longiora, et fiunt inde ciphi ad biben-
5 dum sicut de cornubus bubalorum, et de lateribus pennarum
fiunt arcus validi ad sagittandum.

[f. 67ra] Exinde transitur pluribus dietis per terram Presbiteri
Iohannis qui est magnus imperator Indie, et appellatur terra
sua insula de Pentoxoire. Iste imperator plures patrias habet sub
10 imperio suo, in quibus sunt ciuitates optime et ville satis bone.
In insulas plurimas diuiditur terra illa propter diuersa flumina
ibi existencia de paradiso exeuntia et diuidunt totam terram. . . .
Presbiter Iohannes habet sub se plures reges, plures insulas,
et plures gentes diuersas, et est patria sua valde bona et copiosa
15 diuiciis. . . . [f. 67rb] Iste Presbiter Iohannes filiam magni Chan
semper ducit in vxorem; ille versa vice filiam Presbiteri Iohannis.

In hac terra Presbiteri Iohannis sunt multi lapides preciosi
diuersi generis et tante quantitatis quod faciunt ex eis vasa
diuersa, videlicet ciphos, discos, parapsides, et alia plura que
20 scribere longum esset.

Volo autem aliquid loqui de quibusdam insulis principalibus
ibidem et de statu imperatoris ac eciam de lege eius et populi
terre. Iste igitur imperator Cristianus est cum magna parte sue
gentis, quamquam non omnes articulos fidei ita lucide habent
25 et tenent sicut nos. Credunt namque in patrem et filium et
spiritum sanctum, et valde deuoti sunt et fideles ad alterutrum,
nec vtuntur fraudibus vel cautelis.

Sub imperatore sunt lxxii. prouincie cum totidem regibus

2 insidente] in dente   25 tenent] tenent et teneant

armyd on his bak, or too oxen yokede togedere to his nest. The naylis of hese feet aryn as meche as oxsis hornys, and they make of hem coppys for to drynkyn of, as men don here of bugele hornys, and of the bakkis of here federys they make stronge bowis to shetyn therwith. I say of the bowis with myn eyen.

This eche Emperour of Ynde that men callyn Prestir Ion hath manye dyuers contreis vndyr hi[s]e emperere, in the wheche are manye noble seteis and fayre tounnys and ryche and greete ylis. His lordshepe is de[f. 35rb]partid in manye placis. The wateris that rennyn thour his lond in manye partyes comyn from paradys and departyth al his lond. He hath manye kyngis vndyr hym wonande, manye dyuers men, manye ylis, and mekil and greete plente of rychesse and tresor. This eche rial kyng and emperour Prestir Ion and the Grete Cane of Tartarye arn eueremore allyede togedere thour maryage; eche of hem wedyth otheris systir.

In that lond of Prestir Ion arn gret plente of precious stonys, and therof manye dyuers kyndis of stonys so mechil that they makyn of hem vescellis to etyn of, disshis and dobeleris and coppis and manye othere thyngis that longe it were al the dyuerste for to telle.

Now wole I tellyn and [f. 35va] declaryn and spekyn of the principal ylis of his lond and of the ryalte of his astat and what lawe he and his peple holdyn. Prestir Ion is a Cristen man and the most partie of his lond, al be it so that they han not al the artikele of oure treuthe, ne holdyn hem not so clenly as we do. Neuertheles they trowyn in God, Fadyr and Sone and Holy Gost, and they aryn ful deuoute men and vsyn neythir fraude ne gyle.

Vndyr his subieccioun and his obseruaunce arn lx. and xii. pr[ou]inces, and *in* eche a kyng, that arn his tributaryes, and

---

1 armyd on his bak] *R om.*   togedere to his nest] *R* in a plow3   3-4 as men . . . bakkis] *R* and   4 stronge] *R om.*   5 I say . . . eyen] *R om.*
7 hise] *MS.* hie   8-9 noble . . . ylis] *R* citees and riche touns and iles
10-11 The wateris . . . al his lond] *R* with grete watris and some comen fro paradice   15-16 eche . . . systir] *R om.*   18 therof] *MS.* that of
18-20 and thereof . . . thyngis that] *R* some arn so mochel that they make of hem cuppis and othir dyuers vessellis but   22 and declaryn and spekyn] *R om.*   23-24 of his astat . . . holdyn] *R* and of his estate   26 ne holdyn hem not so clenly as we do] *R om.*   29 gyle] *R* gile ne falsheede amonges hem
31 prouinces] *MS.* princes   in] *MS.* of   31-101. 2 and in eche . . . Ion] *R om.*

eidem tributariis, qui et reges sub se habent minores, omnesque tributa reddunt imperatori. Inter alia mirabilia huius terre est illud mare arenosum quod totum de arena est sine gutta aque. Et habet istud mare accessum sicut *ali*ud mare cum aqua, nec
5 aliquo tempore stat tranquillum sine motu. Nullus hoc mare transire potest nauigio uel alio modo, et ideo incognitum est cunctis qualis terra uel patria est ultra illud mare. Et quamuis non sit aqua in illo mari, ut dictum est, inueniuntur tamen boni pisces in ripis eius, alterius tamen figure et forme quam sunt
10 in alio mari. Sed sunt valde boni saporis et deliciosi ad manducandum.

Et ab illo mari ad tres dietas sunt montes magni, de quibus egreditur fluuius qui venit de paradiso. . . . Vltra fluuium istum versus deserta est vna magna planicies arenosa inter montes. In
15 hac planicie cotidie circa solis ortum incipiunt quasi quedam arbusta crescere usque ad meridiem et fructum videntur portare. Sed nullus audet tangere eo quod sic quasi fantasticum et deceptorium visus, nam ad solis occasum non apparent amplius. Sic contingit omni die, et est satis mirandum.

20   Sunt quoque in illis partibus multi [f. 67ᵛᵃ] homines siluestres qui more bestiarum viuunt in siluis et campis, non loquentes sed grunnientes more porcorum. Sunt et carnes siluestres et aues naturaliter loquentes, et salutant homines euntes per desertum. Et alique ita aperte loquntur sicut essent homines, et tales
25 habent linguam largam et in quolibet pede [quinque] articulos. Istas aues vocant ibi *psitacos*. . . .

Iste imperator, quando pergit ad prelium aduersus aliquem magnum, non habet ante se vexillum sed loco vexilli facit portare

2 terre] terre precipuum   4 aliud] illud   25 quinque] *om.*

they han symplere kyngis vndir hem that they are tributarie to
the Emperour Prestir Ion. Among alle the meruaylis and ferlyes
of his lond that I haue sen thanne is there a gret se al of grauel
withoutyn ony porcioun [f. 35vb] of watyr therin. And that eche
se ebbith and flowyth as othere wateris don and as the Grete Se 5
doth in othere contreis, and neueremore stondyth it stille withoutyn sterynge. That se may no man passe, neythir with seylynge
ne with rowynge ne be non othir slyg[h]te ne queyntyse. And
therfore it is vnknowe to me what skenes thing is on that othir
syde of that ferly see. And thow ther be no watyr in that see, yit 10
are therin gret plente of fischis takyn by the sidys of that see,
and they are goode and seuoury in the mouth, but they arn of
othir shap than othere fisshis in othere wateris, for I Ion Maundevile et of hem. It is soth. Trowe it if ye welyn.

And besydyn this ferly se, toward the desert, is a gret pleyne 15
grauelly a[f. 36ra]mong the mounteynys. In that pleyne eche
day aboute the sone rysynge it shewith as it were treis growende
and berynge freut tyl it be ner ouyrnon. But no man dare come
nygh that freut, for it semyth as it were fantem and disseyuable
thing to syghte, and be that the sone goth doun, there is nothing 20
sene more of al that fare. And thus it farith eche day, and it is
holdyn in that contre an ferly thing.

There is also in that contre a maner of men that wonyn in
the wodys and leuyn eueremore therin as it were bestis. They
spekyn not but grontyn as swyn don here. In some wodys of the 25
lond aryn wilde houndis and neuere comyn to no man, and
foulys kyndely spekyn and salueth men as thei comyn thour
that wildyrnesse and as opynly spekyn as they were men [f. 36rb]
with large tonge and resonable. And in eche foot of the foulys
are fyue clawis, and men callyn the foulys *persital*. 30

This eche grete kyng and emperour Prestir Iohn, whan he
goth to batayle ayens ony othir gret kyng, he doth not beryn

2 and ferlyes] *R om.*   4 withoutyn ony porcioun of watyr therin] *R om.*
5-6 and as the Grete Se doth] *R om.*   8 ne be non othir slyghte ne
queyntyse] *R om.*   slyghte] *MS.* slygte   14 hem] *R* hem harmelees
It is . . . welyn] *R om.*   15 ferly] *R* ilke   18-19 dare come nygh]
R wole take of   19 as it were fantem and] *R om.*   20 that] *MS.* that
that   21-22 more of . . . thing] *R om.*   25-29 In some . . . resonable]
R and ther ben also briddes spekinge vnto men and bryngen men thoruȝ
the desertis   31 eche grete kyng and] *R* rial   32 ayens ony othir
gret kyng] *R om.*

ante se xiii. cruces de auro purissimo. Que cruces grandes sunt et alte, pleneque lapidibus preciosis, et quelibet earum ponitur in vno curru. Et deputantur ad custodiam cuiuslibet crucis x. milia hominum armatorum et plus quam c. milia hominum peditum. Et iste numerus custodum habetur sine principali exercitu et sine scalis ordinatis pro prelio. Et quando pax est et equitat cum priuato consorcio, non portatur ante eum nisi vna crux simplex de ligno sine auro et pictura ob recordacionem passionis Cristi qui passus est in ligno. Portatur eciam ante eum vas plenum terra in memoria incarnacionis sue que in terram reuertetur. Portat nichilominus ante eum vas auro plenum et iocalibus preciosis in signum nobilitatis et dominacionis sue.

Locus habitacionis sue est comuniter apud Susam ciuitatem. Ibi est palacium suum principale, quod tantis habundat diuiciis quod faciliter describi non potest.... [f. 67vb] In tota terra sua non comedunt nisi semel in die, sicut faciunt in curia magni Chan. Et sunt in curia eius comedentes plus quam triginta milia hominum, sed nec isti nec illi de curia magni Chan tantum expendunt sicut x[ii]. milia in partibus istis. Habet eciam iste septem reges continue cum eo ad seruiendum ei, et diuiduntur per menses ita quod quando illi recedunt, alii redeunt. Cum istis regibus seruiunt ei eciam lxxii. duces et ccclx. comites. Omni die comedunt in curia sua xii. archiepiscopi. Patriarcha sancti Thome est ibi quasi papa.... Extenditur autem terra sua in latum quantum transire potest homo in quatuor mensibus comunibus dietis, sed in longum non habet mensuram determinatam....

[f. 68ra] Iuxta predictam insulam de Mulstorak ad sinistram prope fluuium de Phisoun quoddam mirabile cernitur. Est ibi vallis vna inter montes durans spacio quatuor miliariorum. A quibusdam dicitur Vallis Incantata, ab aliis dicitur Vallis Diabolica, a nonnullis vero Vallis Periculosa. In ista valle sepius audiuntur

byforn hym baneris but in the stede of baneris xiii. crossis of
fyn gold, and [thi] aryn meche and heye and ful of preciouse
stonys. And to the kepynge of eche cros aryn asygnyt x.$^{m.}$ men
of armys and mo than an c.$^{m.}$ of foot men, withoutyn the
principal ost and withoutyn lederis that arn ordeynyd for his 5
bataile. And where he ryde in ony place in tyme of pes with
his pryue meyne, thanne is born byforn hym but on cros of tre
withoutyn gold or [f. 36va] ony peynture, in rememorauns of
Cristis passioun that he suffere vpon a cros of tre. And byforn
hym shal ben born a vessel of erthe in tokenyng that he cam 10
of erthe and to erthe shal turnyn. And a vessel ful of gold and
of iewelys shal ben born byforn hym in tokenynge of his grete
lordshepe.

Prestir Ion hath manye noble habytacionys, fayre and delitable to the sight, that longe it were al the nobilte of hym to dis- 15
crye. Thour al hys lond the folk etyn but onys on the day. And,
wete ye wel for sothe, there arn dwellende in his hous ten skore
thousent men. And in his hous arn ay dwellande vii. kyngis for
to seruyn hym, and whan they han dwellid a monyth, thei shul
gon and othir vii. shul come. And with tho kyngis shul [f. 36vb] 20
dwelle ay in the court lx. and xii. dukys. And eche day there
etyn in his court xii. erchebeshopis and xx. bishopis, and the
patriak of Seynt Thomays is as here pope. Trowith wel that
this is soth that I seye, for I was dwellynge in his hous and in his
court long tyme. Prestir Ionis lond contynewith in brede as 25
meche as a man may passe in iiii. woukys continewel iourne, and
in lenthe it may not ben mesoured.

In the lond of Prestir Ion, besyde the yle of Mustorak and
ner the reuere of Pesane, is a wondyr oftyn shewid, for ther is
a valey betwyn too hillis of Doras that cont[i]nuyth iiii. mylyn 30
of lenthe. And some men callen it the Valey of Ench[a]untement,
and some the Deuyllis Valey, and some the Vale Perlious. In
this Vale Perleous arn oftyn herd tempestis and voysis sorweful

1 but] *R* as othir kingis doen but   2 thi] *MS*. ii.   and thi aryn meche and heye] *R om*.   4–6 withoutyn the ... bataile] *R om*.   6 in tyme of pes] *R om*.   13 lordshepe] *R* noblete and lordeshipe   14–16 Prestir Ion ... discrye] *R om*.   17 wete ye wel for sothe] *R om*.   ten skore] *R* xx   19–20 and whan ... come] *R om*.   21 lx. and xii.] *R* xl.   24–25 and in his court long tyme] *R* longe tyme to se alle the manere of that cuntree   28–29 and ner the reuere of Pesane] *R om*.   30 too] *R* the   continuyth] *MS*. contnuyth   31 Enchauntement] *MS*. enchuntement

tempestates ac voces murmurose cum variis tumultibus terri-
bilibus tam noctis quam diebus. Auditur ibi clangor tubarum,
sonitus tympanorum et nacariorum, sicut fieri solebant in festis
magnatum. Vallis hec plena est demonibus et semper fuit.
5 Dicitur quod ibi est vnus introitus inferni. Est ibi copia magna
auri et argenti, pro quibus querendis sepius intrant tam Cristiani quam alii plures sed pauci [f. 68rb] reuertuntur, maxime
de infidelibus; mox enim ut ingressi fuerint vallem causa cupi-
ditatis a demonibus suffocantur.

10   In medio vallis istius sub quadam rupe apparet visibiliter
caput et facies demonis, que facies multum est horribilis
aspectu et vilis. Videtur nisi solum caput [vsque] ad scapulas,
sed non est aliquis in mundo Cristianus qui metum magnum
non incurret aspiciendo faciem illam . . . quod nullus audet
15 appropinquare. De loco illo exit ignis et fumus cum tanto fetore
quod nullus diu ibi sustinere potest. Boni Cristiani stabiles in
fide solidi intrant quandoque vallem et vadunt ibi sine periculo
et metu. Apparent namque visibiliter eis demones circumquaque
comminantes et suscitentes in aere fulgura et tonitrua ac
20 tempestates alias horribiles et inauditas. Ideo multum timent
mali transeuntes, nec mirum, et eciam boni ne forte velit
deus vindicare de malis eorum preteritis.

Noueris quod quando socii mei et ego fuimus in valle ipsa
introeuntes, fluctuauimus cogitacione an ulterius procedere
25 vellemus et committere nos diuine protectioni. Aliqui vero
nostri consenserunt transire, aliqui vero contradicebant. Erant
autem inter nos duo fratres minores de Lombardia qui dixerunt

12 nisi] non nisi   vsque] *om.*   16 nullus] nullius

bothe be day and be nyght. [f. 37ra] And there is herd the vois of trompis, the sound of tympanys and of nakoreris, as it were at a feste of gret lordis. The vale is ful of deuyllis and euere hath ben. Men seyn that ther is on of the entreis of helle or to helle. And in that vale is gret plente of gold and siluyr, and for to 5 getyn therof there comyn oftyn Cristene men and othere and enteryn thedyr in. But there comyn but fewe ageyn out, and the moste party of hem that comyn out aryn myschapyn, for tho that come thedyr because of coueytise arn strangeled and forshapyn and forfarin and wirwid with deuyllis. 10

In the myddis of that vale vndyr a roche shewith opynly the hed of a deuyl orible and foul, that no man dar lokyn theron. Ther is no man in al this world that he shulde haue dred to loke vpon his visage, so oryble and foul [f. 37rb] it is, and forsothe no man dar aprochyn it thedyrward and withoutyn drede. There 15 comyth out of that place a foul fer and a foul roke with so meche foul stynk that no man may sustene hym there. Goode Cristene men and stable in the feith of Crist enteryn thedyr oftyn tyme and comyn ayen withoutyn peril, but fyrst they behouyn to ben clene shreuyn and hoseled, wel blyssid with the signe of the holy 20 cros. And al be it so that they skapyn withoutyn peril of body, yit withoutyn greet dred skape they not, for fendis aperyn to hem opynly and afrayen hem and flyen into the eye with thondyr and fer and othere hidous tempestis that meche dred shal they haue that there forth pasyn, sup[f. 37va]posande that for here 25 olde synnys God wele takyn on hem vengeaunce.

Mynn felawis and I, whan we wer in that vale and herdyn speke therof, some of vs cestyn in oure herte to puttyn vs in the mercy of God al holly and passyn thour that Vale Perlyous, and some forsokyn and seydyn they woldyn not puttyn hem into that 30 peril. So was there amongis vs too freris of Lumbardie that were

1–3 And there . . . lordis] *R om.*   3 ful] *R* euere ful   3–4 and euere hath ben] *R om.*   4 or to helle] *R om.*   5 siluyr] *R* syluere and precious stones vnto mennes si3te   6 Cristene men and othere] *R* manye men   9–10 forshapyn and forfarin and wirwid] *R* born away   11 opynly] *R om.*   12 and foul] *R om.*   13–15 Ther is . . . withoutyn drede] *R* for no man may him se for horryblenesse and foulenesse   16–17 a foul fer . . . stynk] *R* fire, stynke, and smoke   21 And al be . . . body] *R om.*   22 dred] *R* pereille and gret drede   23–24 and flyen . . . tempestis] *R om.*   25 supposande . . . vengeaunce] *R om.*   26 God] *MS.* supposyng that God   27–28 whan we . . . therof] *R om.*   30 forsokyn and] *R om.*

se velle ulterius transire si aliqui de nobis secum vellent iter arripere, ita tamen quod transituri se pararent per confessionem et alias deuociones erga deum. Nos vero, accepta fiducia ex eorum sermonibus et exhortacionibus, fecimus missas celebrari et,
5 factis confessionibus nostris, comunicauimus, et sic intrauimus vallem socii xiiii. numero. Sed in reditu fuimus nisi nouem. Non constabat nobis quid de ceteris factum fuerat, vtrum perditi essent an reuersi, sed nos eos non vidimus vltra. Fuerunt autem ii. Greci et tres Hispanici. Alii autem socii, qui vallem noluerunt
10 intrare, perrexerunt alio itinere ad obuiandum nobis uel ut nos precederent.

Ego [vero] cum sociis relictis vallem transiui. Vidimus autem ibidem in locis pluribus copiam magnam auri et argenti ac lapidum preciosorum et iocalium ex omni parte; vtrum sic erat
15 in rei veritate aut sola apparencia, nescio propter demonum fallaciam qui solent homines aspectu deludere. Nichil tangere voluimus propter periculum et ne impediretur deuocio nostra, quia tunc magis eramus deuoti et orationibus intenti quam vmquam prius uel postea, et hoc propter terrorem demonum
20 qui apparuerunt in diuersis figuris et eciam propter maximam multitudinem corporum mortuorum hominum quibus locus ille habundabat; [f.68va] quod si duo reges magni cum suis exercitibus pugnarent adinuicem et maior pars esset occisa, non esset tantus numerus occisorum sicut ibi, quod satis horribile fuit
25 videre.... Frequenter eramus ad terram prostrati per tonitrua et validos ventorum flatus, sed semper dominus protector factus est nobis, ita quod fauente gracia ipsius transiuimus per vallem ipsam incolumes et illesi.

Vltra eandem vallem habetur insula cuius gens magni corporis
30 est quasi gigantes, sunt enim de longitudine xxviii. uel xxx. pedum. Et vestes non habent nisi de pellibus bestiarum quibus corpora sua tergunt, comedentes carnes crudas et lac bibentes, est enim ibidem copia animalium. Domos non habent ad habitandum. Carnes humanas libencius comedunt quam alias carnes. Hanc
35 insulam nullus peregrinus intrat voluntarie, nam gigantes [illi],

9 ii.] vi   12 vero] *om.*   15 propter] nam propter   16 Nichil] tamen nichil   35 illi] *om.*

Menouris, seydyn they woldyn goon there forth yif that ony of vs woldyn take that weye; so that, thour confert of here wordys and excitacioun of hem, we schreuyn vs clene and resseyuyd oure sacrement, an whan we haddyn herd oure masse, we entered into that vale xiiii. felawis. But at the comynge out 5 we were but ix. left. We wetyn neuere [f. 37vb] whedyr thei were left in the vale or they turned ayen at the entre, but we herdyn neuere more of hem aftyr. To of hem were Grekys and iii. weryn Spanyoles. Oure othere falawys that woldyn not passyn the Vale Perlious wentyn by another wey for to metyn vs. 10

I passed the vale, blyssed be God, and myn felas. And therin we seyen fayre placis and plente of gold and siluyr and of precious stonys on eche a syde, but whedyr it was fantem or non we wete not, but for the grete dred that we haddyn and for it shulde not lettyn oure deuocioun, we woldyn not leyn hond on 15 nothing. But aftir that, what for fered of deuellis that aperedyn to vs in dyuers figure and for the multytude of dede menys bodyis that leye there in oure way (for yif that to grete kyngis [f. 38ra] with here ostis haddyn foutyn togedere and the moste part of bothe sydis haddyn ben slayn, there shulde not ben so 20 gret multitude of dede menys bodiis as there were) we were oftyn streke doun to the erthe with grete hidous blastys of wyndis and thondyr. But thour the grace of Almyghty God we pacede the Vale Perlious hol and fer and in good poynt.

Beside that Vale Perlious is an yle. The men that wonyn 25 therin arn meche of stature of body as thei were ieauntis. They arn xxx. fote of lenthe. Clothis han they none but of the skynnys of bestis. Housis haue they none. They wely[n] gladly etyn menys flesch and leuere than ony othir flesch. And yif thei se a shep in the se with men, they welyn entryn into [f. 38rb] the 30

---

2 of vs] *MS.* of of vs 2–3 of here wordys] *R om.* 4 sacrement] *R* creature and whan we haddyn herd oure masse] *R om.* 6–7 We wetyn ... entre] *R om.* 8–10 To of hem ... metyn vs] *R om.* 11 I passed ... felas] *R* I Ioon Mawndevile and my felawes passid that vale harmelees 11–24 And therin ... good poynt] *R om.* 25 yle] *R* ile be the see 26 of body as thei were ieauntis] *R om.* 28 bestis] *R* beestis and they ete rawe flesshe and raw3 fisshe and drynken watir or mylke welyn] *MS.* wely

si viderint nauem cum hominibus, ingrediuntur mare ad comprehendendum eos. Adhuc dictum erat nobis quod fuit insula ultra illam vbi fuerunt gigantes maiores. Sed non habui voluntatem videndi eos quia nullus intrare potest insulas illas nisi statim deuoretur ab huiusmodi monstris. Inter istos gigantes sunt oues de magnitudine boum, et est lana eorum valde rudis et grossa. Viderunt nonnulli gigantes istos homines interdum capere in mari captosque deferre ad terram duos in manu vna et duos in [alia], comedentes carnes eorum crudas.

Alia insula est ibi pulcra valde et bona, hominibus plena, cuius consuetudo talis est quod nouiter maritata mulier non cubabit nocte prima cum marito suo sed cum alio adolescente qui eam deuirginabit pro mercede sua in crastinum recipienda. Sunt enim constituti tales adolescentes in qualibet villa pro tali seruicio faciendo, quos vocant *Cadeberios*, quod interpretatur fatui desperati.

Dicunt enim ibidem et tenent pro firmo quod valde periculosum est aliquam deuirginare in tantum quod creditur quod ille qui hoc opus aggreditur exponit se periculo mortis. Et si maritus inuenerit vxorem suam virginem nocte sequenti, ita quod ille alius uel causa ebrietatis uel alia causa eam non deuirginauit, habebit actionem suam versus eum coram iudicibus ac si voluisset eum occidere. Sed post primam noctem [f. 68vb] cum fuerint vxores sic deflorate, de cetero tam stricte custodiuntur quod non audent cum alio viro loqui.

Quesiui causam huius consuetudinis, et dictum michi fuerat quod antiquitus quidam mortui fuerant ex deuirginacione iuuencularum que infra se habebant serpentes, et ideo mos iste inoleuit apud eos.

9 alia] manu altera   13 sua] suam

se for to takyn hem to here mete. No man may come into that yle but he be sone wirwid and etyn and fordon with sweche forshapynne bestis. And therfore I hadde no talent for to comyn amongis hem. In that yle among tho ieauntis arn shep as meche as oxsyn ben here, but the wolle of hem is mechil and long. Men han sen the ieauntis takyn men in the see and comyn to londe with too in the ton hand and too in the thothir hand, etande her flesch raw.

Ther is anothir yle and a profitable in that lond of Prestir Ion and ful enabitid with men. Ther is a custom amongis hem that whan a maydyn is amongis hem newe weddyd, she shal not the fyrste nyght lye [f. 38ᵛᵃ] with hyre husbonde but with anothyr man that shal han here maydynhed, takynge vpon the morwe a certayn mone for his trauayle. And in euery toun of that yle arn certeyn men that ben yonge ordeyned for to do that seruyse, the whiche they callyn *Gadiberis*, that is for to say, fol[s] dispered.

They seyn there and affermyn it for soth that it is a ful perlious thing to takyn a virgyne maydynhed, for they seyn ho so doth, he disposith hym to peril of deth. And yif the husbonde of that woman fynde here a maydyn in the nyght aftyr, so he that shulde an had here maydynhed, be it for dronkynesse or for ony othir cause, dede not the ferste nyght his deuer to the woman, thanne here housbonde shal han his accioun to hym byforn the iuge, as meche as he hadde slayn his fadyr. But at the fyrste nyght that the woman be thus de[f. 38ᵛᵇ]foiled, they arn so streytly kept aftyr that they dar speke to no man.

I, Ion Maundeuyle, askid hem what was the cause and the skil whi that swich customys weryn vsed ther. And thei seidyn me that in olde tyme some men in that cuntre weryn dede for they refte yynge maydenys of here maydynhed, for they haddyn withinnyn hem, as longe as they were virgynys, nederis, and therfor they heldyn that custome in that contre.

2–3 and fordon ... bestis] *R om.*   5 mechil and long] *R* stour as it were of a beere   6–8 Men han ... raw] *R om.*   9 and a profitable] *R om.*   10 and ful enabitid with men] *R om.*   15 seruyse] *MS.* seyuyse   16 fols] *MS.* a fol   17 ful] *R* foul and   18–19 for ... deth] *R om.*   21 dronkynesse] *MS.* dronkyensse   24 his fadyr] *R* him   26 so] *R om.*   that they dar speke to no man] *R om.*   27–28 I Ion ... vsed ther] *R* the cause why that they doo so   32 heldyn that custome in that contre] *R* holde ȝit that ilke custome and euermore wolen

Est et alia insula versus austrum in occeano vbi sunt femine pessime et crudeles. Habent in oculis suis lapides preciosos, et sunt talis nature quod si irate respexerint aliquem occidunt eum solo intuitu, sicut facit basiliscus serpens.

5 Est et alia insula iuxta eam vbi mulieres multum dolent quando infans nascitur, et quando moritur valde letantur et festum faciunt cum leticia et mortuum proiciunt in ignem copiosum ad comburendum. Mulieres quoque que viros suos defunctos bene dilexerunt proiciunt se ipsas in ignem cum
10 infantibus suis et ardent. Dicitur enim ibidem, et est opinio eorum, quod sic per ignem purgabuntur ab omni deformitate et vicio ita quod mundi et puri transibunt ad aliud seculum ad suos maritos. Causa autem quare plorant in natiuitate infancium et gaudent d[i]e morti[s] eorum, ista est secundum dictu[m] eorum
15 quod quando infans nascitur intrat inmundum ad laborem et dolorem; quando vero moritur vadit in paradisum, ut dicunt, vbi sunt fluuii manantes lacte et melle et omnium bonorum habundancia sine labore uel dolore. . . .

[f. 69ra] In hac patria ducunt in matrimonium filias suas et
20 sorores aliasque consanguineas suas, et morantur in vno hospicio x. homines uel xii. aut plures. Et vxor cuiuslibet comunis [est] omnibus personis ibidem morantibus et vxores sue alterutrum accipiunt. Sed quando genitus fuerit infans, dabitur ei qui prius cubauerit cum muliere, ita quod nullus scit utrum infans suus
25 sit an alterius. Et si dicatur eis quod isto modo nutriunt puerum alienum, respondent quod ita nutriunt alii suum. . . .

[f. 69rb] Vltra insulam istam inuenitur alia magna satis et bona, plena hominibus bonis et fidelibus ac laudabilis vite iuxta ritum conuersacionis sue. Et quamuis Cristiani non sunt, viuunt tamen

14 die mortis] de morte   dictum] dicta   21 est] *om.*   27 satis] satis opulenta

There is anothir ile there besyde where crewel wemyn and wekede arn dwellende, that han, as men seyn there, precious stonys in here eyne growende, that yif they lokyn vpon a man with an egre wil and a wrothful that thour wertu of that ston they slen that man with a lokyng.

In that eche lond is an yle where that women [f. 39ra] makyn meche sorwe whan they bere a child. And whan the child deyeth, they makyn meche [ioye] and kallyn here frendys and makyn grete festys and takyn the child and brennyn it in a gret fer. And tho women that louyn wel here hosbondys that aryn dede puttyn hemself into the fer to brennyn with here child. They seyn, and is here opynyoun there, that right as they aryn purgyd thour the feer and brent, so that non corrupcioun neuere aftyr shal more comyn of hem, that right so pure and clene they shul passe to here hosbondis into the tothir world. The skyl whi thei gretyn whan here childeryn arn born and makyn ioye whan they deyen is this; that for whan they comyn into the world they come to sorwe and trauayle, and whan they deye they come to the ioye of paradys where abundaunce and plente is of hony and of mylk and of alle maner of othere good withoute trauayle or sorwe.

[f. 39rb] In that contre is an yle where men take to here wyues here doughtryn, here systryn, and here cosynys, and wonyn in an hous togedere, x. or xii. or mo. And euery manys wif is comoun to othere men that wonyn in that hous. And whan a child is born, it shal be youyn to hym that ferst lay by here. So is there non of hem that wot whedyr the child be his or anothyr manys child.

Ther is an yle in that lond nobil and riche and enabitid, ful of goode men and trewe and locable aftyr the maner of here conuersacioun. And thow it be so that they ben none Cristene men, not forthi they leuyn a kyndely lyf and a skilful and ful of

1–2 wemyn and wekede] *R* men and women 2 as men seyn there] *R om.* 4 and a wrothful] *R om.* 5 that man] *R* the man or the woman 6 eche lond] *R* lond of Prester Ioon yle] *R* anothir ile 8 ioye] *MS.* sorwe *deleted* 9 and takyn . . . fer] *R om.* 10 hosbondys that aryn dede] *R* children and the husbondes 12 and is here opynyoun there] *R om.* 13 and brent] *R om.* 18 sorwe] *R* moche sorowe 19 come] *R* seye that they shal goo and plente] *R om.* 20 good] *R* good and tresour 22 In that contre is an yle] *R* and fast beside this forseide ile is anothir ile in Prester Iohnis londe 28 in that lond] *R* faste beside that is callid Ragman 31 ful] *R* arn ful

lege naturali virtutibus pleni, fugientes vicia, maliciam detestantes; non enim sunt superbi, auari, iracundi, gulosi, vel luxuriosi, nec alteri faciunt quod sibi fieri nollent. Non est eis cura de diuiciis vel rebus terrenis. Non menciuntur. Non iuramentum faciunt vlla occasione sed simpliciter 'Est' vel 'Non est'; dicunt enim quod ille qui iurat intendit decipere proximum. Appellatur insula illa insula Bragmanorum. . . .

Terra ista non habet furem nec homicidam, nec est ibi meretrix nec medicus. Numquam ibi aliquis occidebatur. Sunt ita casti et boni ac sancte conuersacionis sicut aliqui religiosi. Non habent ibi tempestates, fulguris tonitrui vel grandinis; famem, pestilenciam, uel guerram non paciuntur sicut nos in partibus istis pro peccatis nostris; vnde verisimile est quod deus eos amat et acceptam habet fidem illorum cum operibus bonis. Credunt namque in deum omnium creatorem, ipsumque adorant et colunt. Pro nichilo ducunt omnia terrena. Et sunt per omnia recte viuentes, ordinate, et sobrie in cibo et potu [ita quod] longius viuunt ceteris nacionibus et plures eorum moriuntur sine morbo, eo quod natura in eis deficit ob nimiam senectutem.

Tempore quondam Alexandri magni misit eisdem idem rex ad gentem istam ad explorandum patriam, quia voluit eam sibi subicere sicut et ceteras.

Illi vero remiserunt litteras in hunc modum: 'Quid sufficere potest homini cui totus mundus non sufficit? Nichil apud nos [f. 69va] reperies propter quod expugnare deberes, non enim habemus diuicias mundi nec cupimus habere. Omnia loca patrie

18 ita quod] ideo

goode vertues, and forsakyn alle maner of [f. 39va] vicious
thyngis, for thei aryn not auerous ne coueytous ne they vsen no
glotenye ne lecherie, ne they don to non othir man but as they
woldyn were don to hem. They settyn not by non richesse of
this world ne by non erthely thing. They makyn none lesyngis. 5
They swere none othis for nothing, but sympelyche seyn it is
or it is not, for they seyn that he that sweryth is aboute for to
begyle and disseyue his neighbore. This yle that this good folk
dwellyn in, it is the yle of *Bragman*.

In that lond is non thif ne non strompet ne non comoun 10
woman ne non lyere ne non mansleere. Thei arn as chaste men
and of as good conuersacioun of alle thynge as it were religious
men. There aryn none tempestis of non maner of wedyr in that
contre, of thondir, ne hail, ne snow; ne hongir, ne pestellence,
ne werre comyth neueremor [f. 39vb] amongis hem as doth to 15
vs in these contreis for oure synne. They trowyn in God that
made alle thynge, and hym they honoure in al here power, and
alle erthely thyngis they sette at nought. They ben rightwise
leuande men and eueremore sobre and mesurable men in mete
and drynk. And forthi thei aryn the lengeste leuande men of alle 20
othere nacionys, for manye of hem deyen withoutyn seknesse
of bodi, that whan kynde faylyth hem for ouergret age they
fallyn r[i]ght doun ded.

Whan Alisaundre the Conquerour regnede and conquerede
al the world, in that tyme he com by that yle and sente his 25
letteris to hem that dwelledyn therinne, and seide he wolde dispolyen here lond but if they woldyn ben vndyr his subieccioun
and hym vndyrloute as othere londis and contreis dedyn.

And they wretyn here letteris ageyn in this maner: [f. 40ra]
'What thyng may suffise to that man that al the world may not 30
suffyse? Thow myght reue from vs nothing, for we han non
richesse of this world ne not coueyte for to haue. Alle the placis
of oure lond aryn comounne to euery man. Alle oure richesse
is mete and drynk, wherewith we susteyne oure bodyis. Oure

1 vertues] *R* werkes   3 don] *R* doen noo skathe   6 othis for nothing]
R grete othis   8 and disseyue] *R om.*   8-9 This yle . . . Bragman] *R om.*
9 Bragman] *MS.* aragman   10 ne non strompet] *R om.*   11 ne
non lyere] *R om.*   14 snow] *R* snows no oueregret reyn   16 trowyn]
MS. trowynge   23 right] *MS.* rght   28 and hym . . . dedyn] *R*
as othir cuntrees were   31 nothing] *R* nothing but our bodies

sunt omnibus comunia. Diuicie nostre sunt esca et potus quibus corpus sustentamus. Noster thesaurus est concordia, pax et dilectio adinuicem. Loco ornatus corporis vilis vtimur panniculo pro cadauere tergendo. Mulieres nostre non sunt compte uel
5 ornate ad apparenciam et complacenciam oculorum, sed talem ornatum stulticiam reputamus ut addatur corpori maior pulcritudo humano studio quam deus ei naturaliter dedit. Nesciunt mulieres nostre maiorem pulcritudinem appetere quam eis concessum est a natiuitate.
10 'Terra nobis duo ministrat, victum dum viuimus et sepulturam post mortem. Huc usque pacem habuimus, de qua nunc nos spoliare et exheredare queris. Et nos regem habemus non pro iusticia alicui facienda, quia apud nos non fit iniuria, sed pro nobilitate nostra conseruanda et pro obediencia nostra pro-
15 banda. Iudex apud nos non habet locum quia nullus facit alteri quod sibi nollet fieri. Nichil a nobis auferre potes nisi pacem que semper nobiscum permansit.'

Et cum legisset Alexander litteras istas, cogitauit penes se quod malum et inquinatum esset talem gentem inquietare, et
20 dedit eis securitatem et pacem, mandans eis quod obseruarent ulterius bonos mores suos et pacem pristinam tenerent in perpetuum, et sic ab eis diuertit.

Est et alia insula nomine Exciadrate et alia que vocatur Tynostriphe, vbi pro magna parte tenent morem Bragmanorum,
25 conuersantes innocenter in fidelitate et mutua dilectione, et vadunt isti semper nudi. Has insulas intrauit Alexander, et ut vidit fidelitatem eorum, dixit eis quod non grauaret eos sed peterent ab eo quicquid vellent et daret eis.

Qui responderunt ei quod diuicias petere nollent nec habere
30 nisi tantum victum simplicem quo corpus sustentari possit, quia diuicie huius seculi fallaces sunt et transitorie. Sed si possit Alexander dare quod essent inmortales, tunc vellent [ei] multum regr[aci]ari.

18 legisset] perlegisset   32 dare quod] quod dare non posset   ei] *om.*
33 regraciare] regrari

tresour is pes and acord, loue and charite that is amongis vs.
Oure wiuys ben not solempnely aparayled to the plesynge of
oure eyen, for swiche maner onourement we holdyn gret folye,
to putte to the wrechede body more beute than God hath
kyndely youe therto.

'Oure contre seruyth vs of ii. thyngis, oure lyflode whil we
leuyn and sepulture whan we ben dede. And euere into this
tyme we [f. 40rb] han led and leuyd in pees, of the whiche that
thow wit now deserityn vs. We han ouer vs a kyng, not for no
right to don to ne fro, for amongis vs no man doth othir wrong
but as he wolde he dede to hym. And therfore from vs mayst
thow reue nothing but pes, that euere yet hath ben amongis
vs.'

And whan the king Alexandir hadde rad here letteris, he
thoughte in his herte that it were ylle and a gret onmanhod to
greuyn or to disesyn sweche men, and yaf pes and reste to hem,
and bad hem contynewe here goodnesse and here goode maneris
and vsyn here customys and goode thewis in ferme pes for
eueremore.

Ner besyde this yle is anothir yle that men calle Exiadras. In
that yle they holdyn for the more party the lawis of the [f. 40va]
Bragmi[n]s, leuande innocently in loue and charyte, but they
gon euere nakyd. Into that yle cam Alexander the Conquerour,
and from that tyme he say here conuersacioun and here goode
leuynge, he seyde that he wolde not greue hem, but bad hem
askyn what they woldyn of hym that myghte esyn hem and he
wolde yeue it hem.

They seydyn that richesse wolde they non aske ne haue but
only mete and drynk wherwith the body may ben sustenyd, for
the goodis of this world is disseyuable and not lastande. But yif
that he myghte yeuyn hem thing that were ay lastande and not
dedly, thanne wolde they thankyn hym meche.

1 and acord] *R om.*   2–3 to the plesynge of oure eyen] *R om.*   4–5 more beute . . . therto] *R om.*   8 led and leuyd in] *R has*   9–10 for no right to don] *R* to riȝt amonge vs nothir   12 pes that] *R* our bodies for   15 ylle and a gret] *R* synne and   16 or to disesyn] *R om.*   17–18 here goodnesse . . . pes] *R* forth her good maners and customes in feerme and pees as they diden bifore   22 Bragmins] *MS.* Arraginis leuande innocently in loue and charyte] *R om.*   24 and from that tyme] *R* at that same tyme and whenne   goode] *R om.*

Ad quod respondit Alexander quod dare non posset quia et ipse mortalis erat sicut [illi. Et 'Quare,' inquiunt] 'tu tam superbus es et presumptuosus quod totum mundum tue vis subdere subiectioni quasi deus esses, nec noscis terminum vite tue neque 5 diem neque horam? Et queris tibi accumulare omnes diuicias mundi, que tamen te dimittent et relinquent, velis no*l*is, vel tu eas sicut et illis contigit qui ante te fuerunt. Tu nichil de mundo tecum portabis, sed vacuus et nudus exibis sicut nudus intrasti, et reuertetur caro tua in terram de qua assumpta est. Cogitare 10 [f. 69vb] ergo debes quod nullus inmortalis est nisi deus qui cuncta creauit.' Hiis et huiusmodi dictis, Alexander stupefactus et compunctus discessit. . . .

In terra eius sunt multi Cristiani bone fidei, habentes capellanos secum qui missas celebrant, sed conficiunt de pane fermentato 15 sicut Greci. Ad missas non dicunt tantum sicut capellani nostri, [f. 70rb] sed tantum dicunt orationem dominicam cum verbis consecracionis prout edocti fuerant antiquitus per sanctum Thomam apostolum. De ceteris autem que ordinata sunt per sedem apostolicam et in ecclesia romana frequentata nichil 20 sciunt.

Versus partes orientales a terra Presbiteri Iohannis est insula bona et magna nomine Thaphane. Regem habet nobilem et diuitem, qui est subiectus Presbitero Iohanni et constituitur iste per eleccionem. In hac insula due sunt estates et due yemes. 25 Duos autumpnos habent, et omni tempore anni sunt prata florida. Gens patrie bona est et bene se gerit. Inter eos sunt plures Cristiani, qui eciam ita diuiciis habundant quod nesciunt quantum habent. . . .

Insula eciam de Thaphane predicta grandes habet montes 30 aureos quos formice custodiunt satis diligenter, que eciam aurum quasi depurant ibidem separantes purum ab impuro. Sunt enim

2 illi. Et 'Quare,' inquiunt] ceteri. Tunc illi quare   5 diem] horam diem   6 nolis] nobis   14 sed] sed non   19 romana] romanana

The kyng Alisaundre answerde therto and seyde that he myghte not don so, for he was dedly hymself as wel as they. And they answerde hym thanne, why he assemblede togedere the richesse of this world that is trans[f. 40vb]cytorye; 'and whethir thow wilt or thow not, thow shalt go ther from, as they dedyn that were before the. And out of this world shat thow bere nothing with the, but nakid as thow come shat thow passe out of this world, and thyn flesch shal rotyn and turnyn ayen to erthe that thow wer mad of. And therfore shat thow thynkyn that nothing may lastyn eueremore but God that made alle thynge.'

In that lond of Prestir Ion aryn manye goode Cristene men, and han with hem prestis that syngyn here messis in alle thynge as oure prestis don. But they sey the *Pater Noster* and the wordis of the consecracioun as Seynt Thomays the Apostil taught hem in old tyme. But of the ordenaunce of the Co[u]rt of Rome knowe thei right nought.

Toward the est from the lond of Prestir Ion is an yle meche and large [f. 41ra] that me callith Taprobane. Ther is a kyng of that yle, riche and noble, that holdyth that lond of Prestir Ion and vndyr his subieccioun. In that yle aryn eueremor to someris and to wyntyris in the yer and to heruestis, and eueremor somyr and wyntir the medewis aryn grene. The men of that yle arn goode men of conuersacioun, and manye Cristene men wonyn in that yle amongis hem that aryn so riche that thei wetyn non ende of here good.

NOTA DE MONTIBUS AUREIS

This eche fayre, riche and nobil yle, Taprobane. In that yle aryn grete hillis of gold, the whiche that the muris, a maner of beste, kepyn and besily puryn the gold and departe the purede from the vnpurede. The muris arn as mech as oure houndys arn

3 answerde] *R* asked of   8 out of this world] *R om.*   rotyn and] *R om.*
9 mad of] *MS.* of mad   11 thynge] *R* thing lastynge and vnlastinge
13 messis] *R* messis in the manere of the Grekes for they seie no3t her messis   15 of the] *MS.* of the the   consecracioun] *R* sacrement but pistille ne gospelle seye they non   16–17 But of . . . nought] *R* also the pope of Rome ne non of his cardenalis   Court] *MS.* acord   21 and vyndyr his subieccioun] *R om.*   23 somyr and wyntir *R om.*   28 This eche . . . that yle] *R* and in that ile of Thaprobane   29 grete] *R* twoo grete   29–30 a maner of beste] *R om.*

ibi formice de magnitudine canum ita quod si quis audeat prope accedere predictis montibus, statim vero insilirent et eum inuaderent formice. Inde tamen adquiritur ingeniose, nam tempore calido solent formice se in terra recondere a tercia hora
5 diei usque ad nonam. Tunc homines patrie in circuitu veniunt cum camelis et equis, et imponunt eis onera predicti auri, et recedunt antequam exeant formice de terra.

Alio autem tempore, cum non habundat calor, vtuntur alio ingenio. Imponunt enim iumentis que pullos habent singulis
10 duo vasa in modum sportellarum, vacua et aperta desuper, et suspendunt ea in dorsis iumentorum hinc inde usque ad terram. Deinde *mittu*nt iumenta ad pasturandum in circuitu montium illorum, pullis eorum domi retentis. Et quando formice vident vasa insiliunt in ea, appetunt enim naturaliter nil vacuum relin-
15 quere iuxta se, nec foramen nec caueam nec aliquid huiusmodi. Et isto modo formice implent vasa illa auro. Cum autem putauerint homines quod iumenta sunt bene onusta, emittunt pullos qui hinniunt pro iumentis. Audito vero hinnitu pullorum festinant iumenta reuerti, et sic adquiritur aurum. Formice enim iste bene
20 paciuntur omnia animalia iuxta se preter [f. 70ᵛᵃ] homines. . . .

De hac regione venitur reuertendo ad aliam terram nomine Ciboth, [f. 71ʳᵃ] et est similiter in subiectione magni Chan. Terra bona est et fertilis de bladis, de vino, et de pluribus aliis bonis. Comunes tamen patrie domos non habent nisi tentoria de
25 feltra nigra. Ciuitas regalis murata est lapidibus albis et nigris, et omnes vici ciuitatis strati sunt pauimento optimo talium lapidum. In hac ciuitate nullus audet sanguinem fundere, siue hominis siue animalis, ob reuerenciam cuiusdam ydoli ibidem quod adorant et colunt. . . .

12 mittunt] intrant

here, and forthy no man dare come thedyr for dred of tho foule bestis. Natheles oftyn men getyn of that gold with queyntyse. The kynde of [f. 41ʳᵇ] the mure is this, that whan the wedir is hot, they wele holdyn hem vndyr the erthe from vndyr[n] of the day tyl aftyr the non. Thanne men of that contre aboutyn comyth with chamaylis and hors and chargith hem with the gold, and hieth hem hom faste and yerne er the murys comyn out.

In anothyr yle, where the wedyr is not so hot as is there, they wonne the gold by anothyr wile. They takyn meris that han yonge folys and leyn vpon the mere to syde vessellis, traylende nigh to the erthe, and letyn hem forth erly at morwe to the pasture aboutyn the hillys where the gold is, and the folys they holdyn stille withinne here housys. And the muris thanne sen the emty uessellis and gon to hem and fellyn hem with gold, for the [f. 41ᵛᵃ] kynde o the mure is this, to leue nothing that is void beside hym that they ne wele sone fyllyn it. And whan the men trowyn the meris ben charged, they letyn forth the folis to here damys, and whan the meris heryn here folis neyen, they hien hem faste to hem, wel charged with the gold. And thus they getyn gret plente of gold. The mure may wel suffere alle maner of besstis besidyn hem but only men.

NOTA DE ILLIS QUI AMPUTARE FACIUNT CAPITA PATRUM
SUORUM SUPER EXCELSUM MONTEM POST MORTEM

Ther is a [reume] that men callyn Giboth vndir the subieccioun of the Greete Cane of Tartarie, a r[i]che lond and a plenteuous of corn and wyn and manye othere thyngis. In that reume is a pryncipal cete that no man therin dare drawe non [f. 41ᵛᵇ] blod, neythir of man nor of beste, and al for reuerence of a maumet that they han there, whiche they honoure in alle thynge as here god.

1 thedyr] *R* thider to fecche of, that golde   1-2 tho foule bestis] *R* hem
4 vndyrn] *MS*. vndyr   6 hors] *R* with assis   7 hieth hem hom faste and yerne] *R* trusse faste awey   11 vessellis] *R* grete vessellis
15 uessellis] *R* vessellis vpon the maris   19 to here damys] *R om.*
and] *R* and thenne anon they wole neyghe and   21 The mure] *R* for the kynde of the mors is that they   25 reume] *MS*. ryuer   *R* kingdome
26 riche] *MS*. rche   27 manye] *R om.*   30 in alle thynge] *R om.*

In hac insula habetur consuetudo comunis quod quando pater alicuius mortuus est, si voluerit filius honorem facere patri, conuocat amicos suos et parentes vna cum presbiteris et copia ministrallorum. Et defert corpus defuncti solempniter ad vnum
5 montem vicinum. Deinde prelatus superior amputat caput defuncti et positum in vase [argenteo], uel aureo si sit diues, tradit filio. Et alii parentes cantant et multas orationes dicunt. Postea presbiteri et religiosi legis uel secte illius concidunt totum corpus in frusta, dicentes quasdam orationes alias.

10   Volucres [vero] patrie, scientes consuetudinem et assue[s]tem ad hoc veniunt volantes desuper, videlicet vultures, aquile, et alie huiusmodi que carnibus viuunt. Quibus presbiteri carnes corporum sic concisas proiciunt. Ille quoque sic volantes sedent non longe deuorantes frusta sibi proiecta.

15   Tunc presbiteri cum ministris cantant, dicentes lingua eorum, 'Considerate quam probus iste fuerat quem sic angeli dei veniunt querere et in paradisum portare.' Hoc ipsi cantant sicut presbiteri nostri cantare solent 'Subuenite sancti dei' et cetera. Videtur autem filio et amicis quod magnus honor exhibetur sibi et
20 omnibus parentibus suis cum deuorauerint aues patrem suum. Et quanto plures fuerint aues, tanto magis gaudent amici.

Deinde reducit filius ad hospicium suum omnes amicos et facit illis grande conuiuium. . . . Coquitur autem caput defuncti

6 argenteo] *om.*   aureo] aures   7 filio] filio suo   10 vero] enim
assuestem] assuetudinem

In that contre is a comoun costome that whan a good man is
ded and his sone wele don ony reuerence to hym, he callyth his
kynrede togedere and the souereynys of here lawe and alle hese
frendis and alle the menstrallis that may be getyn. Thanne they
take the dede body and beryn it vp onto an hey hyl. Thanne 5
shal the souereyn stryky[n] of the dede manys hed and leyn it
vpon a vessel of gold or of syluyr, aftir that his stat askyth, and
takyn it to his eldeste sone. And alle tho that arn hise frendis
shuln syngyn thanne, and manye orisounnys shuln ben seyd.
And thanne the prest of that religious [f. 42ra] of here lawe shal 10
hewe the body al in smale pecis and seyn manye orisonys
therouyr.

Thanne the foulys of that contre that knowyth the maner of
that custome comyn and drawe thedyrward, that is for to say,
botoris, eglis, rauenys, and puttokys, and othere foulis that leuyn 15
by carayn and flyeth ther aboutyn for the blod and the rawe
flesch that thei se. Thanne the prestys castyth vp amongis hem
the smale pecis, and euery of hem hyndit his part who may
fyrst come therto and etyn it. Thus they don til the body, flesch
and bon, be born awey and etyn. 20

Thanne the prestis and the clerkis syngyn loude and seyn in
here langage, 'Takyth entent, goode men, and seth how good he
was, that Godis angellis comyn thus to fech his body and beryn
awoy to paradys.' Thanne alle hese frendys makyn gret ioye
[f. 42rb] therof and thankyn hym gretly that for loue woldyn 25
onoure his body so, and thynkyn that gret reuerence is don to
hym. And ay the more foulis that ther comyn, the more ioye
makyn here frendis.

Thanne the sone takyth the hed of his fadyr and goth hom to
his hous with hise frendis, and makyth hem gret festis, and 30
sethet the hed and partyth the flesch among special frendis. And

1 a good man] *R om.*   2 and his sone] *R* and he haue a sone vnto his heir and 3if he   5 hey hyl] *R* hille that is vsid therfore   6 strykyn] *MS.* stryky   10 prest of that religious] *R* prestis   11–12 seyn manye orisonys therouyr] *R* throwe hem aboute   14–16 that is ... carayn] *R om.*   16 the blod and] *R om.*   17 that thei se] *R om.*   17–20 Thanne ... etyn] *R* and ecche of thoo fowlis takith his part and etith it   21 and the clerkis] *R om.*   22 goode men] *R om.*   23 and beryn] *R om.*   24 awoy] *MS.* awor   25–26 therof ... reuerence] *R* for that reuerence that   27–28 And ay ... frendis] *R om.*   31 sethet the hed] *R* after mete he departith the heede and shereth awey the flesshe therfroo

et diuidit filius carnes eius inter speciales amicos. Et de testa capitis facit sibi ciphum ad bibendum in memoriam patris. . . .

[f. 64rb] Sub firmamento celi non est tam magnus dominus, tam potens, tam diues, sicut iste magnus Chan. Nam Presbiter
5 Iohannes qui est imperator Indie maioris tantus dominus non est, nec soldanus Babilonie nec imperator Persie nec aliquis alius ei comparari potest. Et certe magnum dampnum est et satis dolendum quod Cristianus non est. Libenter tamen vult loqui et audire de deo et bene tolerat Cristianos esse in imperio suo.
10 Nullus enim prohibetur ibi talem legem tenere qualem vult. . . .

[f. 60va] Et scias quod mercatores Ianuenses et de Venesio uel de alia parte Lombardie seu de romanis partibus [isti] vadunt per mare [et] per terram spacio xi. uel xii. mensium uel plus quandoque antequam possint peruenire ad insulam de Cathay,
15 que est principalis regio omnium illic existencium. Huius dominus principalis est magnus Chan de Cathay. . . . Hec est ciuitas copiosissima de serico et aliis mercimoniis diuersis . . . iuxta quam ciuitatem gens Tartarorum fecerunt aliam ciuitatem quam appellant Caydoun. Et habet xii. portas, et inter duas
20 portas est spacium vnius miliaris per totum, ita quod totus ambitus ciuitatis, noue et veteris, plus continet quam viginti miliaria.

Ibi est sedes regia magni Chan in vno pulcherimo palacio, quod tante largitatis est quod circuitus murorum plus quam duo
25 miliaria continet. Infra quos muros sunt alia palacia minora, et in orto magni palacii quidam mons est super quem situatur aliud palacium pulcherimum et ditissimum quod reperitur alicubi in mundo. In circuitu palacii et montis sunt diuersa arborum genera, diuersos fructus afferencia. Sunt eciam in
30 ambitu montis fosse late et profunde, et non longe ab eis sunt

12 isti] qui   13 et] siue

of the panne of the hed he makyth hym a cuppe to drynke of al his lyue in rememoraunce of his fadyr.

NOTA DE STATU ET NOBILITATE MAGNI CANE DE CATHAN

It is for to wetyn that vndyr the fyrmament is not in erthe so gret a lord ne so ryche ne so myghti as is the Grete Cane of Tartarye. Not Prestir Ion, that is Emperour of Ynde the Lasse and the [f. 42ᵛᵃ] More, ne the Soudon of Babylonye, ne the Emperour of Pers, ne non othir may ben comparisounned to hym. Certis it is gret harm and mechil to forthynke that he ne were a Cristene man. Not forthi he wele blethly heryn of Cristenne men and of God, and suffere Cristene men to dwellyn in his empire. No man is forbodyn in his lond to leuyn what lawe hym leste.

The yle of Cathan is the pryncipal reume of alle the reumys that ben in that contre, and therof is the Grete Cane pryncipal lord and kyng, and therof he hath his name. In the prouynce of Cathan aren many fayre ceteis and plenteuous of alle maner of marchaundise, of the whiche ceteis the men of Tartarye madyn a cete that men callyn Gaydon. That cete hath xii. gatis, a[nd] betwyn tho gatis [f. 42ᵛᵇ] [is] the space of a myle so that the circuitude of that cete contynuit more than xii. myle al aboutyn.

That is the chif cete of the Grete Cane in a fayr paleys that is so brod and so long that the compas of the paleys contynewith [ii.] myle. And withinne the wallis of that paleys arn othere lasse paleysis and a mount, on the which manye treis ben stondande that beryn alle manere of freutis plentyuously eche yer. And withoutyn the wallis al aboutyn the paleys arn brode dykis and depe with watyr. And not fer from the watir aryn greete pondis ful of watir in eche side of the paleys and a fayr brege ouer the dich. In the dikis and the pondis arn gret

---

6 myghti] *R* myȝti in Cristendome ne in hethnesse   7–8 the Lasse and the More] *R om.*   8 ne the Emperour of Pers] *R om.*   10 and mechil to forthynke] *R om.*   11 blethly] *R om.*   11–12 of Cristenne men and] *R om.*   17 and kyng ... name] *R om.*   18 alle maner of] *R om.*   20 a] *R* alle but oo   and] *MS.* A   21 is] *MS. om.*   23 cete] *R* see   25 ii.] *MS.* a   of] *MS.* of of   27 plentyuously] *R. om.*   28–29 brode dykis and depe] *R* depe diches   29 fer] *MS.* frer   30 pondis] *R* stankes and pondis   watir] *R* fisshe   31 and the pondis] *R om.*

flumina magna. Ex vtraque parte pons est ibi pulcherimus ad transeundum predictas fossas. In hiis fossis seu viuariis habetur multitudo innumerabilis aucarum siluestrium, anatum, cignorum, et heronum. Circa omnia predicta clausura magna habetur infra quam sunt ferarum diuersa genera et copiosa multitudo, ita quod quando placuerit magno Chan habere solacium de feris et volucribus ad chaceadum eas, potest eas videre et comprehendere ad fenestras palacii sui absque hoc quod exeat cameram suam.

In aula palacii sunt columpne xxiiii. de puro auro. Et omnes muri ipsius aule cooperti sunt coriis rubeis quarumdam bestiarum que appellantur pacies. Et sunt bestie pulcherime et optimi odoris, ita quod propter odorem pellium nullus odor malus uel aer in aulam poterit intrare. Pelles iste rubee sunt ad instar sanguinis. Sunt eciam pulcherimi lucentes contra solem quod vix potest aliquis eas respicere pro fulgore. Plures ibidem in patria illa adorant bestias illas, cum viderint eas, propter earum virtutem et bonum odorem, et pelles earum reputant preciosiores tanto auro.

In medio palacii [f. 60vb] est quoddam ascensorium magni Chan, quod optime fabricatum est de auro et lapidibus preciosis et gemmis, et ad quatuor angulos sunt quatuor serpentes aurei. Sub isto ascensorio uel montorio sunt conductus beueragii vnde bibunt qui sunt de curia imperatoris. Et iuxta illos conductus

noumbre of gees and mathelardis and swannys. And beside
th[o] dichis [arn] gret [f. 43ʳᵃ] plente of heronys and botoris and
manye othere dyuers foulis, and aboutyn alle tho is gret closynge
and strong, withinne the whiche closure is gret multitude of
dyuers maner of wilde bestis. And forthy, whan the Cane lokyth 5
for to haue his solas at the wilde bestis or foulys, he may sen
hem ben takyn at his wil and not comyn out of his chambyr but
lokyn out at an wyndow.

In his halle are xxiiii. peleris of fyn gold to beryn vp his halle.
And the wallis of his halle arn kouerede with rede skynnys of 10
a maner of beste that is callid *patyes*. Tho bestis aryn wondyr
fayre in here kynde and of swete sauour, so that for the swete
sauour of the skynnys and the vertue of hem ther may non ille
sauour entre into the halle ne befelyd [eyr]. The skynnys of the
beste arn as rede as ony blod, and they arn fair [f. 43ʳᵇ] shynande 15
ayen the sonne tha[t] vnethe may ony man lokyn vpon hem for
the grete bryghtnes. The folk of that lond honoure the beste
where euere that they sen it, and they holde the skyn of that
beste more precious than as meche gold.

In mydward the paleys is mad a senserye for the Cane, arayed 20
with gold and precious stonys, and at the iiii. corneris arin made
iiii. dragounys of gold. And vndyr that cencerye arn the condytis of the drynk that tho that ben of the Emperouris court
drynkyn therof. And besyde the condytys arn vessellis of fyn
gold *s*et, that men may drynk of whan hem lest. 25

NOTA DE APPARATU AULE MAGNI CANE DE TARTARE

The halle of the grete worthy kyng and emperour, [f. 43ᵛᵃ] the
Grete Cane of Tartarie, is nobil and worchepfully ordeyned in
alle thynge. Vpon the heye deyn is ordeynyd a trone, in myddis

1–3 gees ... dyuers foulis] *R* swannes, herons, gees, mallardis, dokes   2 tho]
MS. th   arn] *MS. om.*   botoris] *MS.* bototoris   4 and strong] *R om.*
6–8 at the wilde ... wyndow] *R* of huntynge, he may haue it att his owne wille
and come nouȝt into the feelde, and ȝif he wole se hem be taken he may
liggen in his chaumbre and se hem taken   11 a maner of] *R* wylde   14 ne
befelyd eyr] *R om.*   eyr] *MS. om.*   16 that] *MS.* tha   vnethe] *R* nouȝt
17 the grete] *R om.*   17–18 The folk ... sen it] *R om.*   19 as meche] *R om.*
23 of the drynk ... therof] *R* to drynke off   24 arn vessellis of fyn gold
set] *R* stonden cuppis of golde   25 set] *MS.* fet   27–28 of the grete ...
Tartarie] *R om.*   28 and worchepfully] *R om.*   29 ordeynyd a trone]
R a seete

ponuntur plur[im]a vasa aurea, de quibus bibere possunt ad conductum.

Aula est satis nobiliter ornata ac mirabiliter disposita in omnibus. Primo namque in capite aule locatur tronus imperatoris alcius a pauimento vbi sedet ipse ad mensam. Est autem mensa ipsius de preciosissimis gemmis, cuius latera operiuntur auro purissimo, in quo auro inseruntur lapides preciosi. Et gradus quibus ascenditur ad tronum et mensam sunt de lapidibus preciosis aureis laminis decoratis.

Ad sinistram imperatoris est sedes prime vxoris vno gradu inferior a sede imperatoris. Et est de iaspide lateribus deauratis et lapidibus preciosis adornatis. Sedes eciam secunde vxoris adhuc inferiorem tenet locum vno gradu, et est similiter de iaspide. Mensa ipsius ornata ut sedes prioris. Sedes insuper tercie vxoris cum mensa ipsius adhuc inferior ponitur vno gradu et ornatur satis nobiliter; habet enim semper imperator tres vxores secum vbicumque fuerit. Post terciam vxorem ex eadem parte sedent domine et domicelle consanguine regis adhuc inferius, quelibet secundum propinquitatem sanguinis ad regem. Omnes autem femine coniugate habent super caput suum quasi pedem hominis longitudinis vnius cubiti, fabricatum de auro et lapidibus preciosis, in signum subiectionis quod sunt sub pede mariti. Que vero non sunt coniugate predictum signum non portant.

Ad dextram vero imperatoris sedet filius eius primogenitus qui regnare debet post eum, et est sedes eius vno gradu inferior sede imperatoris, et fabricata est ipsa sedes ad modum sedis imperatoris. Post ipsum sedent alii magnates de parentela eius, ut superius dictum est de dominabus. Habent enim omnes mensas per se de auro et lapidibus preciosis vel de cristallo vel amatisto uel de ligno aloes, quod de paradiso venit, vel de ebore, et sunt iste mense laminis aureis ornate in lateribus et extremitatibus suis, ut predictum est, ita quod non est mensa quin valeat magnum thesaurum.

Sub mensa imperatoris sedent quatuor clerici ad pedes eius

1 plurima] plura

of the deis, for the Emperour where he sittyth heyest from that pauuement at his mete. His bord is of precious stonys, and the grecis where he goth vp to his trone arn alle of precious stonys, endentid with gold.

Vpon his left hand is the sete for his fyrste wif, a gre lowere than his trone. Here bord is of iaspere, with the coostis of here bord of gold, set ful of precious stonys. The sete of his secunde wif is yit an gres lowere, and here bord mad honourabli as the othire arn. The sete of the thredde wif is yit a gre lowere than the tothir, and here bord mad wel and honourabli as the othere beforn. The Emperour hath eueremo[f. 43vb]re iii. wiuys wher euere so he ryde in contre fer or ner. Nyst his thredde wif sittyn ladyis and damesellis, eche of hem a gre lowere than othir aftir that they ben nest of blod to the Emperour. Alle the wemyn of that contre that ben weddyd han, stondynge vpon here hed, as it were a manys fot mad of gold and set ful of precious stonys, in tokenynge they aryn vndyr here lordys subieccioun. And they that arn not weddyt beryn not that tokene.

Vpon the ryght han of that Emperour sittyth his eldeste sone that shal regnyn aftyr hym, a gre lowere than hymself, and his bord araied in alle thynge as the Emperouris bord is. Nyst hym sittyn othere grete lordis of the Emperouris kyn, eche of hem a gre lowere than othir aftir that they ben of kyn to the Emperour. Here bordys ben alle of iaspre, amastik, of cristal, and of that [f. 44ra] tre that is callyd aloes that comyth certeyn tyme of the yer out of paradys, and alle here bordis rychely arayed with gold and precious stonys, so that there is none of hem that it ne is worth a gret tresore.

And [vndyr] the Emperouris bord beforn his fet sittyn foure clerkys that wrytyn alle the wordis that the Emperour seyth *at* his mete, whethir that they ben goode or wekke, for al that he

1 deis] *R* trone   3 stonys] *R* stones and the sides thereof arn golde set fulle of precious stones   6 coostis] *R* toftis   9–11 The sete . . . othere beforn] *R om.*   12 ryde in contre fer or ner] *R* be   Nyst . . . Emperour] *R om.*   16–17 and set ful of precious stonys] *R om.*   18–19 And they . . . tokene] *R om.*   21 that shal regnyn aftyr hym] *R om.*   22 in alle thynge as the Emperouris bord is] *R* as his fadres   22–25 Nyst . . . Emperour] *R* and so aftir euery lorde in his degree arn sittynge in his halle euery daie at mete 26–27 certeyn tyme of the yer] *R om.*   27–29 and alle . . . tresore] *R om.* 30 vndyr] *MS. om.*   31 at] *MS.* as

qui redigunt in scriptis quicquid imperator dicit, siue sit bonum siue sit [f. 61ʳᵃ] malum; omne enim quod dicit oportet fieri et obseruari, quia non potest dictum suum mutari uel reuocari. . . . Et omnia vasa quibus seruitur in aula et in cameris, specialiter ad
5 mensas nobilium, sunt de iaspide vel cristallo uel de amatisto aut de puro auro. Sunt ibi cibi de smaragdine, de saphiro, de topazio, et aliis generibus lapidum. Vasa argentea non habentur ibi quia non appreciant argentum, sic quod velint de eo bibere uel alia cibaria sumere, sed faciunt de eo gradus et columpnas ac
10 pauimenta domorum. . . .

[f. 61ʳᵇ] Scias pro certo quod socii mei et ego cum nostris valettis fuimus in seruico istius domini ad stipendia eius per spacium xv. mensium contra regem de Mancy, aduersus quem guerram habuit. Causa nostre more cum eo hec fuit quod
15 desiderauimus videre nobilitatem eius et statum curie sue ac excellenciam omnium diuiciarum, que omnia fuissent nobis incredibilia nisi oculis nostris vidissemus. . . .

[f. 62ʳᵃ] Post hec Chan congregauit exercitum contra eos qui eum sic infestauerant, quos et deuicit et subiecit seruituti.
20 Postquam ergo conquisisset omnes in circuitu naciones et suo subiugasset imperio . . . incidit in infirmitatem et bene sensit quod esset moriturus. Dixit ergo xii. filiis suis quod quilibet eorum sibi vnam de sagittis suis apportaret. Quod cum fecissent, iussit eas simul ligari tribus ligaturis.

8 velint] volunt

seyth, it mot nedys ben holdyn and don in dede, for his word mai not ben ageynseyd for no thing. Alle the vessellis that are seruyd in halle or in chambre byforn ony lord arn of iaspere, or of cristal, or of amastik, of of fyn gold. And alle here coppis ben of saferis and dyamauntis and othere precious stonys, for vessel of syluyr they preise not for they welyn of hem neythir etyn ne drynkyn, [f. 44rb] for they makyn of siluyr grecis, pelerys, and pauuement to here floris of here housis.

It is for to wetyn that I Ion Maundeuyle and mynne felas were wyth hym, in his seruise dwellande and at hese wagis xv. monethis, ayen the Kyng of Mauncy, with whom he hild werre. The cause why that we dwelledyn with hym was to knowe the stat of hym and the nobley of his court and the excilence of his richesse, the whiche we myghte not knowe ne trowyn but we seye with oure eyen.

NOTA QUALITER IPSE MAGNUS CANUS CONQUES*IUI*T REGEM DE MANCY

This iche Grete Cane gaderede his ost and wente forth with a companye innumerable of excellentment, and conquerede the Kyng of Mancy forseid, and put hym vndyr his [f. 44va] subieccioun and vndirloute to hym and to hese eyris for eueremore. Whan he hadde conquerid al that was ab[o]utyn hym and made hem thrallis and vndyr his subieccioun of his empere, he fil in seknesse and felte wel that he shulde deyen. He sente aftir hese xii. sonys, and seyde to hem and bad that eche of hem shulde bryngyn hym an arwe, and thei dedyn as he bad hem. And he bad hem byndyn the arwis togedere, and thei dede so and boundyn hem faste togedere in iii. placis.

And whan thei were so boundyn, he bad his eldeste sone brekyn hem, so boundyn togedere as they were, and he assayede

1–2 in dede... thing] *R om.* word] *MS.* world 3 or in chambre] *R om.*
7 grecis] *R om.* 8 to here floris of here housis] *R* vnto her hallis and chaumbris 9–10 It is... dwellande and] *R* for I Ioon Mawndevile dwellid with the Grete Caan 13 and the nobley] *R om.* 16 CONQUESIUIT] *MS.* conquesunt 18–19 his ost... excellentment] *R* an innumerable oost of man of armes 21 and vndirloute] *R om.* 22–23 Whan he hadde... empere] *R* and aftir this iourney aboutyn] *MS.* abutyn 25 eche of hem] *R* they 26 an arwe] *R* xx arowes 26–28 and thei... placis] *R om.* 30 so boundyn togedere as they were] *R om.*

Deinde dixit filio suo [f. 62rb] seniori quod eas sic ligatas frangeret, qui temptauit nec potuit. Dedit et secundo filio suo nec ipse frangere potuit. Sicque fecit cum ceteris filiis suis, nec potuit eas aliquis frangere. Tandem dixit filio suo minimo, 'Tu fili, solue ligaturas [et frange sagittas] singillatim', qui statim fecit ut ei imperatum fuerat, frangens vnam post aliam.

Dixit ergo pater ceteris filiis, 'Quare non potuistis vos sagittas frangere?' Responderunt, 'Quia simul erant ligate.' Dixitque pater, 'Quare potuit frater vester minor?' Dixerunt, 'Quia dissolute erant et diuise.'

'Sic,' inquit pater, 'erit de vobis, filii mei. Si colligati fueritis vos triplici vinculo dilectionis, fidelitatis, et concordie, nullus preualebit vobis aut nocebit. Si vero fueritis hiis vinculis soluti ac diuisi, cito confusi eritis ac consumpti. Si vero [vos] inuicem dilexeritis, domini eritis omnium nacionum.' Hiis et huiusmodi verbis postquam pater filios suos instruxerat et de regno suo cum senioribus ordinauerat, ad extrema deuictus mortis debitum soluit.

Et regnauit pro eo Octochan, primogenitus eius. Alii autem fratres [eius] perrexerunt conquirere sibi terras alias et regiones usque ad terram de Prussy et de Rossy, et fecerunt appellari Chan. Erant tamen subiecti fratri suo seniori, et ideo appellatur ipse magnus Chan et quilibet successorum suorum post eum.

Post Octochan regnauit Cuno, post quem Ma*ngo* Chan qui fidem Cristi suscepit et baptizatus, deuotus extitit Cristianus. Ipse constituit litteras perpetue pacis in regno suo cunctis Cristianis. Et eciam misit fratrem suum Halaon cum magno exercitu ad recuperandum terram sanctam de manibus Saracenorum et ad destruendum legem Machometi ac eciam ad comprehendendum Calafinum de Baldak, qui tunc fuit imperator et dominus Saracenorum. Qui cum captus esset, inuenerunt magnam

4 et frange sagittas] *om.*   5 statim fecit] cum statim fecisset   15 vos] *om.*
20 eius] *om.*   24 Mango] magnus

and myghte not. He bad his seconde sone, and he myghte not brekyn hem. Righ[t] so he bad to alle hese othere sonys and [f. 44^(vb)] none of hem myghte not brekyn hem. And thanne he bad his yingeste sone onbyndyn tho arwis and brekyn eche by the self, and he dede so and brak eche afty*r* othyr.

And thanne he askede hese othere sonys why they myhte not breke tho arwis, and thei answerdyn ayen and seydyn, 'For they were so faste boundyn togedere.' Thanne answerde the Emperour, 'How myghe youre yingeste brothir brekyn hem?' And thei answerdyn ayen, 'For they were losenyd and departyd ech from othir.'

Thanne seyde the Emperour, 'Right so wele it faryn of yow, for as longe as ye ben knyt togedere with iii. bondys, that is for to seye, the bondis of loue and of bounte and acord, ther may no man of al this [f. 45^(ra)] world stryue with yow. But as sone as the knotte is losenyd, as sone are ye shent and confused. And yif that ye louyn stedefastly togedere, ye shul ben lordis of alle naciounnys.' And from the tyme that he hadde spokyn so to hese sonys and shewid hem this ensaumple, he deyede sone aftyrward.

And aftir regnede his oldeste sone, Octohas, and was Cane. And alle his bretheryn wentyn forth and conqueredyn manye othere rewmys and londis, and eche of hem dede callyn hymself Cane, but alle they were subiect to the eldeste brothir. Forthi he was callyd the Grete Cane of alle hese successouris.

And aftir hym regnede his oldeste brothir, Octo Cane. He was baptised and becam a de[f. 45^(rb)]uout Cristene man and a good. He yaf hem letteris of perpetuel pes to alle Cristen men for to wonyn in his reume. He sente his brothir Alone with his ost for to conquere the Holy Lond out of the Sarasynys hondis and for to distroie the lawe of Macomede and for to takyn Calafernum of Baldok, that thanne was emperour and lord of Sarasynys. He tok hym, and fond with hym gret tresor, and

2 Right] *MS.* righ   othere sonys] *R* sones ecchon aftir othir to breke hem
5 aftyr] *MS.* aftyn   9 hem] *R* hem so wel   10 and departyd] *R. om.*   14 and of bounte] *R* lownes   19 and shewid hem this ensaumple] *R om.*   21 Cane] *R* Grete Caan   23 rewmys and] *R om.*   23–25 and eche ... successouris] *R om.*   26 oldeste] *R* secunde   27–28 baptised ... good] *R* a Cristen man   29 Alone] *MS.* alone   29–30 with his ost] *R om.*   33 tok] *R* wente forth and toke

copiam thesauri apud eum. Dixit autem [ei] Halaon, 'Quare cum isto thesauro non conduxisti tibi bellatores pro defensione patrie tue?' Qui respondit et dixit quod sufficienter habuit bellatores de suis propriis. Et dixit ei Halaon, 'Tu quasi deus fuisti Sarace-
5 norum. Deus autem non indiget manducare vel bibere. Ideo non habebis cibum a nobis, sed comedes si volueris lapides tuos preciosos et thesaurum tuum quem [tantum] amasti.' Et sic misit eum in carcerem cum thesauro suo, vbi et fame moriebatur et siti. Iste Halaon conquisiuit totam terram promissionis ad
10 manus Cristianorum.

Sed interim mortuus est magnus Chan, et ideo negocium in deterius mutabatur. Post M*ango* Chan regnauit Chobila Chan, qui similiter Cristianus [f. 62va] fuit. Ipse fundauit ciuitatem magnam in Cathay que vocatur Ionger, que maior est ciuitate
15 Roma. Alius magnus Chan qui fuit post ipsum deuenit paganus, et ceteri omnes post eum.

Scias quod regnum de Cathay maius est ceteris regnis mundi. Et similiter magnus Chan maximus est inter reges ceteros diuiciis et potencia. Stilus autem litterarum eius talis est: 'Chan,
20 filius dei excelsi, omnium vniuersam terram colencium summus imperator et dominus omnium [dominancium].' Superscriptio autem sigilli sui priuati talis est: 'Dei fortitudo. Omnium hominum imperatoris sigillum.' Et maioris sigilli superscriptio talis est: 'Deus in celo et Chan super terram. Eius fortitudo. Omnium
25 hominum imperatoris sigillum.'

1 ei] *om.*   7 tantum] tu   12 Mango] magnus   13 Ipse] et ipse
17 ceteris] ceteris cunctis   21 dominancium] *om.*

BODLEY VERSION 133

seyde to hym, 'Whi woldist thow not gete the men inowe with thyn tresour for to defendyn thyn lond?' And he answerde ayen and seyde that he hadde men inowe of hese owene. Thanne seide Algon to hym, 'Tho were the god of Sarasynys, and a god hath non myster of non mete. And therfore thow shat han 5 [f. 45va] non mete for vs ne drynk, but yf thow wit etyn thynne preciouse stonys and thyn tresour that thow hast gadered togedere and louyd so meche.' There he put hym in his prisoun with al his tresour, where he deyede for honger and for threst. He, this Alaon, conquerede and wan al the Holy Lond into 10 the Cristenne menys hondys.

And thanne deyede the Grete Cane. Forthi it chaungede aftyr hym into wersse. Aftir hym, that goode Cane and that goode man, regnede anothyr that highte Chabila. He was Cane, a good Cristen man. Also he foundede a gret cete in the reume of 15 Catan that is callid Iung, and it is more than the cete of Rome. Aftir hym cam anothir that was callyd the Grete Cane, he that reneyede his lawe and becam sarasyn, and alle othere aftyr hym into this tyme.

And wete ye wel that [f. 45vb] the reume of Catan is more than 20 ony reume of this world. And so is he that is the Grete Cane the gretteste kyng of alle othere kyngis and the richeste of gold and of tresour and of stat. The stile of hese letteris is this, 'C[a]ne, the hie godis sone and souereyn Emperour ouer alle othere kyngis and lord ouer alle othere men.' The scripcioun of his 25 Priue Sel is this, 'The sel of the Emperour, and of alle othere men the myghty god.' The scripcioun of hese Grete Sel is this, God in Heuene and Cane in erthe. *Eius fortitudo. Omnium hominum imperatorum sig[i]llu[m]*.

The grete Emperour and Cane and alle the men of his lond, 30 thow they ben none Cristen men, yit they trowyn eche one in

2 tresour] *MS.* trosour 4 and] *R* as thou trowest and 7 that] *R* and thy goolde that 9 tresour] *R* tresour and bad him ete and drynke theroff honger and for threst] *R* defaute and myscheef 10 and wan] *R om.* 12 thanne] *R* aftir that iournaye Cane] *R* Caan brothir vnto Aloon 13–14 that goode Cane and that goode man] *R om.* 17–18 he that reneyede his lawe and] *R* but he 19–23 into this tyme . . . of stat] *R om.* 23 Cane] *MS.* Cne 25 lord] *R* lordes and 26–27 and of alle othere men the myghty god] *R* is ouere alle men thoru3 the my3t of God 29 *sigillum*] *MS.* sigllu 31 thow they ben none Cristen men] *R om.* eche one] *R* somdel

Iste imperator cum gente sua sibi subiecta, quamuis Cristiani non sint, tamen credunt in deum inmortalem. . . . [f. 64rb] Et de vxoribus quilibet habet pro libito, alius enim habet c. vxores, alius quadraginta, alius plus, alius minus. Et ducunt ibi vxores consanguineas suas, exceptis matribus, filiabus, et sororibus. Sorores autem de patre, non de matre, ducere solent. Similiter vxores fratrum post mortem eorum et suas nouercas ducunt. . . . [f. 65ra] Quando aliquis mortuus est inter eos, ponunt lanceam iuxta eum, et cum prope mortem fuerit, tunc quilibet fugit de domo quousque mortuus fuerit. Deinde sepeliunt eum in campis.

Quando imperator moriturus est, ponunt eum in cathedra in medio tentorii sui, et ponitur coram eo mensa cum mappa et superponuntur cibi cum cipho pleno lacte iumentorum, et statuitur iuxta eum iumentum vnum cum pullano secum. Equs eciam suus adducitur stratus et frenatus, et ponitur super eum aurum et argentum. Deinde faciunt fossatum grande vbi predicta omnia cum rege sepeliunt in tentorio. Dicunt autem in alio seculo cum voluerit, non carebit hospicio, equo, auro, [f. 65rb] et argento. Iumentum vero, ut dicunt, dabit ei lac et portabit sibi equos alios, ita quod bene erit ibidem prouisus de necessariis. Credunt namque isti quod post mortem in alio seculo erunt comedentes et bibentes et iocantes cum mulieribus sicut hic in vita ista fecerunt. Postquam itaque imperator sepultus fuerit modo predicto, nullus ex tunc aliquid loqui audet de eo in audiencia alicuius amicorum suorum; similiter nec de aliis mortuis. . . .

[f. 58ra] Iuxta istam insulam transeundo per mare inuenitur alia insula larga et bona que vocatur Thalamassi. . . . De pre-

grete God that made heuene and erthe. In his reume they han swiche a custome that it is lefful to eche a man to han as manye wyuys as he wele, some for to haue xl. [f. 46ʳᵃ] and some an hondered, and some more and some lasse as hym list, for they take to here wivis here sisteris by the faderis syde, but not bi the 5 moderis side, here cosynys, and here brotheris wivis whan here bretheryn aryn dede. And whan that ony man is ded that ony stat beryth, they leyn his spere in his graue besydyn hym. And whan they se that a man is nygh ded, they fle echon out of his hous tyl he be ded, and thanne they take hym and graue hym 10 in the feld.

NOTA DE IMPERATORE, VIDELICET CANE, CUM FUERIT MORTUUS

Whan the Emperour that is the Greete Cane is ded, thei settyn hym in his chayer in mydward his graue, and settyn vp a bord 15 byforn hym vpon ii. trostellis and cure it with a cloth, and sette thervpon a fayr [cuppe] ful of mylk. And a mere with here fole and his hors shal ben brout with sadil and brydil [f. 46ʳᵇ] vpon his bak and chargid with gold and syluyr, and al that schal ben don in his graue with hym, the whiche shal ben mad meche and 20 large to resseyue al that is ordeynyd for his sepulture. And al this shal ben grauyd with hym, for they seyn that whan he comyth into the tothir world, he shal not forgon good herberewe ne hors ne gold, and his mere shal yeuyn hym mylk and bryngyn hym forth othere hors, so that he shal ben wel purueyed of al 25 that is nedful to hym in the tothir world. For thei trowyn verrayly that aftyr that thei arn dede, that thei shuln etyn and drynkyn and lyn with women as thei don here. And from that tyme that they ben ded, no man dare spekyn of hem in audience of here frendis. 30

[f. 46ᵛᵃ] Þere is an yle that is callid Calamassus. There

3–4 some for to ... list] *R om.*   16 vpon ... cloth] *R* couered   cure] *MS.* cured   17 cuppe] *MS.* cloth   18 hors] *R* beste hors   18–19 shal ben ... syluyr] *R* sadelid and brydelid and chargid with golde   20 meche and] *R* so   21 ordeynyd for his sepulture] *R om.*   23–26 not forgon ... world] *R* lacke nothing that him nedeth   25 shal] *MS.* shab   28 lyn with women] *R* live   30 of here frendis] *R om.*   31 Þere] *R* beside this ile of Chatan

dictis vero cannis faciunt domos, naues, et alia necessaria, sicut hic nos facimus de quercubus et aliis arboribus magnis. Et non estimet aliquis me ficta uel falsa dicere, nam vidi ego meis oculis [f. 58rb] plures cannas iacentes super ripas lacus, quarum vnam 5 viginti homines de societate nostra non poterant portare uel leuare altius quam ad genua a terra.

Post istam insulam transitur per mare ad aliam insulam que vocatur Alonak, que est satis pulcra et multis bonis plena. Ibi rex tot habet vxores quot voluerit . . . ita quod mille uel plures 10 habet aliquando. . . .

Adhuc habetur ibidem aliud mirabile quod numquam alibi reperitur. Nam omnia genera piscium maris veniunt et proiciunt se in ripis et in fluminibus insule, ita quod in mari vix vnus piscis apparet, et morantur ibidem tribus diebus ut quilibet 15 possit capere quantum voluerit. Et postquam recesserint pisces vnius generis, veniunt alterius generis pisces et similem moram faciunt. Sic vicissim fit quousque omnia et singula genera piscium se presentauerint ordinate vnum post aliud, ut capiat quilibet de patria quantum placuerit. Causa vero nescitur. 20 Dicunt illi tamen de patria, quamuis friuolum sit, quod pisces hoc faciant ob reuerenciam regis sui, qui est dignissimus dominus in terra, eo quod implet dei preceptum prout dictum fuerat ad Adam, *Crescite et multiplicamini et replete terram* et cetera. Nam, quia rex terre multiplicat genus humanum, ut asserunt, 25 per generacionem plurimorum infancium, ut predictum est, ideo mittit ei deus pisces maris ad voluntatem suam. . . .

[f. 58va] De ista patria transitur per Mare Occeanum per quamdam insulam nomine Chaffelles, vbi talis mos est patrie quod

they make here housis and here shepis of redis and alle here othere necessaries, as we don here of okys and of othere treis. For I and myne felas seyen manye of tho redis lyende in oure weye, that xx. of vs myghtyn not leftyn on of hem from the erthe.

And ner besyde is anothir yle that men callyn Calamak, a fayr lond and ful of good. The kyng of that lond takyth as manye wivis as him liste for to haue, that sumtyme he wele haue c.

NOTA DE PISCIBUS MARIS

In that lond is a gret mervayle that I say neuere in no lond but there. For alle maner of fichis that are in that se comyn a certeyn tyme of the yer and puttyn hem into flodys and in[f. 46vb]to reueres of the yle and dwellyn therinne iii. dayes, so that eche man may take of hem as manye as he wele. And whan that maner of fisch is gon, there comyth anothir maner of fich and dwellyth as longe, til eche man hath takyn what he wele. I coude neuere wetyn the skil whi [t]he comyn so thedyr more than into othere londis theraboute. But they of that yle seye that God doth hem that grace at the reuerence of that kyng that takyth so manye wivis and multyplieth the world, as God bad Adam whan He seyde, *Crescite et multiplicamyny, et cetera*, that is for to say, Growith and multiplieth and fulfillith the erthe, and beth lord of fischis in the see. [The] kyng of that lond wele hauyn at onys an c. or cc. of sonys, worthy men and [f. 47ra] grete lordis.

There is an yle that is callid Caffelos. Ther thei han a custom that whan here frendis are greuously sek, they hangyn hem vpon a tre that thei moun ben worwid and etyn with foulys, for thei sey it is betyr for to ben etyn with foulis that ben Godis aungellis than to ben etyn vndyr erthe with foule wermys.

Faste ther besyde is anothir yle where they norysche houndis

1–2 and alle here othere necessaries] *R om.* 2 and of othere treis] *R om.* 4 that xx.] *R and they ben so mochel and so gret that xxx.* 8 for to haue] *R om.* 10–11 that I say neuere in no lond but there] *R om.* 14 of hem as manye as he wele] *R his fille of hem for that 3eer* 15 fich] *MS.* fichc 16–17 I coude neuere wetyn] *R and thus doen al manere of fisshis oon aftir anothir. And I asked* 17 the] *MS.* he 18–19 that God . . . reuerence] *R for nothing ellis but for loue* 23 The] *MS. om.* 23–24 at onys . . . lordis] *R of his owne getinge, worthy men, lordes and ladies, and some of hem wole haue xl. sones, and so is this rewme multiplied* 24 worthy] *MS.* of worthy 29 foule] *R om.*

quando eorum amici grauiter infirmantur, suspendunt eos in arboribus ut possint ab auibus deuorari. Dicunt enim melius esse quod comedantur ab auibus, que sunt angeli dei, quam quod a vermibus turpiter consumentur in terra.

5 De hac insula venitur ad aliam vbi est gens pessimi moris. Nutriunt enim magnos canes, docentes eos iugulare suos parentes et amicos cum fuerint prope mortem, quia nolunt eos mori naturali morte ne paciantur nimiam penam, vt dicunt. Et cum fuerint mortui per morsus canum, comedunt carnes eorum 10 loco venacionis.

Vlterius transitur [de] patria ista per plures insulas maris usque ad quamdam insulam que vocatur Mikke, vbi sunt eciam pessime gentes, nam in re nulla sic delectantur sicut in occisionibus hominum, bibunt enim libenter sanguinem humanum. 15 Et qui crudelior fit in cedibus hominum, honorabilior iudicatur inter eos, vocant enim sanguinem humanum deum suum. Si vero alique persone sint in discordia adinuicem, amici eorum non faciunt inter eos concordiam absque eo quod bibant alterutrum de sanguine suo. . . .

20 [f. 59ra] De ista insula eundo per mare versus meridiem est alia insula longa et larga que appellatur Dondeya. . . . [f. 59rb] Rex huius terre magnus dominus est et potens, et habet sub se quinquaginta insulas grandes cum regibus coronatis, qui omnes obediunt predicto regi. Et habitant in insulis illis plures gentes 25 diuerse condicionis.

In vna illarum habitat gens magne stature quasi gigantes horribiles visu qui vnicum habent oculum in medio frontis. Hii comedunt carnes et pisces crudos.

In alia insula versus meridiem sunt homines deformis figure 30 sine capite qui oculos habent in humeris suis, et os eorum recuruum est ad instar ferri pedis equini, stans in medio pectoris eorum. . . .

11 de patria ista] per patrias istas   23 qui] quia   31 est] est et

for to werwe here frendis whan thei are in poynt of deth, for thei wele not suffere hem deyen kyndely in his bed to suffere meche peine. And thanne, whanne they aryn so dede, they etyn here flesch in stede of venysoun.

There is anothir yle that men callyn Mica, where wikkede 5 men arn dwellande, for in *no* erthely thing haue thei wondyr gret delit as in sloughte of men and for to drynkyn here blod. And who so [f. 47rb] wele gladyest slen men, is best holdyn and worthiest amongis hem and most is honoured, for that is a drynk that thei loue non so wel as the blod of a man. And if ony dis- 10 cord falle amongis hem, there may non acord ben mad til eche of hem haue dronkyn of otheris blod.

NOTA DE REGNO DINDIA

Ther is a reume that is callid Dyndeia, a riche lond and a plenteuous. The kyng is callid Calamak, a gret lord and myghti. 15 He hath vndyr hym liiii. ylis that aryn meche and longe, and of eche of tho ylis is a coronyd kyng, and alle are thei obeysaunt to Kyng Calamak. In tho ylis aryn men of dyuers condicionys, as ye shul here aftyrward.

In on of tho ylis aryn men of gret stature as they weryn 20 geauntis, oryble and foule to the sith, for they han but on eye, [f. 47va] and that is in myddis the forhed. They etyn rau flesch and fych.

In anothyr yle of that contre arn foule men of fygeure with-outyn heuedis. Eyen they haue in eche schuldyr on, and here 25 mouth as rond as an horse sho and stondande in myddis the brest.

There is anothir yle besyden that. In that yle aryn men that here ouere lyppe is as meche that whan they slepe ayen the

---

2–3 to suffere meche peine] *R* ne for to abide to suffre peyne whenne they ligge sike   3 so dede] *R* deed and thus woryed   etyn] *R* take and eten   4 venysoun] *R* venesoun. And this is soth trewely   5 wikkede] *R* wickede and cruel   6 no] *MS.* an   8 slen] *MS.* slon   8–9 and worthiest] *R om.*   9–10 that is ... non so wel] *R* they drynke noo drynk but   12 blod] *R* blode and thenne they waxe frendis   14–15 a riche lond and a plenteuous] *R om.*   15 and myghti] *R om.*   21 oryble and] *R om.*   24 In anothyr yle] *R* and in anothir ile arn men of xii. foote longe and they haue teeth lengere thenne any boor and they goo eyere naked. And in anothir ile

In alia insula sunt [homines] qui habent labium superius tam magnum quod quando dormiunt sub sole, cooperiunt totam faciem suam labio illo. . . .

In insula alia sunt qui grandes habent aures pendentes deorsum magna longitudine.

In alia insula sunt qui pedes habent equinos et sunt fortes et veloces, ita quod bestias siluestres et feras comprehendunt currendo, quas et manducant.

Est alia insula vbi gradiuntur homines super manus et pedes more quadripedum, et sunt pilosi scandentes arbores ita velociter sicut simie.

Est alia insula vbi sunt promiscui sexus, viri et mulieres [f. 59va] habentes membra genitalia vtriusque [sexus], qui eciam habent mamillam in vno latere. Et quando operantur opus virile, generant et inpregnant; quando vero faciunt mulieris opus, inpregnantur et portant. . . .

[f. 71rb] Ab ista terra redeundo x. dietas per terram magni Chan inuenitur insula alia valde bona. Ibi est rex potens et diues. Et inter nobiles ac diuites patrie illius vnus habetur diues valde, nec est tamen princeps, dux, uel comes, sed plures sunt qui de ipso tenent terras suas, et est homo magnarum diuiciarum.

Iste mirabilem ducit vitam, habet enim quinquaginta puellas ei seruientes continue in omnibus que desiderat. Et quando sedet in mensa, iste puelle afferunt ei cibum ac potum et semper simul portant quinque fercula, et portando cantant quasdam cantilenas. Preparant et iste cibum eius, scindendo coram ipso

1 homines] *om.*   13 sexus] *om.*

sonne, they cure al here visage from the mouth vpward with here lyppis.

In anothir yle there besyde aryn men that here eris aryn so grete and so syde that thei hangyn doun a gret lenthe.

In anothir yle aryn men that here fet arn as horse feet, and opon hem they moun rennyn so faste that they wele go to the wode and takyn wilde bestis thorw swiftnesse of here feet and bryngyn [f. 47vb] hem hom to here mete.

In anothir ile aryn men that gon on hondys and on feet, and they aryn rowe, and they wele clymbe vp to the crop of a tre a[s] lyghtely as ony ape.

In that reume is anothir yle where bothe men and wemen han bothe the ton harneys and the othir, and eche of hem hat a pappe vpon the on syde. And whan they werkyn the manys werk, they getyn childeryn, and they that werkyn the womanys werk, they beryn chylderyn.

NOTA DE PUELLIS SEMPER CANTANTIBUS AD MENSAM REGIS

Ther is a kyngdom beside the Grete Cane of Tartarye and therof is an kyng ryche, rial, and noble. Among alle the grete lordis of the lond ther is a strong, ryche, and a myghty man, and yit is he neythir duk, prince, ne erl, but there ben manye grete lordis that holdyth here londis of hym, [f. 48ra] and he hymself a lord of gret rychesse.

This cche greete lord ledyth a wondyrful lyf, for he hath eueremore l. damesellis that arn entendaunt to hym and to seruyn him bothe day and nyght at his wil in alle thynge that he wele han don. And whanne he syttyth at his mete, these

1 from the mouth vpward] *R om.*   3-4 here eris ... lenthe] *R* haue eren hangynge doun as doggis   6 opon hem] *R om.*   7-8 thorw ... mete] *R om.*   10 rowe] *R* row3 as beris   10-11 vp to ... ape] *R* into trees and rochis as apis doen   11 as] *MS*. a   12 that reume is] *R om.*   13 harneys] *R* privee harneys   14-16 And whan ... beryn chylderyn] *R* And in anothir ile arn men and women that haue even like to doggis and they speke no3t. Al othir shappe they haue aftir vs. And in anothir ile arn men that haue oon heede and two facis, oon bifore and anothir byhynde. They haue also two nosis, two mouthis, two tungis, two neckes, and foure eyen, in ecche face two eyen. And they speke on her manere. And alle thes men goen naked euerychon.   19-20 beside ... kyng] *R* that is   21 strong, ryche, and a myghty] *R* riche   23-24 and he hymself a lord of gret rychesse] *R om.*   26-28 that arn ... han don] *R* to serue ny3t and daye   27 him] *MS*. hem

et in ore mittendo ac si infantem cibarent; ipse enim cibum non tangit digitis suis sed sedet in pace tenens manus suas ante se super mensam, et hoc propter longitudinem vnguium suarum, quia eum non permittunt aliquid digitis tenere uel accipere.
5 Hec autem prolixitas vnguium reputant ibi pro magna nobilitate et dignitate, non enim amputant vngues suas sed permittunt crescere quantum possunt. . . .

Predicte quoque puelle coram predicto domino [suo] quando sedet in mensa pene semper sunt cantantes. Et cum satis
10 comederit de ferculis allatis, iterum afferunt coram eo alia quinque fercula cantantes ut prius, et sic faciunt usque ad finem prandii. Talis est modus istius diuitis omni die. Atque in hunc modum ducit vitam suam ex antiqua consuetudine antecessorum suorum. Quam [et] consuetudinem successores
15 eius obseruant, ita quod nichil probitatis vel virtutis facit progenies illa sed viuit modo predicto in requie et deliciis quasi porcus reclusus ad impinguandum. . . . .

Noueris autem et pro constanti teneas quod de omnibus terris, regnis, regionibus, et nacionibus, vnde superius retuli, exceptis
20 hiis populis que racione non vtuntur, non est gens aliqua que non teneat [f. 71va] aliquem articulum fidei nostre. Generaliter omnes vero credunt in deum mundi creatorem quem deum nature vocant. Sicque verificatur illud propheticum, 'Et metuent eum omnes fines terre'; item, 'Omnes gentes seruient ei.' Sed
25 nesciunt perfecte loqui de deo, precipue de trinitate, eo quod non habent doctorem. De filio et de spiritu sancto nil nouerunt. Locuntur tamen de sacra scriptura, specialiter de libro Genesis et de aliis libris Moysi ac eciam interdum de dictis prophetarum.

       8 suo] *om.*   14 et] *om.*   27 specialiter] et specialiter

damesellis seruyn hym bothe of mete and of drynk, and they settyn hym v. mes of mete at onys, syngende. These maydenys cuttyn his mete beforn hym, syngende. They puttyn the mete in hese mouth, syngynge, for he shal hymself leyn non hand on no mete but syttyn stylle and holdyn his hondis byforn hym vpon the bord. And that is for hese naylis are so longe, for hese naylis fallyth not to ben kytte neuere more. For the custom is there that no man shal kyttyn hise naylis, but letyn hem growyn of lenthe as they wele, and that [f. 48rb] gyse thy rettyn for gret nobley and gret dignete.

The damesellis arn ay syngende beforn hym, and whan he hath etyn of that mete that hym lykyth, thei settyn hym anothyr maner mete with long song and real. And thus they don ay tyl the endyng of his mete. Swich is the maner of that ryche man eche day to do. In this maner he ledyth his lyf thour elde custome of hese elderis, that non bounte ne non vertu ne comyth from that progenye but in reste leuyth and in delycis, as swyn that is fed for to be slayn.

Wete ye wel for certeyn that of alle reumys and londis and naciounnys that I haue of spokyn of byforn, outakyn [hem] that han non resoun with hem, there arn none maner of men that [f. 48va] thei ne holdyn manye artikellis of the feyth, for generally thei trowin alle in God that made the world, whom they honoure and clepyn to for helpe. And ther thour is the prophesie verified where it is said, *Et metuant eum omnes reges, omnes gentes seruient ei*, and that is for to say, Alle kyngis shuln dredyn hym and alle men shul seruyn hym. They connot spekyn parfitly *of* God and specially of the Trinite, for they han none techeris to shewyn hem of the Sone and of the Holy Gost. Nouth forthi thei speke of holy scripture and of the Bok of Genesis and of othere bokis of Moyses and of the lawe of holy cherche, *id est* of holy prophetis.

1-2 and they settyn hym v. mes of mete at onys, syngende] *R om.*   4-6 on no mete ... bord] *R* therto   8-10 that no man ... nobley and] *R* men of gret estate therby haue   11 The damesellis ... real] *R om.*   15 elde] *R om.*   17 from that progenye] *R* of him but fewe   in reste leuyth and] *R* thus he liveth   18 for to be slayn] *R* euere   19-20 reumys and londis and naciounnys] *R* thes cuntrees   20 hem] *MS.* ii   24 for helpe] *R om.*   26-27 and that ... seruyn hym] *R om.*   27 of] *MS.* to   27-28 of God and specially] *R om.*   31-32 of the lawe of holy cherche, *id est* of holy prophetis] *R* holi prophecies

Et dicunt quod creaturas quas *ad*orant non sunt dii, sed eos honorant et colunt propter virtutem magnam que reperitur in eis ex dei dono, quod vtique donum non haberetur nisi ex speciali gracia dei. Et de similacris dicunt quod non est gens que similacra non habeat. Hoc maxime dicunt quia vident Cristianos ymagines crucifixi et sanctorum venerari. . . . Dicunt preterea quod angeli locuntur eis in ydolis et mira operantur. Verum dicunt quod angeli Sathane locuntur eis. . . .

[f. 59ra] Est alia insula longa et larga que appellatur Dondeya, in qua habitat gens mirabilis condicionis, ibi enim pater comedit filium, filius patrem, maritus coniugem, et coniux maritum. Nam si contingat aliquem de amicis infirmari, si pater fuerit, filius pergit statim ad presbiterum legis terre illius et rogat eum consulere ydolum an debeat pater conualescere de infirmitate sua. . . . Si autem ydolum respondeat quod eger morietur, tunc vadit presbiter cum filio et cum vxore egroti ad ipsum et ponunt pannum vnum super os eius ad suffocandum eum, et sic illum occidunt. Tunc totum corpus in frusta scindunt et faciunt vocari omnes amicos defuncti, comedentes illud cum magna solempnitate. Et postquam carnes comederunt, colligentes ossa sepeliunt more suo, can[f. 59rb]tantes cum magna melodia. Si quis de parentibus vel amicis non se presentauerint huic festo et solempnitati, a ceteris reprobatur quasi notam criminis incurrisset, et de cetero non computabitur inter amicos. . . .

[f. 71va] Multe quidem et alie sunt patrie, aliaque plura mirabilia que non vidi in partibus illis. Sunt eciam que vidi plura alia que non refero, esset enim longum nimis et laboriosum cuncta referre. Et ideo ista ad presens sufficiunt. . . .

Et ego, Iohannes de Maundeuile supradictus, qui discessi de istis partibus et mare transiui anno gracie m.ccc.xxii. et multas

1 adorant] honorant   6 sanctorum] aliorum sanctorum

And they seye that the criaturis that they honure are none goddis, but they honoure hem for the [f. 48ᵛᵇ] gret vertues and the sothfastnesse that is foundyn in hem thour the yifte of God. And thei sei ther is non nacyoun that thei ne han ymagis and honoure hem, and thei [seye] forthi that Cristen men honoure the crucifix and othere ymages of halwyn. They seyn that angellis spekyn to hem thour here ymagis and ydolatrie and werkyth manye wondris. And there thei seyn soth, for the deuillis angellis spekyn to hem.

In that reume of Dundya is swich a custom that the fadyr etith the sone, and the sone the fadyr, and the man the wif, and the wif here husbonde, whan they deyen. And if ony man se his frend that is sek in poynt to deye, they takyn hym a cloth and cast it vpon hym and quesemyth hym to the deth. And whan he is ded, thi [f. 49ʳᵃ] take the body and hewyn it al in pecis, and [callyn] alle hese frendys and alle the mensterallis that mowe ben foundyn and makyn hem a solempne feste and etyn the dede manys body. And whan the flesch is al etyn, they gadere alle the bonys togedere and grauyn hem in her manere with gret solempnete and loud song. And if that it be so that onye men of hese frendis or of his kyn holde hym awei and come not to the solempnete, al the kynrede wele reprowyn hym as of a notabele blame and neuere aftyr that tyme shal he ben acountyd amongis hise frendis.

Manye cuntreis and ferlies there ben, the whiche that I saw, and many I saw that I spek not of, for it were long and ouer gret trauaile to shewin al that I saw. And forthi this mai suffise at this tyme.

I, Iohan Maundevile beforn[f. 49ʳᵇ]said, that wente out of Yngelond and pased the se in the yer of grace m. and ccc. and xxii., and manye londis and regeounys passid thoure with good

---

2 the gret] *R om.*   4 thei sei] *R om.*   5 thei seye] *MS.* that thei
6 of halwyn] *R* in her chirchis   8 And there thei seyn soth] *R om.*
9 hem] *R* hem in her mawmettis   11 etith] *MS.* ethith   13 cloth]
R wollen clooth or a lynen   14-15 whan he is ded] *R om.*   16 callyn]
MS. allyn *deleted*   20 gret solempnete and loud] *R* solempne   21-22 or
of his kyn ... solempnete] *R* lacke at that feest   28 tyme] *R* tyme.
And also, for men wolde nou3t haue trowed al in certayn, I saw3 manye thingis
that I wolde nou3t haue trowed myself til I saw3 hem in dede   29-147.3 I,
Iohan Maundevile ... constreynede me therto] *R om.*

terras et regiones adiui cum bono comitatu, multis probitatibus virorum strenuorum et actibus militaribus presens interfui [quamuis indignus]; et iam ad *quie*tem perueni quasi inuitus propter certas causas vrgentes. Ista redigi in scriptis prout ad
5 memoriam recurrebant anno gracie millesimo ccc.lvi., videlicet tricesimo quarto anno postquam recessi a partibus istis, scilicet Anglie, iter arripiendo.

Omnes autem hec legentes deprecor quatinus pro me peccatore preces fundant ad dominum. Ego vero pro eis vice versa libenter
10 orabo prout dominus dederit cunctis insuper fidelibus qui pro me dixerint orationem dominicam cum salutacione angelica mente deuota. Concedat eis Cristus, et ego quantum in me est concedo participacionem peregrinacionis mee et omnium [f. 71vb] aliorum bonorum que feci uel sum facturus, vlterius deum
15 exorans, a quo omnis gracia descendit, quod ipse omnes fideles hoc audientes vel legentes sua gracia repleat et incolumes custodiat atque post hanc peregrinacionem ad patriam perpetue pacis perducat, qui est trinus et vnus sine principio et sine fine, sine qualitate bonus et sine quantitate magnus, vbique presens,
20 omnia continens, cui nullum bonum prodesse, nullum malum obesse potest, qui in trinitate perfecta viuit et regnat per omnia secula deus. Amen.

    EXPLICIT ITINERARIUM DOMINI IOHANNIS
    DE MAUNDEUILE MILITIS DE MIRABILIBUS
    MUNDI, ET CETERA.   DEO GRACIAS.

3 quamuis indignus] *om.*   quietem] etatem

cumpanye with worthi straunge folk, and at dedys of armys was, thow I be vnworthi; and now I am comyn to reste as a man disconfitid for certeyn cause that constreynede me therto. This bok I haue mad and wretyn as it is comyn to myn mynde in the yer of grace of oure lord m.ccc.lvi, that is for to say in the xxxiiii. yer aftir that I departid out of this lond and tok myn viage thedirward.

Wherfore I prei entierly to alle tho that this bok redyn or writyn that thei redyn no more ne writyn than I haue wretyn, for that I haue wretyn is trewe. And [f. 49va] also I preye to alle tho that this bok redyn or heryn that thei welyn preie for me a *Pater Noster* and an *Aue*, and I shal preie for hem in as meche as I am worthi. And ho so preie for me, I graunte hem part of alle myn pilgrymage and of alle othere goode dedis that I haue don or may don in tyme comynge, preyinge to God, from whom alle grace and goodnesse comyth, that he of hese grace souereyne saue and kepe alle tho that this bok redith or herith it to be red, and aftir this lif brynge hem thedir where ioye is endeles and reste and pes. Amen.

EXPLICIT IOHANNES MAUNDEUYLE,
CUIUS ANIME PROPICIETUR DEUS.

5–7 that is . . . thedirward] *R* and in the Holi Londe I was trauelynge xxxiiii. ʒeer   8 entierly] *R* vttirly   9–11 that thei redyn . . . this bok redyn] *R om.*   13 as I am] *R* as they arn   15 or may don in tyme comynge] *R om.*   17 kepe] *R* kepe in clennes   18 it to be red] *R* and writeth   19 endeles and reste and pes] *R* and euermore pees and euerelastynge reste withouten ende

COMMENTARY

The main sources of *Mandeville's Travels*, cited below, are:
Albert of Aix, *Historia Hierosolimitanae Expeditionis*, 1125.
Haiton, *Fleurs des Histoires d'Orient*, before 1308.
Odoric of Pordenone, *Itinerarius*, 1330.
Vincent of Beauvais, *Speculum Naturale* and *Speculum Historiale*, c.1250.
Jacques de Vitry, *Historia Hierosolimitana*, before 1240.
William of Boldensele, *Itinerarium*, 1336.
William of Tripoli, *Tractatus de Statu Saracenorum*, c. 1270.

For an excellent discussion of the use of these sources see G. F. Warner, *The Buke of Iohn Maundeuill* (Roxburghe Club, 1889), pp. xv–xxviii. Further information may be found in M. Letts, *Mandeville's Travels*, Hakluyt Society, Series II, vol. ci, 1953, and P. Hamelius, *Mandeville's Travels*, E.E.T.S., o.s. 154, 1923.

3/9 None of the English Mandevilles is known to have been *born and norisched* at St. Albans. This absence of historical record is one of the most persuasive arguments for believing that the Sir John Mandeville of the book is entirely fictitious. Its ascription to John de Bourgogne, a physician who died at Liège c. 1372 and who was referred to as *Mandavele ly cheualier dengleterre* as early as 1459 in a document quoted by T. Gobert, *Les Rues de Liège* (1884–1904), vol. iv, p. 202, is doubtful; and the more traditional views of the authorship, e.g. Letts, pp. xvii–xxvii, and Mrs. J. W. Bennett, *The Rediscovery of Sir John Mandeville* (1954), pp. 189–204, are unconvincing. Cf. note to 147/13 below.

3/11 Attempts have been made to infer from this date, 29 September 1322, and a circumstantial story told by the Liège notary Jean d'Outremeuse in his *Myreur des Histors*, that the author was one of those who fled the realm after Edward II crushed the revolt against the Despensers in 1321. But in fact the date is derived from a corrupt copy of William of Boldensele's dedicatory letter to Cardinal Talleyrand-Périgord, *datum Avinione anno domini m.ccc.xxxvii. in die sancti Michaelis*.

3/15 All geographical names outside Europe necessarily refer to ill-defined regions. *Lesser Armenia* was the small kingdom on the northeast shore of the Mediterranean around Tarsus, and *Greater Armenia* extended eastwards from the Kingdom of Trebizond on the Black Sea. *Lesser India* probably represents the Middle India of medieval cartographers, a coastal area extending from southern Arabia to the Indus delta; *Greater India* is then the sub-continent proper.

5/1 This overland route to Constantinople, followed by the First Crusade in 1096, is described by Albert of Aix, from whom this account is substantially derived.

5/6 The territorial expansion of Hungary reached its peak under Louis I (1342–82), who concluded his Bulgarian campaign shortly before he was crowned King of Poland in 1370. The seemingly accurate knowledge of contemporary events displayed here does not, however, solve the problem of dating the book, *pace* A. Steiner, 'The Date of the Composition of *Mandeville's Travels*', *Speculum*, ix (1934); cf. note to 147/5 below. The scribal confusion of Cumania and Bulgaria and the corruption, also in R, of *ioynes* to an otherwise unrecorded country *Iaynes* are corrected by reference to the Latin text, which also shows *Doros* (R. *Dorews*) to be a corruption of *Prussie*. Such scribal corruption of place-names is a common feature of all versions of *Mandeville's Travels*.

5/13 The *gret toun in the ende of Hongry* is Maleville, the modern Zemun, near Belgrade. In Sub-Group A of the Insular Version, from which the Latin text was translated, the original *Maleville* is corrupted to *la male ville* 'the evil town'. To this or a similar corruption the readings *quandam villam* (4/12) and *gret toun* are undoubtedly traceable. Though a variant *magnam villam* is not found in any of the six extant Latin manuscripts, it seems likely that it did exist in the manuscript from which the Englisher worked.

5/15 The reading *it rennyth thorw Almayn*, accurately rendering *vadit in Alemanniam* (4/14), reflects a corrupt variant in the Insular Version, some manuscripts of which have *vient en Almayne* instead of the better *naist en Almaigne*, i.e. rises in Germany.

5/27 The stone bridge crossing the Maritsa, *not* the Morava, at Kermen is mentioned by Albert of Aix, who also speaks of the *Pincenarii qui Bulgariam inhabitant*. These Pincenarii, the Petchenegs of history, settled along the lower Danube, i.e. *the lond of Pyncemacert*. They were finally crushed in 1091 by the Emperor Alexius I, and it is doubtful whether even their name survived outside written sources when *Mandeville's Travels* was written.

7/1 The huge bronze statue of Justinian, erected in 543, originally held in the left hand a gilt orb, the *appil of gold*, surmounted by a cross. This cross was blown down in 1317 and restored in 1325. The legend recorded here, in an account otherwise derived from William of Boldensele, probably stems from this accident. The confusion of the cross and the orb, said to equal a fifteen-gallon jar in size, proves that the author was not writing from personal observation.

7/13 In the manuscript this section carries the rubric *Nota de montibus super nubes* which recurs more appropriately at 11/6. The rubrics were inserted in a distinctive red ink after the manuscript had been written

COMMENTARY 151

—towards the end of the manuscript are blank spaces left for rubrics which were never added—and the scribe has here mistaken his place.

7/19 The fragment of wood, supposedly of the cross of Dismas, was preserved as a famous relic at the monastery of Stavro Vouni, near Larnaca. William of Boldensele claims to have seen it.

7/27 The Sainte Chapelle was built in Paris by St. Louis (1226–1270) as a repository for the holy relics which the Emperor Baldwin presented to him in 1239. The author's claim to have seen these and other relics and to possess *on of the thornys* is an obvious attempt at authenticity.

8/14 A short note on the Enidros marble which perpetually drops water is omitted. It and the details of Constantinople and Troy which follow, with the exception of the translation of St. Luke, are found in William of Boldensele.

9/21 The phrase *toward the west*, found also in R, is almost certainly corrupt, cf. *versus occeanum vel magnum mare* (8/21). The Black Sea, sometimes thought to be part of the Ocean or Great Sea, contrasted with the West or Mediterranean Sea, lies east of the site of Troy. Cf. note to 101/5 below.

9/23 At this point R inserts the last two paragraphs found beginning at 11/21. The effect of this change, to bring together details about Constantinople, is slight but noteworthy as the first of many such deliberate divergences from the sequence of MS. e Musaeo 116 and all other related manuscripts.

9/24 Excessive scribal contamination prevents the precise identification of all these names, though the general reference to the Cyclades is clear. *Meleta Ypateia* is the result of a false scribal division of *Melo Caipateia* (8/26) written as one word in the manuscripts of the Latin text and concealing the separate identities of Melos and Scarpanto.

9/26 *Caucasis*, according to Warner 'the desperate remedy of a scribe', has the cloud-topping quality which Vincent de Beauvais, whose account is here followed, ascribes to Mount Olympus. The corruption, cf. the better *Athos* of the Insular Version, occurs in the Latin text as well as in R and the Egerton Version.

9/33 Aristotle died at Chalcidice but is said to have been buried at his native Stageirus on the Strymonian Gulf, where the yearly festival of Aristotelia was celebrated in his honour. It is this festival which is referred to as *here conseyl*.

11/7 This legend comes ultimately from Solinus, who records that both Mount Athos and Mount Olympus tower so high above the clouds that the ashes of the altars on their summits were never disturbed by rain. The story is also found in Vincent de Beauvais.

11/11 The obviously corrupt manuscript reading *pleyinge*, paralleled in R, is corrected by reference to the *gracia contemplacionis* (10/12) of

COMMENTARY

the Latin text. The first two syllables of an earlier *contempleyinge* could both have been written in a contracted form, which would make their omission more likely.

11/22 The palace of Boukoleon adjoined the Hippodrome, but neither is mentioned by William of Boldensele, from whom much of the information about Constantinople is taken. The source of the passage has not been traced.

11/31 The immediate source of this story of the mythical Hermes Trismegistus, named in other versions of *Mandeville's Travels*, is unknown, but the legend is told by Oliver Scholasticus, *Historia Damiatina*, and Roger Bacon, *Metaphysica*. In other versions of *Mandeville's Travels* the discovery of the tablet is made when the emperor is entombing the body of his father, not himself, but the Bodley Version exactly follows the distortion already present in the Latin text (10/26).

13/8 The account of the Greeks which follows is taken from Jacques de Vitry, with the obvious exception of the story of Pope John XXII (1316–34) whose attempts to establish his suzerainty over the Byzantine Church were rebuffed by the Emperor Andronicus III. The facts were notorious, and this fictitious Greek reply, with its reference to Pope John's known avarice, circulated widely after his death.

13/23 The manuscript reading *vs*, paralleled in R, is clearly unsatisfactory, but its origin may lie in a copyist's error in the Latin text where the original *tuos* (12/17) may, through the omission of initial *t*, have been misread as *nos*.

14/28 The names of the Greek alphabet are here omitted. The Latin manuscripts do not give the Greek characters.

15/9 *Latynys*, i.e. priests of the Roman Church. The translator has misunderstood *latinos* (14/9) and attempted to explain it as a foreign name, cf. *papoynes* (23/20).

16/2 A brief reference to the island of Chios and its mastic-bearing trees is omitted.

16/6 A reference to the Turkish occupation of Ephesus and the miraculously moving tomb of St. John is omitted.

17/16 *in diserd*, i.e. in the desert. The translator has apparently mistaken the ablative adjective *deserto* (16/16) as a noun.

17/20 The legend of the daughter of Hippocrates, the physician of Cos, otherwise Lango, was current in the eastern Mediterranean in the fourteenth century, but the immediate source of this account has not been traced. Unlike much of the preceding and succeeding details of the itinerary at this point, it is not derived from William of Boldensele.

19/4 In the Insular Version it is the horse, not the rider, that flees at the sight of the dragon and subsequently leaps into the sea. The Bodley Version exactly follows the Latin text (18/4), which undoubtedly

COMMENTARY 153

reflects a confusion of *cheual* and *cheualier* in its Insular source. The same error is found in all English prose versions of *Mandeville's Travels*, but in no extant manuscript of the Insular Version.

20/11 A brief reference to the older name of Rhodes, *Collos*, which is mistakenly associated with St. Paul's Epistle to the Colossians, is omitted.

21/15 The Hospitallers occupied Rhodes from 1309 until their expulsion by the Turks in 1523. The passage is derived from William of Boldensele but, here as elsewhere in medieval itineraries, the distances expressed are suspect, partly because of the great corruptibility of roman numerals by the scribes, partly because of a lack of a recognized standard of measurement in the Middle Ages. For example, *leucas* (20/12) are continental leagues and not, as the translator always rendered the word, English miles. Both the Insular and Latin texts give the number as *viii.$^{c.}$*, thus supplying grounds for the emendation, but the distance between Rhodes and Constantinople is approximately 500 English miles.

21/22 This story of necrophily has its origin in the classical myth of the Gorgon's Head, but it is heavily overlaid with local legend. It was probably brought from the East by the Crusaders and in various forms it is recorded by Benedict of Peterborough, Roger Hoveden, Walter Map, and Gervase of Tilbury. However, its immediate source here is not known. The Gulf of Satalia, the modern Adalia, is noted for its storms and whirlpools, but there is no record of a natural catastrophe overwhelming the old town.

21/29 Neither *a yer* nor *tres menses* (20/22) is a satisfactory reading. The Insular Version gives *ix. mois*, which is clearly correct.

23/8 The distance from Rhodes to Cyprus is, in fact, 250 miles. The correction of the manuscript reading is made by reference to the Latin text (22/6). Cf. note to 21/15.

23/19 Trained hunting leopards, first used in the East, were imported to Europe during the thirteenth century. Frederic II sent three to Henry III in 1235, and William of Boldensele, whose account is here followed, reports their presence in Cyprus. The use of the term *papoynes* for such beasts is peculiar. Jacques de Vitry speaks of *papiones*, a kind of jackal or hyena, immediately after describing hunting leopards in the East, and it is probable that a confused reminiscence of this passage is responsible for the presence of the word here. Cf. A. C. Moule, *Quinsai and other notes on Marco Polo* (1957), pp. 65–66.

23/22 This curious custom, probably a distorted reference to the Cypriot habit of sitting crosslegged while eating, is reported in *The Voyage of Master Laurence Aldersy to Jerusalem*, printed by Hakluyt. Manuscript *ladderys*, a scribal alteration inspired by the reference to pits, is corrected from R, cf. *mensas* (22/23).

23/32 Tyre was captured by the Crusaders in 1124 and became one of the chief cities of the Kingdom of Jerusalem. It was recaptured and destroyed by the Saracens in 1291 after the fall of Acre.

24/6 A few brief details of the itinerary, including a reference to Elijah and the widow's son, are here omitted.

24/16 A larger passage, containing an account of the Fosse of Memnon as well as details of the itinerary, is omitted.

25/9 The ancient port of Jaffa was supposed, by false etymology, to have been founded by Japhet, son of Noah. *Adamis*, also in R, is a scribal corruption, cf. *Noe* (24/11). The passage is taken from William of Boldensele.

25/15 This confusion of Andromeda and the sea-monster, the *ieaunt* from which Perseus rescued her, is found in all versions of *Mandeville's Travels*. It was, in fact, a common error, but it is avoided by Vincent de Beauvais from whom this account is otherwise derived.

25/18 *Babylonye*, i.e. Cairo, is not to be confused with *the grete Babilonye* (31/23) of biblical fame. The site of the town Bab-al-yun, founded by Cambyses in 525 B.C., lay a mile to the south of Cairo, founded in A.D. 969, and the two cities eventually merged. Almost inevitably the name *Bab-al-yun* passed into Europe as *Babilonye* and its ruler became known as *the Soudon of Babylonye* (27/22). However, Cairo retained its identity at least till the time of William of Boldensele, from whom these details are taken, cf. *Chathre* (35/17) and *Chayre* (35/22).

25/20 Darum Castle, 9 miles south of Gaza, was founded by Amalric (d. 1174) to assist his invasions of Egypt. It fell to Saladin in his drive to Acre, and was recaptured by Richard I in 1192. See R. C. Smail, *Crusading Warfare* (1956), p. 61.

25/22 The emendation *helful*, made on reference to R, does not seem to make sense at first sight. Yet it is undoubtedly right. The Latin *vie sabulose* (24/21), i.e. sandy ways, which accords with the sense of all other versions of *Mandeville's Travels* at this point, has been misread by a copyist or even the translator as *vie salubres*, i.e. *helful weyes*.

26/20 A brief reference to Saladin's father is omitted.

26/23 Further details of Egyptian history, including the ill-starred campaign of St. Louis, are omitted.

27/2 Meshach, Shadrach, and Abednego were, of course, not children except in the special sense of children of the Lord. This misconception, which was widely prevalent, is traceable to Daniel i. 4, *children in whom there is no blemish*.

27/5 The citadel El Kalah, built by Saladin in 1166, is mentioned by William of Boldensele, and the extent of the Sultan's possessions is described by William of Tripoli.

COMMENTARY 155

27/19 The dignity of Caliph is here confused with that of Sultan. The Fatimite caliphate became extinct in 1171, but Saladin and his successors then paid a nominal deference to the Caliph of Baghdad, never themselves assuming the title.

27/24 This information about the sultans and their army is taken from Haiton. Saladin (d. 1193) was sultan during the time of Richard I. Baibars (*Melyk Darre*) was sultan during the crusade from which Edward I was recalled to ascend the throne in 1272; he died in 1277. After Baibars' death his son Baraqa reigned until deposed by Qalawun (*Elphi*) in 1279, and it was he who captured Tripoli in 1289. On his death in 1290 his son al-Ashraf Khalil (*Mellechi Madrabon*) became sultan; he was murdered by his emirs in 1293. It was during his reign that 'Mandeville' claimed to have left Egypt, i.e. some thirty years before he claimed to have started his travels (3/12)!

28/3 Brief details of six other sultans are here omitted.

29/22 *for myschef of mone*, also in R, is apparently an expansion of an earlier phrase *for mischeeffe*, given in the Egerton Version (Warner 20/12). The phrase, which has no parallel in the Latin text, was possibly introduced by the translator, and *myschef* may then be a corruption of an earlier *myster*, i.e. need, which better suits the context.

29/23 This colourful account of the Sultan's wives and concubines is developed from a short reference by William of Tripoli, supplemented by the Book of Esther.

31/22 This description of Babylon and its Tower is taken from William of Boldensele. The association of Nimrod with Assyria stems ultimately from Micah v. 6.

32/2 A brief reference to the image of his father which Nimrod raised as an idol is here omitted.

32/3 A short reference to the size and site of Babylon is omitted.

32/21 Much detail of geography and itinerary, including an account of the Nile's seasonal flooding, is here omitted.

32/28 A brief account of the five provinces of Egypt is omitted.

33/5 Cyrus, the founder of the Persian empire, was killed in 528 B.C. According to Herodotus, *Hist.* i. 189, he was crossing the river Gyndes, the modern Diala (not the *Eufrates*), on his way to attack Babylon in 538 B.C. when one of his sacred white horses plunged into the river and was drowned. Cyrus thereupon swore vengeance, which he achieved by digging 180 canals to disperse the torrent.

33/17 According to 'Mandeville', almost every distant land is an *yle*. The Great Khan, whose existence was authenticated by Marco Polo in 1299, exercised a vast sway over the ill-defined regions of Cathay. The legendary Prester John, whose forged letter began to circulate in

Europe in the thirteenth century, was thought by some to rule the empire of India, but cf. notes to 85/10 and 99/6.

33/26 *toun*, i.e. two, cf. R *tweyne*. The word has no parallel in any related version of *Mandeville's Travels*, and is possibly corrupted from *ston*, cf. *many grete cragges of stane* of the Egerton Version (Warner 24/3).

33/28 *Costantyn the Noble*, also in R, is corrupted from *Costoun* (32/24) in the Latin and Insular versions. It is tentatively identified by Warner as Kus on the east bank of the Nile, but it is not mentioned by William of Boldensele, on whom this account of Egypt is based.

34/12 An account of the Phoenix is omitted. Although this marvel is an integral part of *Mandeville's Travels*, the account given in R (footnote to 37/29) is an interpolation not directly connected with the passage here omitted in the Latin text.

34/14 A brief reference to precious stones found in Egypt is omitted.

35/4 The story of St. Paul's meeting with a satyr is told by St. Jerome, *Vita Sancti Pauli*, and reproduced in the Golden Legend, from which much similar information in *Mandeville's Travels* is derived, cf. note to 37/19.

36/9 A long passage, containing *inter alia* an account of balsam, a description of the Saracen alphabet without characters, and a reference to the gates of Hell, is here omitted.

36/18 A brief reference to the Saracen custom of whitewashing walls of former Christian churches to hide the mural paintings is omitted.

36/21 A few minor details of the itinerary are here omitted.

36/26 A brief reference to a four-day journey through the Red Sea is omitted.

37/8 The *applis of paradys*, more prosaically the fruit of the plantain which is very similar to the banana, are mentioned by William of Boldensele. The superstition that the core of the banana, when cut transversely, represents the True Cross is still current.

37/19 The translation of St. Mark is described in the Golden Legend. According to St. Jerome, St. Mark died a natural death at Alexandria. His body was later stolen by two Venetian merchants and shipped to Venice during the reign of the Emperor Leo I (d. 474).

37/23 The wood *lignum aloes*, which was supposed to float down the Nile from Paradise, is mentioned by William of Boldensele, on whom this account is based. The *aloes*, the resin and wood of the leguminous agalloch, was used for incense and ornament as well as medicine. Its name possibly derives from the Arabic *al 'ud*, i.e. the wood.

COMMENTARY

38/12 A brief reference to the need for translators in these desert journeys is here omitted.

39/5 *the West See*, i.e. the Mediterranean. But this reading is apparently the translator's error, cf. *Maris Occeani* (38/2). A similar mistake occurs at 9/21.

39/27 This story of the olive-bearing birds is not in William of Boldensele and its immediate source is unknown, though a similar account is found in Thietmar, *Peregrinatio* (1217), who reports that St. Catherine gave the monks an inexhaustible jar of oil. Vincent de Beauvais has a similar story without the reference to the birds.

41/14 The reading *Moyses seyde*, also in R, is clearly unsatisfactory in the context, which requires a reading like *Godd said to Moyses* of the Egerton Version (Warner 37/3), which is wholly dependent upon the lost translation of the Latin text (from 26/7 to 44/3 in this edition) at this point. See above, p. xiii.

41/29 *Ich a monk . . . brennende*. This clause is found in the Egerton Version (31/16) at this point. In the Latin text it occurs in the next sentence (40/28). The change must have been made by the translator.

42/10 Further arguments against the monks' failure to make known this marvel of divine election are omitted.

42/20 Brief details of another church of St. Mary, the chapel of Elijah, and a vine planted by St. John are omitted.

43/14 The legend of St. Catherine and the vermin is given by William of Boldensele, who also notes the location of the biblical sites mentioned in the following paragraph.

44/3 A description of the burial-place of St. Catherine is here omitted.

45/10 This account of the Bedouin is derived from William of Boldensele and Jacques de Vitry, neither of whom mentions the highly imaginative detail of roasting meat in the sun. But cf. Vincent de Beauvais, who reports the solar roasting of fish.

46/13 Further brief details about the Valley of Hebron are omitted.

46/17 An account of the sepulchres of the Patriarchs is omitted.

46/26 A short note on the kamala spice, a dust-like substance obtained from a powdered shrub, is here omitted.

47/6 The city of *Bersabe*, the modern Beersheba, which is mentioned by William of Boldensele, has of course no connexion with Bathsheba, as this passage claims.

47/29 This account of the legend of the Dry Tree, widely current in the Middle Ages, is taken from the *Liber de Terra Sancta*, falsely attributed to Friar Odoric. For the history of the legend see G. V. Smithers, *Kyng Alisaunder*, vol. ii, E.E.T.S., o.s. 237, p. 146, note

to l. 6755 and the authorities cited there. The prophecy alluded to derives ultimately from the Book of Sirach and for a time was thought to relate to the Emperor Frederic II (d. 1230). Although the miraculous properties of the Dry Tree are well attested (e.g. in Vincent de Beauvais), it is only in *Mandeville's Travels* that they include a preservative against *the fallynge euyl*, i.e. epilepsy; elsewhere this preservative refers to the evils attendant on falling off a horse! Such an error could only have arisen through the author's following a written source.

48/17 Further details of the itinerary and the story of the virgin miraculously saved from the fire are omitted.

49/19 This sentence is not found in the Latin text or any other related version of *Mandeville's Travels*. It was presumably inserted by the redactor to conceal the omission noted at 48/17.

49/21 This story of the Magi, like the subsequent references to the charnel of the Innocents, the tomb and chair of St. Jerome, and the church of St. Nicholas, is derived from the pseudo-Odoric, *Liber de Terra Sancta*. The legend concerning the Virgin Mary associated with the church of St. Nicholas is a superstitious explanation of the deposits of white porous stone scattered in the neighbouring soil.

50/18 A brief reference to certain Saracen prohibitions about the eating of flesh is here omitted.

50/21 Further details about the itinerary, including a false account of the etymology of Jerusalem, are omitted here.

50/25 Brief details of the church of the Holy Sepulchre are omitted at this point.

51/13 These details of the Koran and the Prophet are derived from William of Tripoli.

51/24 This account of the church of the Holy Sepulchre is based on William of Boldensele. He does not mention the annual miracle of the holy fire, but it is reported by Albert of Aix among many others.

52/30 A short explanation seeking to reconcile the apparent discrepancy between the actual age of Jesus and the age of the Messiah prophesied by David is here omitted.

53/12 The reading *fote*, also in R, is curious, cf. *capitis humani* (52/10). It seems that, in some way no longer discoverable, *capitis* has been corrupted to *pedis* in the Latin manuscript from which the Bodley Version derives. For a somewhat similar corruption involving the loss of initial syllables, cf. note to 11/11.

53/20 A skull, said to be Adam's, was seen by the pseudo-Odoric (*c.* 1325) and le Seigneur Ogier d'Anglure (1395). It was a notable relic, and the author's failure to see it—and to say that he had seen it—is added proof that he did not visit Jerusalem.

COMMENTARY

53/24 The tombs of Godfrey of Bouillon (d. 1100), the leader of the First Crusade, and his brother Baldwin (d. 1118) were ransacked by the Turks in 1244 and finally destroyed by the Greeks in 1808. They are mentioned by almost all the historians of the Holy Land.

53/30 The immediate source of this passage is unknown. The first of the two inscriptions, the Septuagint Version of Psalm 74, verse 12, which in the Insular and other versions of *Mandeville's Travels* is given in Greek characters, is found in Peter Comestor, *Historia Scholastica*, but the second is not otherwise recorded until the fifteenth century. The Latin text of the first and the English translation of the second inscription appear to have dropped out of the Bodley Version.

54/20 A brief reference to hermits, mentioned in *Vitas Patrum*, is here omitted.

54/21 A short reference to the certainty of Christian reconquest of the Holy Land when God wills is omitted.

56/1 Further brief details concerning the imprisonment of Christ at this place are omitted.

56/2 More details of the holy places near the Church of the Holy Sepulchre are omitted.

56/7 A short reference to the original Hospital of St. John is omitted.

56/10 Further brief details of the Temple are here omitted.

57/1 That Jerusalem was the centre of the world, a widely held belief in the Middle Ages, is stated in the opening paragraphs of the longer versions of *Mandeville's Travels* and repeated in the discussion of the rotundity of the earth. Both these references are omitted in the Bodley Version. The precise location of the centre, however, was in doubt.

57/3 The *Porta Aurea*, the more southern of the two east gates, was only opened on Palm Sunday and on the Feast of the Exaltation of the Holy Cross. It is mentioned by all pilgrims, including William of Boldensele and the pseudo-Odoric.

58/4 A brief reference to Charlemagne and the *responsum Cristi*, a corrupt reading paralleled in the Insular Sub-Group A where an original *le prepuce de Nostre Seignur* has been distorted, is here omitted.

58/22 A reference to the wall which was built to include the church within the city is omitted.

58/28 More details of the church of the Holy Sepulchre, with a reference to the Jewish *Sancta Sanctorum*, are omitted here.

59/5 *aftir the tenour of hym*, i.e. after their import. Cf. *secundum earum tenorem* (58/3).

59/7 This account of the Temple is ultimately derived from a variety of sources, but it is likely that the author followed a single compilation which has not been traced. Titus (emp. A.D. 79–81) captured

Jerusalem in A.D. 70 during the Jewish War (Josephus, *De Bello Judaico*, vi. 9). The story that he sold Jewish captives is found in St. Ambrose, *De Excidio Hierosolymitanae*, v. 47. The earthquake, which destroyed the repairs of Julian (emp. 361–3), and the earlier restorations of Hadrian in A.D. 136 are mentioned by Ammianus Marcellinus, xxii. 1.

60/13 A long passage, wholly concerned with places of biblical significance in and near Jerusalem, is omitted at this point. This omission is neatly concealed by the redactor where he interpolates the clause *In that contre is a watyr that is callyd the Dede Se* (61/16), cf. *Istud Mare Mortuum* (60/14).

61/16 This description of the Dead Sea is ultimately derived from Josephus, but Peter Comestor, *Historia Scholastica*, gives a very similar account. According to Josephus, the water changed colour thrice daily, and Vespasian threw bound men into the Dead Sea as an experiment to see whether they would sink.

62/10 A brief reference to the statue of Lot's wife, an account of the legendary descent of the Jews from Isaac and of the Saracens from Ishmael, and a lengthy description of places near the river Jordan are omitted here.

62/14 Another large passage, chiefly concerned with the itinerary and including a description of the Samaritans and the names of the characters of the Hebrew alphabet, is omitted.

62/18 A brief reference to Mount Tabor is omitted here.

63/1 The apples of Sodom, which were probably the fruit of the colocynth, according to Warner's note 'fair to look at but nauseous beyond description to the taste', are mentioned by Josephus.

63/14 The descriptions of Nazareth and Mount Tabor are derived from William of Boldensele, who did not visit the Dead Sea.

63/25 *mountis*, i.e. Mount Tabor, which is named in the Latin text immediately beforehand, viz. *de Nazareth ad montem Thabir sunt quatuor miliaria* (see note to 62/18).

64/7 A short passage, containing further details of the itinerary, is omitted at this point.

64/16 Another short passage detailing the itinerary is omitted.

65/11 This account of the Sea of Tiberias is derived from William of Boldensele.

65/23 Most historians of the crusades (e.g. Albert of Aix) mention the carrier pigeons. The misunderstanding by which the pigeons are said to fly in two directions is also found in the Latin text (64/25) and the Egerton Version (Warner 58/20) but in no other related version of *Mandeville's Travels*.

COMMENTARY

66/19 A brief reference to other Christian sects is omitted.

66/22 A very long passage, almost wholly concerned with the details of the itinerary, is here omitted.

66/24 From this point until 70/26 the Latin text is printed from Hunterian Museum MS. T. 4. 1, here identical with Durham Univ. MS. Cosin V. iii. 7, and not from B.M. MS. Royal 13 E. IX which at this point differs in detail from all other related versions of *Mandeville's Travels*, including the Bodley Version. It seems as though at an earlier stage a page containing this part of the account of the Koran was lost and a substitution, taken from an unknown source, was written into the exemplar of the B.M. manuscript. It is perhaps worth noting that a similar occurrence involving the rewriting in a different hand of the outside bifolium of a quire (f. 52 and f. 63) is also found in B.M. MS. Royal 13 E. IX.

67/5 These notes on various Christian sects are derived, chiefly and confusedly, from Jacques de Vitry. The *Jacobites* were founded by Jacob Baradaeus, a monk of Constantinople, in the sixth century, but there is no record of their disuse of auricular confession, supported here by quotation of Psalm 3, verse 1 and Psalm 118, verse 28. The *Surrany* or Syrians were, according to Jacques de Vitry, Arab converts who used the Greek liturgy. The *Barbaryes* are the creation of the translator who possibly had before him a corrupt variant of *Barbas nutriunt* (66/12). There is no historical connexion between the *Gorgicy*, an Arian sect following the persuasions of George the Cappadocian (d. 361) and St. George. The saint, whose martyrdom at Lydda *c*. 300 was reported in the Golden Legend, inherited the veneration due to the pagan Perseus whose fight with the sea-monster supposedly occurred at Joppa near Lydda. He became the patron saint of England in the reign of Edward III.

67/28 This account of Saracen beliefs is derived, almost word for word, from William of Tripoli. Similar accounts are also found in Vincent de Beauvais and Higden's *Polychronicon*.

69/2 From this point until the author's account of his colloquy with the Sultan (77/3) the sequence of the material in R is deliberately rearranged. Cf. note to 9/23.

69/29 The name *Tagyna* (*Taquius* in William of Tripoli) has its origin in a misunderstanding of the Arabic *taki*, i.e. God-fearing, which thus distorted the account of the Annunciation contained in the Koran.

71/12 *Ion te ewangelist*, also in R, is an obvious scribal contamination, cf. *Iesum* (70/12). The mistake is either accidental, through a misreading of a contracted *Iesum* as a contracted *Iohannem*, or a deliberate *correction* of the statement that Jesus made the Evangel (70/13).

162   COMMENTARY

71/14 William of Tripoli does not mention the *Missus est* (Luke i. 26). It is, however, found in the account of the Saracens given by Jacques de Vitry.

74/9 A further brief reference to the belief, stated in the Koran, that Jesus is the Word of God is here omitted.

75/14–15 *Godis sone and Godys word* is apparently a scribal expansion, cf. R which has merely *Goddis worde*. However, the Latin text reads *verbum et spiritum dei* (74/11), and the reading *Godis sone* may reflect a corrupt variant of *spiritum*. Cf. Egerton (Warner 68/21) *þe worde and þe gaste of Godd*.

75/28 This paragraph, without parallel in any related version, is clearly an interpolation, cf. 91/19. Scribes of all versions of *Mandeville's Travels* often felt a need to support its marvels with some interpolated statement of authenticity, but this example is curious in that it vouches for something which is historically accurate.

77/3 This colloquy is based on a very similar incident in the *Dialogue on Miracles* by Caesarius of Heisterbach where an emir complains to Brother William of Utrecht about the shortcomings of Christians. The themes of lechery, greed, and vanity are common to late medieval satirists and homilists, cf. *Piers Plowman*, B. v.

77/20 *for to swere othis falsely*, paralleled in R and the Egerton Version, does not translate *inuicem iniuriari* (76/17), i.e. to harm each other. The English reading probably derives from a corrupt Latin variant like *inuite iurare*, but the steps by which the original phrase was contaminated are not recoverable.

77/21 The change from third to second person, which begins with *ye wetyn*, is not paralleled in the Latin text and is probably of scribal origin.

77/22 The balanced phrasing of this part of the indictment is a stylistic improvement on the Latin text, *nunc curtis, nunc longis, nunc largis*. It may well be an echo of the *Prick of Conscience* (ll. 1534–5),

> for now wers men short and now syde,
> now uses men narow and now wyde.

78/17 A lengthy passage, containing anecdotes of Mahomet's life and further details of the itinerary, is here omitted.

79/23 This paragraph represents an attempt to effect a smooth transition from the account of the Saracens to the tale of the Castle of the Sparrowhawk after the redactor has omitted much intervening material (see note to 78/17).

79/29 The metamorphosis of the ruler of *Cruk* (the ancient *Corycus*) from prince into town is probably a blunder by a scribe, not the translator or the redactor, neither of whom would have had reason to omit in the previous line words corresponding to *Persipie que est domini* (78/25).

COMMENTARY 163

Korgos (*Cruk*) and Ayas (*Layays*) were important coastal towns in Lesser Armenia, but the source from which the author derived this information and the legend that follows is unknown. The Tale of the Castle of the Sparrowhawk is associated with the French romance of *Melusine*, compiled, from sources now lost, by Jean d'Arras after 1387; an English version is edited by A. K. Donald, E.E.T.S., E.S. 68. This romance, however, in its extant form was written after *Mandeville's Travels* and it records only the history of the king of Armenia, not the *symple manis sone* or the *knyght of the Temple*. The *fayr lady* is Melior, the sister of Melusine.

81/21 *ferme pes* is possibly a mistranslation of *forma pacis* (80/19) or, more likely, derived from a corrupt Latin variant *firma pace* or an uncontaminated English reading *forme of pes*. Confusion between *e* and *o* is a characteristic of this manuscript.

83/8 The story of the Amazons is part of the Alexander epic cycle, but the immediate source of this account is unknown. Vincent de Beauvais, in his description of the Amazons, refers to the king Scolopitus, of which *Cholophenus* is probably a corrupt scribal form.

84/8 A brief reference to the twelve cities of Alexander and the two parts of Ethiopia is here omitted.

84/20 A brief reference to Ethiopian youth and the city of Saba is omitted.

84/21 A short reference to the tripartite division of India (cf. note to 3/15) is omitted. Besides Greater and Lesser India, another region, roughly comparable to modern Tibet, is described.

84/25 A brief comparison of Indian diamonds and inferior kinds in Arabia and Cyprus is here omitted.

85/10 The marvellous fountain and the Sciapodes are mentioned by Vincent de Beauvais among many others. *Ethiopia*, over which the legendary Prester John ruled, was thought to be a large eastern empire, stretching from Egypt to India and Cathay. Cf. note to 99/6.

85/24 *contynuel frost* is apparently a mistranslation through the misreading of the ablative *gelu* as a contracted accusative *gelum*. In the Latin text *continuum* (84/23) qualifies *frigus* and not *gelu*, which modifies *congelatur*.

85/26 The diamond, the *adamas*, is described by many writers, including Vincent de Beauvais on whom this account is based. He, however, does not mention the fanciful idea of male and female. The Late Latin loanword *adamas*, used also by Trevisa, is derived from the Arabic *al-mas*, cf. *admiral*.

The author's interest in precious stones was probably no greater than the normal medieval curiosity but, according to Jean d'Outremeuse, 'Mandeville' was the author of a Latin lapidary, translated

into French as *Le Lapidaire en françoys composé par Messire Jehan de Mandeuille cheualier* and printed at Lyons *c.* 1530. This ascription has complicated the vexed question of the authorship of *Mandeville's Travels*. See Mrs. J. W. Bennett, *The Rediscovery of Sir John Mandeville*, pp. 123–33, and d'A. Goosse, 'Les lapidaires attribués à Mandeville', *Les Dialectes belgo-romans*, xvii (1960), pp. 71–85.

86/7 A short reference to the vastness and diversity of India is omitted.

86/18 Descriptions of the magnetic rocks and the island of Thana are omitted.

86/21 A short reference to the Pepper Forest is omitted. The Latin text is probably defective itself at this point, for in the Insular Version the Forest and the nature of pepper are described at length.

87/11 The great heat and its effect on the testicles are reported by Odoric, and the custom of total immersion is described by Marco Polo.

87/24 The source of this story of the Fountain of Youth is the *Letter of Prester John*, but its location at Quilon (*Polyne*) on the Malabar Coast is due to the textual proximity, in the longer versions of *Mandeville's Travels*, of the Pepper Forest which, Odoric says, is near Quilon. See above, note to 86/21.

89/9 This account of ox-worship is based on Odoric, but the reference to *the moste souereyn prelat*, the *Archioprothopapaten* of the Latin text (88/14), which was a title sometimes used to denote the chief prelate of the Nestorian Church, is supplied from the *Letter of Prester John*.

90/1 A brief reference to the malignant voice within these idols is omitted.

91/10 Unlike the rest of this passage, the account of the disgrace accorded to women who refuse suttee is not found in Odoric.

91/18 This reference to unnatural shaving is traceable to a corrupt reading, still extant in some manuscripts of Odoric, where the original report that women shave their foreheads and men do not shave their beards is distorted.

91/22 This account of St. Thomas's shrine at Mailapur (*Calomy*) on the Coromandel coast is mainly derived from Odoric, but he does not mention the miraculous judgements of the saint's hand. Where the author found this legend is unknown, but versions of it are widely reported, eg. in the *Letter of Prester John* and Gervase of Tilbury.

93/19 This reference to the shrine of *Seynt Iamys* at Compostella is the only important detail in this account which is not found in Odoric. At this point he refers to St. Peter's, Rome. The alteration supports the fiction that the author of *Mandeville's Travels* was an Englishman. See Letts, pp. xxiv–xxv.

94/7 A short account of the procession of the enthroned idol is omitted.

94/17 A brief reference to the minstrel attendants of the idol is omitted.

COMMENTARY

94/20 A description of the immortal glory given to these self-immolators is omitted at this point.

94/21 A brief reference to the length of the journey is omitted.

95/25 *Lamore*, the *Lamori* which Odoric reached after a journey of fifty days, was one of the dependent kingdoms of Sumatra. Its location here within the *lond of Ethyope* is due to the redactor, who was presumably trying to keep some geographical coherence in his abbreviated account of the marvels of the East. The descriptions of the nakedness, promiscuity, and cannibalism of the islanders are derived from Odoric.

96/20 At this point occurs the long digression concerning the rotundity of the earth. The Bodley Version now diverges from the sequence of the Latin text, which is hereafter printed to correspond to the sequence of the Bodley Version.

97/20 At this point the manuscript, which, unlike R, has hitherto followed the sequence of the Latin text, introduces a lengthy description of lands, peoples, and the court of Prester John, which in other versions of *Mandeville's Travels* follows a similar description of the Great Khan. As this latter potentate is later described as the greatest earthly lord (123/6), the deliberate transposition of the account of Prester John is clearly intended to heighten the climax of the book, the description of the Great Khan. See my note, 'A Medieval Redactor at Work', *Notes and Queries*, ccvi (1961), pp. 169-71.

97/22 These marvels in the land of Bactria (*Baldasdor*), the cotton-bearing trees, the hippopotami, and the griffons, are all mentioned in the apocryphal *Letter of Alexander*. This work, supplemented by Vincent de Beauvais's description of the beasts, provides the basis of this account, but the confusion here of the hippopotamus and the hippocentaur is unique.

98/13 A brief reference to the capital city of *Nisa* is omitted.

98/15 A passage, chiefly concerned with the difficulties and dangers, particularly the magnetic rocks, that beset merchants who wish to trade in the riches of Prester John's land, is here omitted.

99/6 This account is almost wholly derived from the apocryphal *Letter of Prester John*, allegedly sent by him to the Emperor Manuel c. 1165. It describes the marvels and magnificence of the land of Prester John, and the existence of this mighty ruler was never seriously doubted. When Odoric reached the court of the Khan of the Keraits, he thought that he had found Prester John, and soberly reported that not one hundredth of the things said about him were true. Prester John, however, was an elusive figure, said to reign variously in India and Ethiopia. An admirably succinct account of the legend is Yule's article on Prester John in the *Encyclopaedia Britannica*. See also

166 COMMENTARY

V. Slessarev, *Prester John, The Letter and the Legend* (Minnesota, 1960).

99/24 Much of the attraction of the legend for medieval Europe lay in the belief that Prester John was a Christian prince of the Nestorian persuasion, living in Asia and ready to join the Crusaders in crushing the Saracens. Cf. L. Olschki, *Marco Polo's Precursors* (1943).

100/13 A short account of the river of precious stones, which flows from Paradise into the Sandy Sea, is omitted.

100/26 A brief reference to another kind of parrot is omitted.

101/3 The Sandy or Gravelly Sea, probably identical with Odoric's Sea of Sand, and its delicious fish are described in the *Letter*. The origin of the marvel probably owes much to the shifting sands of the desert, cf. the phantom fruit which, reported also in the Alexander romances, appears to be a confused reminiscence of a desert mirage.

101/5 A precise meaning for the scribally contaminated phrase *the Grete Se*, which clearly refers to tidal seas generally, cf. *aliud mare*, should not be pressed. The *Great Sea* usually indicated the whole Mediterranean, cf. the Prologue to the *Canterbuty Tales*, l. 59, but it was often confused with the *Great Sea Ocean*, which was thought to surround the known land mass of the eastern hemisphere before the discovery of the Americas, through the scribal omission of *Ocean*. Its identity is still further obscured, in the fuller versions of *Mandeville's Travels*, by a similar scribal confusion with the *Great Sea of Maure*, i.e. the Black Sea. Cf. note to 9/21.

101/21 *of al that fare*. This curious reading, unparalleled in any other related manuscript, is undoubtedly an interpolation, and *fare* may be a corruption of an earlier *ferly*. But cf. O.E.D. s.v. Fare sb.[1] II. 7.

101/30 These parrots are described by, *inter alios*, Vincent de Beauvais and Haiton. The form *persital* is a false scribal expansion, cf. *psitacos* (100/26), in which the initial *ps-* was thought to represent a contracted *pers-*.

102/15 A detailed description of the riches of the palace, particularly the royal throne and bed, is omitted here.

102/24 A short account of the household duties undertaken by the prelates is omitted.

102/26 A long account of the Crusader story of the Old Man of the Mountains, the chief of the Assassins, is here omitted.

103/2 The emended reading *thi* (MS. *ii.*) is conjectural but cf. the unstressed forms *the* and *thi* of the pronoun *they* at 17/27, 23/25, &c.

103/14 The alteration of the sense here, cf. 102/13, neatly conceals a large omission by the redactor of the description of the imperial palace at *Susa*, which appears, on the evidence of the *Letter of Prester John*, to be the biblical *Shushan*.

COMMENTARY 167

103/23 For an interesting discussion of the relationship between the legend of Prester John and that of St. Thomas, see Slessarev, op. cit., pp. 9–31.

103/23 This interpolated claim of authenticity is not unique, cf. note to 75/28.

103/28 This account of the Valley Perilous is an imaginative elaboration of an incident reported by Odoric on his way to Tibet. Like Bunyan's description of the Valley of the Shadow of Death, which an early printed English edition of *Mandeville's Travels* probably inspired, this passage is remarkable for its descriptive force. The reference to the *freris of Lumbardie* (i.e. Odoric himself) 105/31 is probably a skilful attempt to meet a possible charge of plagiarism by implying that 'Mandeville' travelled with Odoric on the latter's genuine journey.

103/30 The *hillis of Doras* is either a mistranslation of *montes durans* (102/29) or an exact rendering of a corrupt Latin variant, a contracted *durās* having been misread as a proper name.

104/14 Further brief details about the monstrous face are here omitted.

106/12 This paragraph, abridged in the Insular Version but not in the Continental Version (see above, p. xvi), here indicates that the Latin text derives from the former of the two French versions of *Mandeville's Travels*. See Guy De Poerck, 'La tradition manuscrite des Voyages de Jean de Mandeville', *Romanica Gandensia*, iv (Ghent, 1956), pp. 138–54.

107/25 Tales of giants are reported by Isidore and Vincent de Beauvais, but the immediate origin of these cannibals has not been discovered. The *shep as meche as oxsyn* are undoubtedly yaks, which were reported by Marco Polo.

109/7 This strange custom and the title of *Gadiberis* are not found elsewhere, but Vincent de Beauvais reports a similar practice, without reference to serpents, among the Augylae. Such anthropological curiosities are well authenticated, cf. N. M. Penzer, *Poison Damsels* (1952), p. 37.

109/24 The curious reference to *his fadyr* is clearly of scribal origin, cf. R and 108/23. At this point the Egerton Version (Warner 141/4) reads *als fortherly as he had been aboute for to slae him*, and it seems likely that the adverb *fortherly* is the ultimate source of a scribally corrupt noun *fadyr*.

110/18 A short account of the office of kingship in these islands is omitted.

110/26 A lengthy description of various wild beasts found in these lands, such as the crocodile, is omitted.

111/1 These evil-eyed ones are the Bithyae of Scythia, described by Vincent de Beauvais. Like his sources Pliny and Solinus, he says that

the women have *pupillas geminas*, i.e. double pupils. By an obvious error *geminas* has become *gemmas* and thus passed into *Mandeville's Travels* as *precious stonys*.

111/6 This account of apparently unnatural mothers is mainly derived from Vincent de Beauvais, who quotes Solinus's report of the Thracians. He, however, does not confuse the burning of the dead child with the custom of suttee (see above, note to 91/10), nor does he give any explanation of this unnatural grief and joy.

111/22 The immediate source of this paragraph is again Vincent de Beauvais, but its ultimate source is *De Bello Gallico*, v. 12, where Caesar describes the Britons!

111/28 This account of the Brahmans is mainly derived from Vincent de Beauvais and the *Letter of Prester John*, but the ultimate source is the Dindimus correspondence between Alexander and the Brahman king. It is possible that the author may also have consulted this.

111/29 *locable* is either a mistranslation or, more likely, derived from a corrupt Latin variant, cf. *laudabilis vite* (110/28), i.e. of praiseworthy life. The gen. sing. *laudabilis* has been misread as an abl. pl. and its governing noun omitted.

112/7 Another name for this land and a reference to the river *Terhebe* which flows through it are omitted.

113/11 *lyere* is not a translation of *medicus* (112/9), i.e. doctor. The translator has either misread the word or had before him a corrupt variant *mendax* or *mendaces*.

113/12 *of as good conuersacioun* is apparently a scribal contamination, cf. R and *et boni ac sancte conuersacionis* (112/10). It is, however, possible that the translator interpreted the nom. pl. *boni* as a gen. sing. qualifying *conuersacionis*.

115/20 The historical Oxydracae (*Exiadras*) were a tribe of the Punjab, on the banks of the Hydaspes, who opposed Alexander's advance. Like the Brahmans, they become an *yle*, not a people, in *Mandeville's Travels*.

116/12 A large passage, chiefly concerned with establishing the claim of the Brahmans to the mercy of God and with an account of the origin of Prester John's name, is here omitted.

116/28 A short reference to the length of the voyage between Ceylon and the land of Prester John and the isles and stars to be observed *en route* is omitted.

117/2 In the Latin text and other related versions direct quotation begins here. The clumsy attempt at indirect relation, almost immediately abandoned, is undoubtedly of scribal origin.

COMMENTARY 169

117/28 Apart from the reference to Prester John and the Christians, this description of Ceylon (*Taprobane*) is derived immediately from Vincent de Beauvais and ultimately from Pliny. Elsewhere, in the longer versions of *Mandeville's Travels*, the author gives another account of Ceylon, under the name *Silha*, which he found in Odoric.

117/28 This unrelated phrase at the beginning of the paragraph, without parallel in any related manuscript, is either a remnant of a lost English rubric or a scribal expansion, originally part of the next sentence and now detached in error.

117/29 This account of the giant ants is derived from Vincent de Beauvais, ultimately from Herodotus. They are also found in the *Letter of Prester John*.

118/21 A description of Paradise, which the author did not claim to have visited on account of his unworthiness, is here omitted.

118/29 A brief reference to the Grand Lama is omitted.

119/25 The description of Tibet (*Giboth*), including the account of the funeral rites, is based on Odoric. The Tibetan practice of using skulls as religious drinking-cups survived until the present century.

120/23 A brief reference to the delight of the mourners in counting the number of birds who ate the body is omitted.

121/10 *the prest of that religious of here lawe* is apparently a mistranslation, cf. *presbiteri et religiosi legis* (120/8), where the nom. pl. *religiosi* has been rendered as a gen. sing. adjective qualifying *legis*.

122/2 The sequence of the Latin text here diverges from that of the Bodley Version. See below, note to 123/5.

122/3 This paragraph is deliberately placed out of context in this edition to correspond to the alteration of sequence made by the redactor at 123/5 (q.v.).

122/16 A brief reference to the city of *Sugarmago* is omitted.

122/17 A reference to an unnamed city near Peking is omitted.

123/5 At this point the redactor begins the description of the Great Khan which, in the Latin text and other versions of *Mandeville's Travels*, precedes the account of Prester John (see above, note to 97/20). This first paragraph, however, is not an introductory one in the Latin text where it occurs, in context, after the account of the Khan's manner of going on progress and before a more general description of his peoples. Its placing here is a deliberate and successful attempt to make the larger transposition of the accounts of Prester John and the Great Khan the more effective by giving the latter an emphatic introduction.

123/20 *Gaydon*, the *Taydo* of Odoric and the *Taidu* of Marco Polo, is the Tartar *Ta-tu*, i.e. the great court, built in 1267 by Kublai Khan near Peking, which was captured in 1215 by Jengiz Khan and made the chief Tartar city in 1264.

125/11 Odoric mentions the red, sweet-smelling skins, which he calls leather, but he does not refer to the panther (*patyes*). This detail is apparently taken from Vincent de Beauvais, who relates the ancient notion that the panther exuded a sweet odour to attract its prey.

125/14 The MS. *ne befelyd*, omitted in R, is a crux. The Latin text gives a double subject to this sentence, *nullus odor malus uel aer* (124/13), which suggests the addition of *eyr*; a similar phrase, *odor bonus uel aer nociuus*, occurs in the passage omitted at 102/15. If this correction is valid, then *befelyd*, i.e. fouled, is an addition by translator, redactor, or scribe.

125/20 The *senserye* (*ascensorium* in the Latin text 124/20, *ascensory* in the Egerton Version, cf. *mountour* in the Insular Version) corresponds to the *magna pigna* of Odoric. This great jar was made of jade, hooped with gold, and drink was conveyed into it by conduits. The misunderstanding which ultimately produced the corrupt form *senserye* and similar readings in other versions probably stems from a confusion of *pigna*, i.e. jar, and *pinna*, i.e. pinnacle.

125/27 This description of the hall of the Great Khan is taken mainly from Odoric, with some details added from the account of Prester John's palace given in the *Letter of Prester John*. A similar description is found in Marco Polo, lxxxvi (ed. L. F. Benedetto, 1928).

127/16 The decoration of the *manys fot* on the women's head-dress, which the author, after Odoric, claims to be a symbol of subjection, is probably the long tail, called a *gu-gu* and fashioned like a duck's tail, which hung from the caps of the Tartar women.

128/3 A short account of the mechanical birds and other details of the Tartar court is here omitted.

128/10 A brief reference to the guards about the hall is omitted.

128/17 A long passage, chiefly concerned with the legendary rise of Jengiz Khan, is omitted.

129/9 Odoric states that he lived for three years at the court of the Great Khan, and this personal reference no doubt suggested the author's claim to have served the Great Khan as a mercenary. The Sung dynasty of Manzi was overthrown and the kingdom submitted to the overlordship of the Great Khan in 1278, some forty-years before 'Sir John Mandeville' left England! Cf. note to 27/24.

129/19 The *companye innumerable of excellentment* is apparently a scribal alteration, cf. R. The whole sentence is an expansion of the

Latin text (128/18), and the reference to the king of Manzi is undoubtedly interpolated by the redactor to make a smooth transition after a lengthy omission (see above, note to 128/17), for the Latin text refers to an unnamed enemy of Jengiz Khan. The redactor's hand is also noticeable in the following sentence, which is formed from parts of two sentences separated in the Latin text by an account of the Tartar veneration of the number nine, omitted at 128/21.

129/24 The legend of the death-bed of Jengiz Khan and the tale of the captured Caliph of Bagdad are taken from Haiton. He, however, reports them in the third person.

131/21 Ogotai (*Octohas*) was the third, not the eldest, son of Jengiz Khan and ruled from 1227 to 1241. He was succeeded by Kuyuk (*Octo*), his eldest son, not his brother, who died in 1248. Because of the omission of the reference to Mangu his successor in the Bodley Version, cf. 130/24, everything that follows must be read as relating to Mangu, not Kuyuk.

According to Haiton, Mangu was baptized by a bishop who accompanied his kinsman Hethum I, King of Lesser Armenia, on a mission to the Tartar court 1254–5. Undoubtedly the *letteris of perpetuel pes to alle Cristen men* refer to a clause in the treaty concluded at the same time. Cf. C. Dawson, *The Mongol Mission* (1955), p. xxv.

131/29 In 1258 Hulugu (*Alone, Algon, Alaon*) savagely stormed Baghdad and murdered the Caliph Mostassim (*Calafernum of Baldok*) in the way which would not violate the Tartar reluctance to shed royal blood.

133/10 After taking Aleppo and Damascus, Hulugu was about to advance upon Jerusalem when he was recalled by the news of Mangu's death in 1259. Thus, he did not win *al the Holy Lond* and, despite the nominal baptism of Mangu, his campaigns were certainly not motivated by Christian considerations, a naïve belief which may have been prompted by the wishful thinking inspired by the *Letter of Prester John*. See above, note to 99/24.

133/14 Kublai Khan (*Chabila*) reigned from 1259 to 1294. He established his chief residence at Yen (*Iung*), now Peking, in 1264 and built near by his famous palace. See above, note to 123/20.

133/15 Both Kublai and his successor Timur, like all later khans, were professed Buddhists, not Mohammedans. *sarasyn* (133/18) is here used in its wider sense of 'pagan, heathen', cf. *paganus* (132/15).

133/23 It seems likely that the Bodley Version once gave the Latin as well as the English forms of these inscriptions, and that the former, in the first two instances, were omitted by later scribes; the inscription of the Privy Seal being a corrupted translation of the Latin text (132/19), and that of the Great Seal being an incomplete translation. Haiton does not mention these styles, but Carpini gives the inscription of the

Great Seal, and that of the Privy Seal is identical with the exordium of Kuyuk Khan's letter to the Pope (printed by D'Avezac in his edition of Carpini). The origin of the formula given here as *the stile of hese letteris* is unknown.

134/2 A lengthy description of the manner of celebrating the principal Tartar feasts and of the Great Khan's going on progress is here omitted. The passage ends with the paragraph which is printed, out of context, 122/3. Cf. note to 123/5.

134/7 Another lengthy passage, describing the customs of the Tartars, is omitted here.

134/26 The sequence of the Latin text is here discontinued. See below, note to 135/31.

134/28 An account of trees which bear flour and others which produce poison, as well as huge reeds, is here omitted.

135/1 The author, following Haiton, is referring to the Buddhism of the Tartars.

135/2 These marital and funeral practices are described by Vincent de Beauvais, who took them from Carpini.

135/28 *lyn* is probably translated from a Latin variant *iacentes* (as in Hunterian Museum MS. T. 4. 1, f. 322), rather than an idiomatic paraphrase of *iocantes* (134/27).

135/31 At this point, having concluded the account of the Great Khan, the redactor reverts to an earlier passage which, in context in the Latin text and related versions, precedes the description of that potentate. All the fabulous marvels that are mentioned in the following pages are, however, to be found within his empire, and their presence in this last part of the Bodley Version is doubtless intended by the redactor to heighten the climax of the work (see above, note to 123/5).

Calamassus (the *Thalamasyn* of Odoric) is identified by Yule, *Cathay and the Way Thither* (revised ed. 1913), ii, p. 156, as Banjarmasin on the Borneo coast.

Calamak (137/6, the *Zampa* of Odoric) is similarly identified as Tchampa in Indo-China. When Marco Polo visited the country (not an island) in 1285, the royal progeny numbered 362. When Odoric visited it, c. 1323, the number exceeded 200.

136/9 A reference to the manner of recruiting the royal harem is omitted.

136/10 A short account of the elephants which the king uses in battle is omitted.

136/26 A brief description of large snails and white worms in this land is omitted here.

137/10 The story of the fish is taken from Odoric, but he does not give it a biblical explanation. Such phenomena of spawning are

reported throughout the world, e.g. the annual running of pilchards along the Natal coast.

137/25 This account of island marvels is based on Vincent de Beauvais, but he does not mention names. *Caffelos*, the ancient Theodosia, is Kaffa, a Genoese trading centre in the Crimea; the last syllable of the scribal form represents the French definite article *les* which, in all manuscripts of the Insular Version, was attracted to the proper name from the following phrase *Les gens de ce pais*. For a contemporary description of Kaffa see M. Letts, *Pero Tafur* (1926), pp. 131–7.

138/19 A lengthy passage, describing other marvels to be found in other islands on the way, is omitted.

138/21 In the Latin text there follows the account of necrophagy which is printed out of context at 144/9. See notes to 139/14 and 145/10.

138/32 A short description of men with eyes in their shoulders and others without eyes or nose, living in other islands, is omitted.

139/5 *Mica* is tentatively identified with Malacca. Though Vincent de Beauvais gives no name for this land, Pliny, one of his authorities, refers to *Malichu insula* which may equally well be the ultimate source of *Mica*.

139/14 The description of the fabulous monsters of antiquity, which begins here, is based on Vincent de Beauvais and Isidore of Seville. Such creatures are a notable feature of bestiaries and early world maps, e.g. the Hereford *Mappa Mundi*, and their inclusion in *Mandeville's Travels* was undoubtedly one of the reasons for its popularity.

139/14 *Dyndeia* (the *Dondin* of Odoric) is tentatively identified by Yule, op. cit., p. 173, with the Andaman Islands. In the Latin and other versions there follows an account of necrophagy, which in the Bodley Version begins at 145/10 (q.v.). This account closely resembles Marco Polo's story of the people of Dagroian in Sumatra, and it is therefore possible that Odoric's *Dondin* is identical with this kingdom.

The name *Calamak*, here used twice to indicate the king of *Dyndeia*, is not found at this point in any other version of *Mandeville's Travels*. The scribal form is identical with that of the name given to the island of Tchampa at 137/6 (cf. *Alonak* 136/8), but this sheds little light on the present occurrences. It must be assumed either that the name is the invention of redactor or scribe, or that it is the result of successive scribal corruptions of an earlier interpolation.

The empire, here attributed to *King Calamak*, is described in terms used by Odoric of India, where he speaks of 24,000 islands and 64 kings. Its ascription to *Dyndeia* is common to all versions of *Mandeville's Travels*.

140/3 A brief account of dwarfs in another island is omitted.

140/16 In the Latin text there now follows the long description of the Great Khan and his empire which, in conformity with the rearrangement effected by the redactor of the Bodley Version, is printed on pp. 122 et seq. See above, notes to 123/5 and 135/31.

141/19 This story of the rich Chinaman, which is taken from Odoric, occurs in the Latin text immediately after the account of necrophagy which, in the printed Bodley text, begins at 145/10. For an explanation of its transposition, see below, note to 145/10.

142/7 A brief reference to the esteem accorded to small feet is omitted.

142/17 A short account of the palace of the rich Chinaman is here omitted.

144/9 The sequence of the Latin text is here interrupted by the extra-contextual account of necrophagy, for which see above, note to 141/19 and below, note to 145/10.

144/25 With the end of the interpolated account of necrophagy the printed Latin text reverts to the sequence of the manuscript.

144/28 A brief statement that the author has not related all the marvels that he saw, so that other travellers may have new tales to tell, is omitted.

145/10 This account of necrophagy at *Dundya* (otherwise *Dyndeia*, 139/14) interrupts the sequence of the epilogue and is clearly out of context. See above, note to 139/14. In R the account immediately follows the story of the rich Chinaman, cf. the Latin text where it immediately precedes that story. This suggests that the redactor, having first decided to omit it, almost immediately changed his mind and inserted it after the story of the Chinaman; and that the transposition of the passage in the printed Bodley Version is due entirely to a later scribe.

145/14 *quesemyth*, i.e. suffocate, cf. *ad suffocandum eum* (144/17). This word is first recorded in *O.E.D.* s.v. *Queasom* from 1561.

146/7 At this point Durham University MS. Cosin V. iii. 7, f. 83^v, gives a unique Latin account of 'Sir John Mandeville's' visit to the Pope. This story corresponds, very generally, to similar English accounts in the Cotton, Defective, and Egerton Versions, and it is undoubtedly linked in some way with them. It is not, however, a translation of any of those passages.

The story is obviously an interpolation, since for thirty years after the return of the papal curia from Avignon in 1377 the papal succession was in dispute, and the notoriety of this dispute kept alive the memory of the 'Babylonish Captivity' (1309–77). Thus the anachronism by which 'Sir John Mandeville' is said to have visited the Pope *in Rome* in 1356 could hardly have occurred much before 1400. See K. Sisam, *Fourteenth Century Verse and Prose* (Oxford, 1921), pp. 239–40.

As this interpolation is important in determining the interrelation-

ship of the English versions of *Mandeville's Travels*, I print the account in MS. Cosin V. iii. 7:

Et quia nonnullis est credibile mirandis faciliter fidem exhibere preter hiis quibus corporalibus oculis aperte conspexerint, ideo in rediundo versus Romam peregrinacionis gracia iter arripui; et causa aliqualiter istum libellum summo pontifici demonstrandi, eoque diuersorum nacionum gentes ibidem mundi vniuersalis tunc temporis extiterant commorantes, ab hiis comprobandi causa an experta vel friuola agnoscerent ea que in dicto libello fuerant exarata.

Quem cum benigne acciperat et [f. 84ʳ] diligenter cum bona deliberacione examinauerat, die quadam per armigerum suum causa mutue collocucionis ad cameram suam in palacio Sancti Petri fecit me venire. Quod cum venissem et prostratus super terram humiliter adorassem, in presencia duorum cardinalium hiis verbis michi affatus est, 'Quod est tibi nomen?' Ad quem ego, 'Iohannes.' Ac ille inquit, 'Librum tuum perspexi atque per librum alium maiorum mirorum examinaui.'

Tunc asportari fecit quemdam librum magni voluminis quem appellauit *Policronica*, et fecit in eo legi multa maiora et mirabiliora ac etiam plura qu*am* in libro meo continebantur. Et fecit cardinalem michi demonstrare quoddam instrumentum rotundum curiose et modo mirifico compositum, in eo continens per sculpciones vel depicturas pene omnia regna et genera nacionum, mirificum quod appellauit *Speram Mundi*. Et dixit quod instrumentum fuerat compositum secundum disposicionem et formam predicti voluminis michi premonstrati. Et ibi inueni omnia genera tam virorum quam bestiarum contentorum in libello meo prenotato, valefaciensque domino Pape optinens ab eo suam benediccionem, asserenti et confirmanti ea in libro meo descripta esse vera.

147/3 The *certeyn cause* that allegedly enforced the author's retirement was arthritic gout (*goutes artetikes* in the Insular Version, a phrase which was understandably outside the vocabulary of the translator responsible for the Latin text).

147/5 The precise date of the composition of *Mandeville's Travels* is unknown. The best manuscripts of the Insular Version give this date as 1356, while those of the Continental Version read 1357. Jean le Long's translations, which the author used, were completed in 1351, and the earliest dated manuscript of *Mandeville's Travels* was written in 1371. A study of the scribal tradition suggests a date *c.* 1357. For a brief discussion of some of the problems involved, see J. D. Thomas, 'The Date of *Mandeville's Travels*', *M.L.N.* lxxii (1957), pp. 165–9.

147/13 The traditional disposing of *part of alle myn pilgrymage* was one of many contemporary customs associated with the pilgrim which were censured by the Lollards. This reference in *Mandeville's Travels*, quite apart from problems of date and provenance, is sufficient to

refute the theory, advanced by Hamelius in the E.E.T.S. edition of the Cotton Version, that the book was an anti-papal Lollard pamphlet in disguise.

Other, no less erroneous, interpretations of *Mandeville's Travels* require a more detailed refutation than may be given here. But it may be of interest to set down briefly the conclusions of a forthcoming study:

(a) *Mandeville's Travels* was written on the Continent, in French, by an unknown hand *c.* 1357.

(b) The author was probably not an Englishman, and the existence of 'Sir John Mandeville' is completely fictitious.

(c) The interpolations in the Liège Version (a French recension of the original Continental Version) which first claim that the book was written at the instigation of Jean de Bourgogne, *alias* Jean à la barbe, who died *c.* 1372, were probably inserted after the Truce of Bruges in 1375.

(d) The apocryphal story that Jean de Bourgogne was the pseudonym of a genuine Sir John Mandeville was the invention, based on the earlier interpolations, of Jean d'Outremeuse, the Liège notary, which gained currency after 1386.

(e) The subsequent acceptance of d'Outremeuse's fictions is reflected and amplified by the epitaph, the later chroniclers, documents in the Liège archives, and the ascription of a plague tract and a lapidary.

These conclusions do not solve the problem of the authorship of *Mandeville's Travels*, but at least they restore to the book that decent anonymity which the author desired.

GLOSSARY

This select glossary gives words and forms in the English text which are not immediately intelligible. Generally the forms and references are those of the first occurrence. Exceptionally, where more than one form is listed, the reference is to the first occurrence, which is not necessarily the headword.

The scribe uses these letters in free variation: a/o; c/ch/k; c/s; i/y; ch/ss/sh/sch/; t/th; u/v; vn/on.

a *aux.* have 11/14.
abasched *pp.* abashed 69/26.
accion *n.* lawsuit 109/23.
acord *n.* harmony 131/14.
adamas, adamaundes *n.* diamonds 85/26.
admirale, amerel *n.* commander 29/16.
adrad *pp.* frightened 19/4.
afrayen *pr. 3 pl.* terrify 105/23.
agenseyd *pp.* denied 129/2.
algate *adv.* at least 29/14.
aloes *n.* fragrant wood 127/26.
amastik *n.* mastic wood 127/25.
amerous *adj.* amorous 19/1.
anow, inow *adv.* enough 77/16.
aparayled *pp.* dressed 115/2.
aperyn *pr. 3 pl.* appear 105/22; aperede *pt. 3 s.* 57/2; aperedyn *pt. 3 pl.* 107/16.
arayed *pp.* adorned 11/23.
ark *n.* wooden coffer 61/4.
arwe *n.* arrow 129/26.
asayed *pt..3 s.* tried 7/9.
aschis *n.* ashes 63/3.
aseur *n.* azure 51/28.
as faste *adv. phr.* immediately 71/2.
astat *n.* estate 99/23.
as tyd *adv. phr.* immediately 23/6.
asyngnyt *pp.* assigned 103/3.
auansyn *inf.* promote 29/19.
auter *n.* altar 11/1.
ayen *adv.* back 19/23; *prep.* against 21/1.

bakkis *n.* spines (of feathers) 99/4.
batayle, batyle *n.* battle 55/19.
baumme *n.* balsam 41/22.
baumyd *pp.* perfumed 31/3.
befelyd *pp.* fouled 125/14.

begilyn, begyle *inf.* deceive 77/19; begilede *pt. 3 s.* 69/28.
beheste *n.* promise 3/7.
behouyn *pr. 3 pl.* are obliged 23/32; behouyt(h) *pr. 3 s.* 31/7, *pr. 3 pl.* 23/29.
belewe *n.* belief 73/20.
benefisys *n.* benefices 15/24.
bere *inf.* carry, give birth to 49/8; bere, beryth *pr. 3 s.* 49/14; beryn *pr. 3 pl.* 37/3; bar *pt. 3 s.* 25/4; boryn *pt. 3 pl.* 53/7; born *pp.* 3/10.
berthe, byrthe *n.* birth 51/4.
besege *pr. 3 s.* besieges 65/25.
besily *adv.* carefully 117/30.
bet *adv.* better 89/3.
betyd *pp.* chanced 81/24.
beute *n.* beauty 17/23.
bey *inf.* buy 87/10; beyen *pr. 3 pl.* 97/17; bought ageyn redeemed 53/22.
blethly *adv.* gladly 123/11.
blewe *inf.* blow 65/3.
bordes *n.* tables 23/27.
borw *n.* city 37/16.
botoris *n.* bitterns 121/15.
bounte *n.* goodwill 131/14.
bowis *n.* bows 99/5.
bowys *n.* boughs 39/14.
bred *n.* bread 13/28.
brede *n.* breadth 33/29.
brege *n.* bridge 5/27.
brekyn *inf.* break 129/30, *pr. 2 pl.* 77/28; brak *pt. 3 s.* 131/5.
brennyn *inf.* burn 111/11, *pr. 3 pl.* 111/8; brennande, brennynge *pr. ppl.* 39/28; brend *pt. 3 s.* 59/9; brende, brent *pp.* 41/28.
brode *adj.* broad 123/28.
brom *n.* broom (the shrub) 41/12.

GLOSSARY

brout *pp.* brought 135/18.
bugele *n.* ox 99/3.
by *prep.* by 3/29.
by *pr. 3 s.* be 25/22.

camelys, chamele *n.* camel(s) 39/14.
carayn *n.* carrion 121/16.
carnacioun *n.* incarnation 69/15.
cencerye, senserye *n.* drinking fountain 125/20.
cepulcre, cepulture, sepulcre *n.* tomb 9/32.
cerkle, serkele *n.* compass 3/18.
certis, sertis *adv.* certainly 19/19.
cestyn *pt. 1 pl.* considered 105/28.
chargith *pr. 3 pl.* load 119/6; **charged** *pp.* 119/18.
chaungith, chongith *pr. 3 s.* changes 61/19.
chauntement *n.* enchantment 69/28.
chayer *n.* chair 51/1.
clepid *pp.* called 65/11; **clepyn** *pr. 3 pl.* 143/24.
clerkys *n.* clerics 67/22.
closid *pp.* enclosed 85/6.
closure *n.* enclosure 125/4.
closynge *n.* surrounding wall 125/3.
code *n.* cud 15/19.
comounys *n.* common people 23/23.
comparisounned *pp.* compared 123/9.
condicionys *n.* conditions 139/18.
condytis *n.* conduits 125/22.
confert *n.* comfort 107/2.
coniourrede *pt. 3 s.* adjured 69/30.
consecracioun *n.* consecration of the Elements 117/15.
conseil, conseyl *n.* council 11/2, advice 11/4.
conseyl *adj.* secret 43/11.
conseyue *inf.* conceive 69/19, *pr. 3 pl.* 85/31.
contempleyinge *n.* contemplation 11/11.
continewel, contynuel *adj.* continuous 85/24.
contynewe *inf.* continue, contain 115/17; **continuyth, contynuit, contynewith** *pr. 3 s.* 93/6; **contynuede** *pt. 3 s.* 31/30; **contynued** *pp.* 65/21.

conuersacioun *n.* disposition 113/12.
coostis *n.* sides 127/6.
coppys *n.* cups 99/3.
corneled *pp.* cornered 85/28.
corone, coroun *n.* crown 7/2.
coronyd *pp.* crowned 139/17.
cors *n.* body 55/14.
cottyn *see* **kyttyn.**
coueyte *pr. 3 pl.* desire 113/32.
craftyly *adv.* skilfully 51/27.
crewel *adj.* cruel 39/21.
criaturis *n.* creatures 145/1.
Cristente *n.* Christendom 13/16.
crop *n.* top (of a tree) 141/10.
croun *n.* crown of the head 67/22.
cure *pr. 3 pl.* cover 135/16.
cyte *n.* sight 31/9.

dampnen *inf.* condemn 71/10; **dampned** *pp.* 73/8.
dedliche, dedly *adj.* mortal 15/3.
defaute *n.* lack 15/25.
defendid *pp.* forbidden 51/12.
defoiled *pp.* deflowered 109/25.
deis, deyn *n.* dais 127/1.
dele *inf.* have to do (with) 85/14.
delitable *adj.* delightful 9/18.
deluuie *n.* the Flood 25/13.
delyces *n.* joys 69/7.
departe *pr. 3 pl.* separate 117/29; **departedyn** *pt. 3 pl.* 33/7.
derthe *n.* famine 29/21.
deserityn *inf.* disinherit 115/9.
deuer *n.* duty 109/22.
dewis *n.* dews 87/5.
dich *n.* ditch 123/31.
differens *n.* diversity 67/26.
disconfitid *pp.* in ill health 147/3.
discrye *inf.* describe 103/15; **discriede** *pt. 3 pl.* 79/14.
diserd *n.* desert 17/16.
disesyn *inf.* discomfort 115/16.
dispered *pp.* despaired 109/16.
dispolyen *inf.* ravage 113/26.
disportyn *inf.* amuse 19/11.
disseyuable *adj.* deceitful 101/19.
disseyue *inf.* deceive 113/8.
distruccioun *n.* destruction 83/2.
dobeleris *n.* large dishes 99/19.
dokys *n.* ducks 35/25.
dolue *pp.* buried 37/19.

GLOSSARY

doum *adj.* mute 75/4.
doutyest *superl.adj.* most valiant 85/1.
dowis *n.* doves 65/26.
dredist *pr. 2 s.* fearest 65/13.
drenk *pp.* drowned 33/10.
drewy *adj.* sluggish 85/13.
dykis *n.* ditches 123/29.
dyuers *adj.* various 3/6.
dyuersete *n.* diversity 5/1.

eche, iche *adj.* same 5/6.
egele *n.* eagle 97/30.
egre *adj.* savage 111/4.
eld *n.* age 63/19.
eld *adj.* old 17/16; **eldere** *comp.* 21/19; **eldeste** *superl.* 25/12.
ellis *adv.* otherwise 11/14.
elys *n.* eels 87/7.
emperere *n.* domination 99/7.
enabytid *pp.* inhabited 47/7.
endentid *pp.* edged 127/4.
endorid *pp.* gilded 7/2.
ensample, exaumple *n.* example 71/6.
ensens *n.* incense 93/34.
entendaunt *adj.* attendant 141/26.
entent *n.* heed 121/22.
ere *pr. 3 pl.* err 67/3; **erryn** *pr. 1 pl.* 13/29.
ermyte *n.* hermit 35/4.
erthedene *n.* earthquake 59/19.
eryn *n.* ears 75/29.
esement *n.* shelter 39/12.
esyn *inf.* comfort 115/26.
euangelye, ewangeilis *n.* the Gospel(s) 71/21.
euyn *n.* evening 71/18.
exitacioun *n.* exhortation 107/3.
exite *inf.* incite 43/12.
eyen *n.* eyes 63/11.
eyr *n.* air 11/9.
eyren *n.* eggs 35/24.
eysel *n.* vinegar 7/15.

fallynge euyl *n. phr.* epilepsy 49/15.
fantem *adj.* ghostly 101/19.
fare *n.* display 101/21.
faryn *inf.* fare, happen 131/12; **farith** *pr. 3 s.* 101/21; **ferdyn** *pt. 3 pl.* 77/7.
fech *inf.* fetch 121/23.
fedyr *n.* feather 61/26.

feis *n.* fees 85/4.
felas *n.* fellows 19/22.
felaushepe *n.* company 81/5.
felle *adj.* cruel 39/22.
fellyn *pr. 3 pl.* fill 119/15.
fendis *n.* devils 105/22.
fer *n.* fire 63/5.
fer *adj.* far 31/12; **fertheste** *superl.* 73/29.
fer *adj.* sound 107/24.
fered *n.* fear 107/16.
ferly *adj.* wonderful 101/10.
ferlyes *n.* marvels 101/2.
ferme *adj.* firm 81/21.
ferst, fyrst *adj.* first 21/12; *adv.* 7/6.
fich, fysch *n.* fish 45/22.
fier *adv.* far 51/2.
filysofris *n.* philosophers 11/10.
fleen *inf.* fly 65/28; **fleit, flye** *pr. 3 s.* 65/29; **flyeth** *pr. 3 pl.* 121/16; **fley** *pt. 3 s.* 23/4; **flyende** *pr. ppl.* 41/2; **floun** *pp.* 23/5.
fletyn *inf.* float 61/26.
flix *n.* dysentery 85/17.
flyen *n.* flies 43/14.
folye *n.* lust, folly 21/22.
folys *n.* foals 119/11.
fordede *pt. 3 s.* destroyed 23/6; **fordon** *pp.* 109/2.
foregoere *n.* forerunner 75/14.
forfarin *pp.* destroyed 105/10.
forme fadyr *n. phr.* forefather 53/20.
fors *n.* force 5/21.
forschapyn *pp.* deformed 23/4.
forsokyn *pt. 3 pl.* left 105/30.
forsothe *adv.* truly 19/21.
forthi *adv.* therefore 11/10; ~ **that**, *conj.* because 3/4.
forthynke *inf.* cause regret 123/10.
forwhy *adv.* therefore 39/9.
foul *n.* bird 37/1.
foule *adj.* evil 57/13.
foutyn *pt. 3 pl.* fought 47/2.
foysoun *n.* abundance 61/10.
freseth *pr. 3 s.* freezes 85/25.
freut *n.* fruit 35/16.
frosche *adj.* fresh 51/29.
ful *adv.* very 3/26.
fulfille *inf.* satisfy, possess thoroughly 13/25; **fulfyllid** *pp.* 45/11.
fygeure *n.* stature 139/24.
fylde *pt. 3 s.* felled, overthrew 59/19.

180   GLOSSARY

gendere *pr. 3 pl.* engender **85**/31.
getyn *pr. 3 pl.* beget **141**/15, *pt. 3 pl.* **47**/22, *pp.* **21**/31; **gat** *pt. 3 s.* **47**/10.
got *n.* goat **35**/6.
gouernayle *n.* government **83**/33.
gradde *pt. 3 s.* wept **71**/1.
grauyn *inf.* bury **17**/5; **graue** *pr. 3 pl.* **135**/10; **grauyd, grauyn** *pp.* **9**/15; **grauyd** *pt. 3 pl.* **41**/26.
gre, gres, greces *n.* step(s) **11**/26.
grefonys *n.* griffons **97**/29.
grette *pt. 3 s.* greeted **69**/25.
grettynge *n.* weeping **47**/15.
gretyn *pr. 3 pl.* weep **111**/16.
greue, greuyn *inf.* annoy, harm **43**/26; **greuede** *pt. 3 s.* **51**/5.
greuaunce *n.* annoyance **43**/23.
Grew *n.* Greek **13**/1.
grond *n.* bottom **61**/27.
grontyn *pr. 3 pl.* grunt **101**/25.
gyle *n.* guile **99**/29.
gyrdelis *n.* garlands **93**/15.

haluyndel *n.* half **7**/17.
halwis, halwyn *n.* saints **9**/16.
hardy *adj.* bold **19**/1.
harneys *n.* genital organs **141**/13.
harneysid *pp.* decorated **93**/16.
hedous *adj.* hideous **23**/5.
hedyrward *adv.* up to this time **83**/20.
helede *pt. 3 s.* healed **71**/24.
helful *adj.* sound, wholesome **11**/4.
helle *n.* salvation **53**/28.
herberewe *n.* lodging **135**/23.
heryn *inf.* hear **3**/6.
heuedis *n.* heads **139**/25.
heylere *comp. adj.* healthier **89**/3.
heyte, hyght *n.* height **9**/27.
hien, hieth *pr. 3 pl.* hasten **119**/7.
hight *pt. 3 s.* was called **17**/22.
ho *pron.* who **5**/1.
hol *adj.* whole **11**/18.
holdyn *inf.* hold **3**/29, *pr. 3 pl.* **99**/26, *pp.* **13**/6; **haldyth, holdyth, holde** *pr. 3 s.* **5**/7; **hild** *pt. 3 s.* **129**/11.
hond, hondys *n.* hand(s) **7**/10.
hondys *n.* hounds **23**/21.
hoselyn *pr. 3 pl.* administer the Communion **13**/31; **hoseled** *pp.* **105**/20.

hosyn *n.* stockings **41**/13.
hym *pron.* them **3**/22, him **9**/33.
hyndit *pr. 3 s.* seizes **121**/18.

iaspre *n.* jasper **127**/25.
iche *see* **eche.**
ieaunt *n.* giant **25**/15.
ilke *adj.* same **5**/24.
inow *see* **anow.**
ioynes *pr. 3 s.* adjoins **5**/11.
iuge *inf.* judge **65**/10.
iuge *n.* judge **65**/5.
iugement *n.* judgement **93**/1.
iurne *n.* a day's journey (about 20 miles) **25**/10.
iustyng *n.* jousting **11**/24.

kallyn *pr. 3 pl.* call **111**/8.
kepyn *inf.* keep **29**/31; **kepyth** *pr. 3 s.*; **kepande** *pr. ppl.* **81**/3; **kept** *pp.* **35**/15.
kepynge *n.* guarding **27**/8.
keuere *inf.* cover **85**/21; **kouerede** *pp.* **125**/10.
knaue *adj.* male **83**/22.
komenly *adv.* commonly **45**/20.
konyng *n.* wisdom **75**/21.
kynde *n.* nature **61**/27.
kyndely *adj.* natural **111**/31; *adv.* **101**/27.
kynrede *n.* family **121**/3.
kyrke *n.* church **5**/32.
kyttyn *inf.* cut **143**/8; **cottyn** *pr. 3 pl.* **37**/9; **kytte** *pp.* **143**/7.

lastyth, *see* **leste.**
latsom *adj.* slow, sluggish **11**/9.
Latynys *n.* Latins **15**/9.
lebbard *n.* leopard **23**/20.
lef, leuys *n.* leaf, leaves **47**/30.
lefful *adj.* lawful **73**/32.
leman *n.* lover **19**/20.
lene *adj.* thin **97**/18.
lerid *pp.* taught **69**/16.
leste, lestyth *pr. 3 s.* lasts **5**/4.
leste, luste, liste *pr. 3 s. impers.* it pleases **29**/26; **lestyn** *pr. 3 pl.* **85**/8.
lesynges *n.* lies **75**/31.
lettered *adj.* educated **75**/20.
leue *n.* permission, leave **25**/19.
leue *pr. 3 s.* leaves **41**/5.

GLOSSARY

leue *inf.* live 21/13; **leuyth** *pr. 3 s.* 47/1; **leue, leuyn** *pr. 3 pl.* 39/25; **leuede** *pt. 3 s.* 63/21; **leuande** *pr. ppl.* 113/19; **leuyd** *pp.* 19/15.
leuere *adv.* rather 97/28.
leuyn *inf.* believe 71/27.
lewede *adj.* lay 67/22.
lightere *comp. adj.* easier 75/19.
locable *adj.* praiseworthy 111/29.
logis *n.* tents 45/12.
lordshep *n.* suzerainty 79/25.
losenyd *pp.* loosened 131/10.
luxuriouse *adj.* lascivious 77/24.
lyere *n.* liar 113/11.
lyflode *n.* livelihood 115/6.
lyghtely *adv.* easily 85/15.
lykyngest *superl. adj.* most attractive 31/1.

maieste *n.* majesty 33/22.
mamettis, maumet *n.* idol(s) 91/3.
manas *n.* threat 7/12.
mansleere *n.* murderer 113/11.
marchaundye, marchaundyse *n.* trade 81/28.
marche *n.* frontier district 39/10.
marchid *pr. 3 s.* borders 33/19.
massage *n.* embassage 31/12.
massanger *n.* envoy 31/11.
mathelardis *n.* mallards 125/1.
maumetterye *n.* idolatry 93/11.
maysteris *n.* officers 95/4.
meche, mechil, mekyl *adj.* great 11/7.
mede *n.* reward 73/24.
medewis *n.* meadows 117/23.
menere *comp. adj.* meaner 83/30.
Menouris *n.* Friars Minor 107/1.
menstrallis *n.* musicians 121/4.
menstre *n.* church of monastic foundation 51/1.
meris *n.* mares 119/10.
merour *n.* mirror 19/14.
meruayle *n.* marvel 35/15.
mes *n.* courses of food 143/2.
meselrye *n.* leprosy 71/24.
mesoured *pp.* measured 103/27.
mesurable *adj.* temperate 113/19.
metisynable *adj.* healing 37/23.
mo *adj.* more 29/8.
mok *n.* dung 89/18.
mone *n.* money 25/24.

mot *pr. 3 s.* must 25/8.
moun, mowe *pr. 3 pl.* may 5/12.
muris *n.* ants 117/29.
murmuracioun *n.* complaint 39/1.
myngynge *n.* mingling 5/23.
myschapyn *pp.* deformed 105/8.
mysdoeris *n.* evil-doers 7/12.
myster *n.* need 57/19.

nakoreris *n.* kettle-drums 105/2.
nederis *n.* serpents 31/27.
neghen *inf.* approach 53/9.
nest, nyst *adj.* nearest 71/13.
neyen *inf.* neigh 119/19.
nobley *n.* nobility 129/13.
non *n.* noon 119/5.
norysche *pr. 3 pl.* breed 137/30; **norisched** *pp.* 3/10.
not forthan, not forthy, nouth forthi, nevertheless 23/26.
nouyl *n.* navel 35/6.
nygh *adv.* near 135/9; *prep.* 45/21.
nytheborgh *adj.* neighbouring 33/19.

obesiound, obeysaunt *adj.* obedient 9/28.
ocupien *pr. 3 pl.* pass (time) 77/14.
onde *n.* breath 11/14.
onmanhod *n.* shame 115/15.
onoure *inf.* honour 121/26.
onourement *n.* adornment 115/3.
onymentis *n.* ointments 87/15.
onys *adv.* once 35/4.
operemore *adv.* farther inland 9/20.
ordenaunce *n.* direction, ordinance 13/20.
ordeyne *pr. 3 pl.* appoint 65/26; **ordeyned** *pp.* 11/26.
orisounnys *n.* prayers 121/9.
ost *n.* host 27/25.
ouermeche *adj.* excessive 9/2.
outakyn *prep.* except 85/6.
outh *n.* anything 31/14.
ouyrnon *n.* midday 101/18.
owyn *pr. 1 pl.* ought 41/9.

pace, passyn *inf.* pass 3/28; **passyn** *pr. 3 pl.* 105/29; **pacede** *pt. 1 pl.* 107/24; **passed** *pp.* 3/26.
panne *n.* cranium 123/1.

GLOSSARY

papoynes *n.* leopards 23/20.
pappis *n.* breasts 51/5.
parteynyn *pr. 3 pl.* appertain 61/14.
Pask *n.* Easter 15/8.
patyes *n.* panthers 125/11.
pauuement *n.* floor, paving 129/8.
peler *n.* pillar 55/2.
perchaunce, perschauns *adv.* perhaps 77/14.
perke *n.* perch 81/2.
perlious *adj.* dangerous 23/7.
pert *adj.* open 43/12.
pes *n.* peace 81/21.
peyne, pyne *n.* torment 69/5.
peynture *n.* painting 103/8.
plenteuous *adj.* abundant 139/15.
pors *n.* purse 81/32.
poudyr *n.* dust 63/3.
pouste *n.* power 5/7.
preise *pr. 3 pl.* value 129/6.
prent *n.* impression 43/31.
prest *n.* priest 63/26.
priuite *n.* secrecy 63/24, privacy, private parts 77/6.
proferedyn *pt. 3 pl.* offered 65/15.
proprist *pp.* annexed 27/15.
prys *n.* esteem 49/11.
pryue meyne *n. phr.* bodyguard 103/7.
puppliche *inf.* make known 43/12.
purchasyn *inf.* obtain 25/19.
purueyed *pp.* provided 135/25.
puryn *pr. 3 pl.* refine 117/29.
puttokys *n.* kites 121/15.
pyned *pp.* tortured 7/26.
pyttyn *pr. 3 pl.* put 23/25.

queke, quik *adj.* living 61/23.
quere *n.* choir 55/27.
quesemyth *pr. 3 pl.* suffocate 145/14.
queyntyse *n.* cunning 101/8.

raddere *comp. adj.* redder 39/7.
rapyd *pt. 3 s.* hastened 19/31.
ratonys *n.* rats 87/20.
rau, raw *adj.* raw 139/22.
real, rial *adj.* royal 57/22.
rechellis *n.* incense 49/23.
recure *inf.* recover 79/4.
red *n.* reed 7/14.
rehersed *pp.* related 51/13.

rekenede *pt. 3 pl.* rehearsed 79/13.
rekkyn *pr. 3 pl.* consider 45/26.
rem, reume, rewme *n.* realm 3/8.
rememorauns *n.* remembrance 103/8.
reneyede *pt. 3 s.* renounced 133/18.
renne, rennyn *inf.* run 85/19; **renne, rennyth** *pr. 3 s.* 5/15; **rennyn** *pr. 3 pl.* 99/10; **rennande, rennede** *pr. ppl.* 5/21.
reparacioun *n.* repairing 95/5.
reparayle *inf.* repair 59/16; **reparayledyn** *pt. 3 pl.* 59/22; **reparailed** *pp.* 59/18.
repayryth *pr. 3 pl.* go 23/13.
replenishit *imp. pl.* fill 97/6; **replenyshed** *pp.* 37/5.
reprouable *adj.* sinful 57/13.
resoreccioun *n.* resurrection 57/2.
resseyue *inf.* receive 89/4; **resceyuyth** *pr. 3 s.* 5/17; **resseyuyn** *pr. 3 pl.* 59/2; **resseyued** *pp.* 57/20.
rettyn *pr. 3 pl.* account 15/13; **rettid** *pp.* 91/12.
reue *inf.* take, deprive 113/31; **refte** *pt. 3 pl.* 109/30; **reuyn** *pp.* 87/3.
reuel *n.* entertainment 11/27.
reysede *pt. 3 s.* raised 71/24.
robbyth, robith *pr. 3 s.* rubs 89/24.
rod *pt. 3 s.* lay at anchor 19/10.
roke *n.* smoke 105/16.
rokys *n.* rooks 41/1.
rond *adj.* round 139/26.
roste *pr. 3 pl.* roast 45/22; **rostid** *pp.* 65/15.
rotyn *inf.* rot 117/8, *pp.* 37/11.
rotys *n.* roots 87/4.
rowe *adj.* rough 141/10.
ryalte *n.* magnificence 99/23.

saferis *n.* saphires 129/5.
salueth *pr. 3 pl.* greet 101/27.
samelet *n.* rich silken stuff 31/7.
sauory *adj.* tasteful 21/20.
schekenys *n.* chickens 37/1.
schild *n.* shield 83/30.
se, sen *inf.* see 11/28; **sau, say** *pt. 1 s.* 3/13; **sewyn** *pt. 1 pl.* 59/30; **sen** *pp.* 9/6.
segit *pt. 3 s.* besieged 59/8.
sekyrly *adv.* safely 25/19.
sel *n.* seal 133/26.

GLOSSARY

seld *pt. 3 s.* sold 59/12, *pp.* 37/24;
  selde *pt. 3 pl.* 59/13.
semonye *n.* simony 15/5.
sethet *pr. 3 s.* boils 121/31.
seylynge *n.* sailing 101/7.
shat *aux. 2* shalt 19/27.
shent *pp.* ruined 131/16.
shep *n.* ship 19/10.
shep *n.* sheep 109/4.
shere *pr. 3 pl.* cut away 83/28.
shete *inf.* shoot 83/31.
shetynge *n.* shooting 83/32.
shon *n.* shoes 41/14.
shop *pt. 3 s.* transformed 17/23.
sith *n.* sight 139/21.
sithe, sythis *n.* time(s) 3/26.
sithyn *adv.* since 9/23.
skape, skapyn *pr. 3 pl.* escape 105/21.
skathe *n.* harm 17/18.
skenes *adj.* kind of 101/9.
skil *n.* reason 59/31.
skilful *adj.* reasonable 111/31.
skole *n.* school 63/21.
skore *n.* score (twenty) 29/13.
skornyn *pr. 3 pl.* scorn 95/27.
skrowe *n.* scroll 43/7.
sle, slen *pr. 3 s.* kills 77/18; **slayn** *pp.* 143/18; **slowyn** *pt. 3 pl.* 83/18.
sloughte *n.* slaughter 139/7.
slyghte *n.* craft, cunning 101/8.
soffere *pr. 3 pl.* allow 83/22.
solas *n.* entertainment 125/6.
solempne *adj.* splendid 5/32.
sond *n.* sand 11/17.
sonde *n.* sending 59/18.
sondis *n.* messengers 79/18.
sothe *n.* truth 95/16.
sothe *adj.* true 73/10.
sothfastnesse *n.* truth 71/21.
sotyl *adj.* thin 11/9.
soudeouris *n.* soldiers 29/21.
soudon *n.* sultan 27/4.
souereyn *adj.* excellent, complete 13/22.
souereynte *n.* monopoly 13/24.
souke *n.* suck 25/5.
sparhauk *n.* sparrowhawk 81/2.
spekere *n.* prophet 75/14.
sperid *pt. 3 s.* shut firmly 21/27.
spoyle *inf.* harrow 65/9; **spolyede** *pt. 3 s.* 65/7.

spryngyn *pr. 3 pl.* sprinkle 91/2.
stalthe *n.* stealth 53/7.
stalworthy *adj.* brave 45/23.
stedis *n.* places 35/16.
sterre *n.* star 49/21.
sterynge *n.* motion 101/7.
steryth *pr. 3 s.* moves 41/20.
stile *n.* inscription 133/23.
strekyn *inf.* strike 31/15; **strok** *pt. 3 s.* 43/27; **streke, strekyn** *pp.* 37/18.
streyte *adj.* narrow 77/22.
streytly *adv.* closely, strictly 25/1.
stronge *adj.* strange, foreign 23/27.
stroyed *pp.* destroyed 9/23.
sundery *adj.* various 33/8.
syde *adj.* large 119/11.
sympelyche *adv.* simply 113/6.
symplenes *n.* innocence 89/10.
symplere *comp. adj.* minor 101/1.
synet *n.* signet 57/29.
swerly *adv.* surely 85/32.

table *n.* tablet 11/32.
talent *n.* desire 85/16.
taris *n.* rich silken fabric 31/7.
te *def. art.* the 5/18.
tende *adj.* tenth 95/19.
tenour *n.* import 59/5.
the, thy *pron.* they 17/27.
thedyr, þedyr *adv.* thither 11/17.
thef *n.* thief 7/20.
thene *adv.* thence 9/11.
theth *n.* teeth 89/24.
thewis *n.* customs 115/18.
tho *dem. adj.* those 11/15; *pron.* 15/22.
thorw, thour, thourw, þoure *prep.* through 3/13.
thous *adv.* thus 37/4.
thredde *adj.* third 29/25.
threst *n.* thirst 39/2.
thryes *adv.* thrice 87/27.
thynkyth *pr. s. impers.* it seems 11/19; **thoughte** *pt. 3 s.* 13/19.
to, too *adj.* two 65/24.
ton *adj.* one 7/4.
tothyr *adj. and pron.* other 9/8.
trauayle *n.* labour 109/14.
trauaylyn *pr. 3 pl.* labour 45/19; **trauayled** *pp.* 27/12.
traylende *pr. ppl.* hanging down 119/11.

GLOSSARY

tren, treis *n.* trees 97/22.
tresorye *n.* treasury 13/6.
trompis *n.* trumpets 65/3.
trone *n.* throne 125/29.
trostellis *n.* trestles 135/16.
trowe *pr. 1 pl.* believe 13/23; **trowith** *imp. pl.* 75/28; **trowyn** *pr. 3 pl.* 13/12.
turmentyd *pp.* tormented 43/18.
turnement *n.* tournament 11/24.
twey *adj.* two 93/4.
tympanys *n.* drums 105/2.
tynt *pp.* lost 21/22.

vmbelappid *pp.* enfolded 75/8.
vnderyn *n.* mid-morning 87/18.
vndyrloute *inf.* submit 113/28; **vndirloute** *pt. 3 s.* subjugated 129/21.
vnethe, vnnethes *adv.* with difficulty 95/18.
vnkynde *adj.* unnatural 91/12.
vnwemmyd *pp.* unharmed 11/19.

varyen *pr. 3 pl.* differ 13/9.
vekyr *n.* vicar 13/17.
venym *adj.* poisonous 31/28.
vertu, wertu *n.* virtue 49/9.
very, verray, verry *adj.* true 15/25.
veuer *n.* fishpond 95/1.
veyn *adj.* empty 77/21.
viage *n.* journey 147/5.
visage *n.* face 105/14.
vytailis *n.* foodstuffs 25/24.

wasche *inf.* wash 15/11; **wesch** *pt. 3 s.* 55/30; **waschyn** *pp.* 31/3.
waxen *inf.* grow 49/8; *pr. 3 pl.* 87/6; **wex** *pt. 3 s.* 21/2.
waynys *n.* wagons 95/11.
wedewis *n.* widows 83/17.
wedyr *n.* weather 63/10.
wekede, wekke, wikkede *adj.* wicked 65/10.
wende *pt. 3 s.* thought 19/14.

were *inf.* wear 97/24; **werith** *pr. 3 pl.* 31/8.
wermys *n.* worms 91/5.
werre, werris *n.* war(s) 27/11.
wersse *n.* worse 133/13.
werwe *inf.* kill 139/1; **wirwid, worwede** *pp.* 21/1.
wetene, wetyn *inf.* know 13/8; **wete** *imp. pl.* 31/22; **wete, wetyn** *pr. 3 pl.* 43/2; **wot** *pr. 3 pl.* 73/1; **wiste, woste** *pt. 3 s.* 19/8; **wiste** *pt. 3 pl.* 79/20.
wit *aux. 2* wilt 23/1.
wondirly *adv.* wonderfully 71/1.
wondyn *pp.* wound 41/25.
wondyr *n.* wonder 75/31.
wone, wont *adj.* accustômed 7/3.
wone, wonyde, wonyn *pr. 3 pl.* dwell 17/20; **wonede** *pr. 3 s.* 17/16; **wonede, wonedyn** *pt. 3 pl.* 63/13; **wonande** *pr. ppl.* 3/19.
wonyn *pp.* won 19/16; **wan** *pt. 3 s.* 133/10.
wonyng *n.* dwelling 27/4.
wordely *adj.* worldly 81/29.
wouke, wokys *n.* week(s) 15/20.
wrethe *n.* wrath 63/4.
wrothe *adj.* wrathful 65/24.
wyndyth *pt. 3 s.* went 19/30.

yat *n.* gate 57/4.
yede *pt. 3 s.* went 19/11.
yerde *n.* rod 43/28.
yerne *adv.* eagerly 119/7.
yeue, ȝeuyn *inf.* give 3/21; **yeuyth** *pr. 3 s.* 15/23; **yeue, yeuyn** *pr. 3 pl.* 7/15; **yeuyn, youe, youyn** *pp.* 7/31; **yaf** *pt. 3 s.* 13/18.
yif *conj.* if 15/8.
yifte *n.* gift 15/15.
Yol Euyn *n. phr.* Christmas Eve 15/8.
yong, yynge *adj.* young 17/21; **yingeste** *superl.* 131/9.
yre *see* **eyren**.
yryn *n.* iron 7/16.

INDEX OF NAMES

The scribal forms of the names of persons and places mentioned in the English text are listed with their page references and their modern forms where these differ from the scribal forms. Biblical names are identified by the forms of the Authorized Version, and names occurring in crusading history by the forms preferred by S. Runciman, *A History of the Crusades* (1951–6). Scribal variants which differ only in their use of *i* and *y*, or their retention or omission of final *e*, are not recorded. Scribal forms where initial *I* corresponds to modern *I* are listed before those where initial *I* corresponds to modern *J*. The addition of *n*. indicates a reference in the Commentary.

The best maps for locating the places mentioned in the text, with much additional information and some excellent photographs, may be found in the series of translations of continental works published by Nelson, viz. L. H. Grollenberg, *Atlas of the Bible* (1957), A. A. M. van der Heyden and H. H. Scullard, *Atlas of the Classical World* (1959), F. van der Meer and C. Mohrmann, *Atlas of the Early Christian World* (1959).

Aaron, Aron, 61.
Abel, 47.
Abraham, 47, 53, 63, 75.
Adam, 25 n., 47, 53, 95, 137.
Adrian, Hadrian, 59.
Adromedis, Andromeda, 25 n.
Alaon, Algon, Alone, Hulagu, 131 n., 133.
Alape, Alopi, Aleppo, 27, 55.
Albonys, St. Albans, 3.
Aldama, Admah, 63.
Alexandir, Alisandir, Alisaundre, Alexander the Great, 9, 113, 115, 117.
Alheylek, Alihet, desert of, 25.
Almayn, Almaynne, Germany, 5, 9.
Alysander, Alexandria, 35, 37.
Amason, Amazon, Amazonia, 3, 83 n., 85.
Andrew, St. Andrew, 65.
Andropolyn, Adrianople [*now* Edirne], 5.
Anne, St. Anne, 9.
Arabye, Arrabye, Arabia, 3, 7, 27, 31, 37, 39, 45, 55, 61.
Aristotyl, Aristotle, 9 n., 11.
Arrabitis, Arabs, 39.
Aserye, Assyria, 91.
Askalon, Ascalon, 29.
Assie, Asye the Lesse, Asia Minor, 7, 55.

Babilonye, the Grete, Babylon, 31, 33.
Babiloyne, Cairo, 25 n., 27, 31, 33, 37, 39.
Baldasor, Bactria, 97 n.
Baltasar, Balthasar, one of the Magi, 49.
Barbare, St. Barbara, 25.
Barbaryes, *see note to* 67/5.
Baudewen, Baldwin I, 53 n.
Bedlem, Bethelhem, Bethlem, Bethlehem, 49, 51.
Bernabe, St. Barnabas, 23.
Bersabe, Bathsheba, 47 n.
Bersabe, Beersheba, 47 n.
Betanye, Bithynia, 9.
Bragman, yle of, land of the Brahmans, 113, 115.
Bugres, Bulgary, Bulgaria, 5.

Caffelos, Kaffa, 137 n.
Calafernum of Baldok, Caliph of Baghdad, 131 n.
Calamak, an Eastern king, 139 n.
Calamak, Tchampa, 137 n.
Calamassus, Bandjarmasin, 135 n.
Calde, Caldes, Chaldaea, 3, 83.
Calomy, Mailapur [*now* Madras], 91.
Caluerye, Caluorye, Mt. Calvary 7, 53, 55.
Calysta, Thera, 9 n.

INDEX OF NAMES

Cane, the Grete, the Great Khan, 33, 97, 99, 119, 131, 133, 141, 149.
— court of, 123, 125, 127, 129.
— seals of, 133.
— death rites of, 135.
Catan, Cathan, Cathay, 33, 123, 133.
Cathalay, Satalia [*now* Adalia], 21.
Caucasis, Mt. Athos, 9 n.
Caym, Cain, 47.
Cecile, Cilicia, 65.
Chabila, Kublai Khan, 133 n.
Charchie, Thrace, 5.
Chathre, Chayre, Cairo, 35.
Chetheuettoun, Chiethus, Civetot, 15.
Cholophenus, Scolopitus, king of the Amazons, 83 n.
Choos, Cos, 17 n.
Cipre, Cype, Sypre, Cyprus, 7, 21, 23, 25, 37.
Cirie, Cirry, *see* **Surry.**
Comagyn, Cumania, 5.
Costantyn the noble, Constantinople, 5, 7, 9, 11, 21, 33 n.
— emperor of, 5, 7, 9, 11, 15, 55, 79.
Crist, *see* **Iesu.**
Cruke, Corycus, 79 n.
Cypron, Sopron, 5.
Cyrrye, *see* **Surry.**

Damask, Damascus, 27, 29.
Danby, the Danube, 5.
Darry, Darum Castle, 25 n.
Dauyd, King David, 47, 51.
Dede Se, Dead Sea, 61 n.
Dismas, the good thief, 7.
Doras, *see note to 103/30.*
Doros, Prussia, 5 n.
Dundya, Dyndeia, Andaman Islands, 139 n., 145 n.
Dyane, Diana, a goddess, 17.

Ebron, Hebron, 47.
Edward, Edward I, 27 n.
Effesym, Eiffrasim, Ephesus, 17.
Egip, Egipt, Egypt, 3, 7, 25, 27, 29, 33, 35, 37, 55.
Elene, Elyne, St. Helena, 7, 9, 55.
Elphi, Qalawun, sultan, 29 n.
Elye, Elijah, 63.

Ermonye, Armenia, 3 n., 55.
— king of, and the hawk, 81.
Erodis, Herod the Great, 25.
Ethiope, Ethiopia, 3, 85 n., 87, 89, 91, 95.
Eue, Eve, 47, 95.
Eufrates, the Euphrates, 33.
Exiadras, Oxydracae, 115 n.

Famagost, Famagusta, 23.
France, 7.
Fynpap, Philippopolis [*now* Plovdiv], 5.

Gabriel, the archangel, 69.
Galile, Galilee, 65.
Gaydon, Daidu, Mongol city, 123 n.
Gaza, 25.
Gene, Genoa, 87.
George, Iorge, St. George, 67.
— **Bras of,** the Bosphorus, 9, 15.
Giboth, Tibet, 119 n.
Godfrey de Boloyne, Godfrey of Bouillon, 53 n.
Gomore, Gomorrah, 61, 63.
Gorgicy, Georgians, 67 n.
Grece, Gres, Greece, 5, 7, 9.
— **ile of,** Crete, 17.
Grekis, Greeks, 13, 15, 39, 67.
gret toun, Zemun, 5 n.
Grete Se, 101 n.

Hermonye, *see* **Ermonye.**
Hongery, Hongry, Vngarye, Hungary, 5.
Hospitaleris, Knights Hospitallers, 21 n.

Inde, Ynde, India, 3 n., 33, 85, 87, 99.
Irland, Ireland, 5.
Isak, Isaac, 47.
Iung, Peking, 133 n.

Iacob, Jacob, 47.
Iacobites, Jacobites, 67 n.
Iamys, St. James, 63, 65, 67.
— shrine of, 93 n.
Iaph, Jaffa, 25 n.
Iaph, Japheth, 25 n.
Iasper, Gaspar, one of the Magi, 49.
Ierom, St. Jerome, 49, 51.

INDEX OF NAMES 187

Ierusalem, Jerusalem, 3, 23, 25, 27, 29, 37, 39, 45, 47, 51, 53, 55, 59, 61, 63.
— holy places in, 49–57.
Iesu, Iesus, Jesus, 7, 13, 23, 25, 35, 41, 43, 47, 49, 53, 55, 57, 59, 61, 63, 65, 67, 69, 71, 73, 75, 91.
Iewes, Jews, 7, 49, 57, 59, 71, 73.
Iohan, Ion, St. John the Evangelist, 17, 63, 65, 67, 71 n.
Iohan, Pape, Pope John XXII, 13 n.
Iohn Crisostamus, St. John Chrysostom, 9.
Iorge, *see* **George.**
Iosep, Joseph, son of Jacob, 25.
Iosep of Aremathie, Joseph of Arimathea, 55.
Iosephath, Jehosaphat, vale of, 65.
Iuda, Judaea, 7, 25, 61, 65.
Iudas Skariot, Judas Iscariot, 71.
Iulianus, Julian the Apostate, 59.

Kateryn, St. Catherine of Alexandria, 37, 41, 43 n.
— church of, 39.

Lamore, Sumatra, 95 n.
Layays, Ayas, 79 n.
Leo, the Emperor Leo I, 37 n.
Libie, Libya, 3.
Limites, Limasol, 23.
Lonbardye, Lombardy, 5, 105.
Longo, Cos, 17 n., 21.
Loth, Lot, 47, 63.
Luk, St. Luke, 9.
Lympyna, Lemnos, 9 n.

Mabron, a district on the Coromandel Coast, 91 n.
Macomede, Makamede, Mahomet, 51, 69, 73, 75, 131.
Mancy, Mauncy, Manzi, 129 n.
Mandevile, Maundeuyle, Sir John Mandeville.
— begins his travels, 3.
— sees holy relics, 7.
— serves the Sultan, 27.
— visits Mt. Sinai, 43.
— given passport by the Sultan, 57.
— visits Jerusalem, 57, 59.
— sees the ruins of Sodom, 63.

Mandevile (*cont.*)
— speaks with the Sultan, 77 n., 79.
— sees diamonds, 87.
— visits the Well of Youth, 89.
— eats fish from the Gravelly Sea, 101.
— serves Prester John, 103.
— crosses the Valley Perilous, 105, 107.
— avoids man-eating giants, 109.
— questions islanders, 109.
— serves the Great Khan, 129 n.
— sees the spawning fish, 137 n.
— takes his leave, 145 n.
Mariak, roche of, the Holy Rock of Bethel, 61.
Marie Maudelyn, St. Mary Magdalen, 57.
Mark, St. Mark, 37 n.
Marro, the Morava, 5 n.
Marye, St. Mary the Virgin, 9, 13, 25, 43, 51, 63, 69, 71, 73, 75.
— church of, 25.
Mechel, Michal, wife of King David, 51.
Melchior, one of the Magi, 49.
Melchisadek, Melchisedech, 63.
Melchisak, Baraqa, sultan, 29 n.
Meleta, Melos, 9 n.
Mellichi Madrabon, al-Ashraf Khalil, sultan, 29 n.
Melyk Darre, Baibars, sultan, 27 n.
Mesopotanye, Mesopotamia, 55, 91.
Messodonye, Macedonia, 9.
Mica, Malacca, 139 n.
Mincafla, Minca, 9 n.
Mirre, Myra, in Lycia, 17.
Moyses, Moses, 37, 41 n., 43, 45, 61, 63, 75, 143.
Mustorak, Malazgirt, 103.

Nabagodonosor, Nebuchadnezzar, 27.
Nazareth, 63.
Nembrok, Nimrod, 33.
Neuke, Nicaea, 15.
Nicholas, St. Nicholas, 15, 17, 51.
Norwey, Norway, 5.
Noscelawe, Livonia, 5.
Nundynea, Numidia, 33.
Nyli, the Nile, 37.

INDEX OF NAMES

Octo Cane, Ogotai Khan, 131 n.
Octohas Cane, Kuyuk Khan, 131 n.

Palestyn, Palestine, 39, 65.
Panouns, Pannonia, 5.
Parthi, Parthia, 7.
Parys, Paris, 7, 9.
Patenos, Patmos, 17.
Patran, Patara, in Lycia, 17.
Pers, Perside, Persia, 3, 33, 55, 123.
Pesane, the Ganges, 103.
Petyr, St. Peter, 13, 63, 65.
Pharao, Pharoo, Pharaoh, 39, 61.
Poleyne, Poland, 5.
Polyne, Quilon, 87 n.
Prestir Ion, Preter Ion, Prester John, 33, 67, 79, 99, 101, 123.
— his court and his empire, 99, 101, 103, 109, 117.
Pyncemacert, land of the Petchenegs, 5 n.

Rede Se, Red Sea, 33, 39, 61.
Richard, Richard I, 27.
Rodis, Roodis, Rhodes, 17, 21, 23.
Rome, 7, 9, 13, 59, 61, 117, 133.
Ros, Russia, 5.

Saladyn, Saladin, sultan, 27 n.
Salomon, King Solomon, 47.
Sarazynys, Saracens, 23, 25, 47, 49, 51, 55, 57, 59, 65, 131.
— beliefs of, 67, 69, 71, 73, 75.
Segor, Zoar, 63.
Set, Seth, 47.
Sipre, *see* **Cipre.**
Sirrye, *see* **Surry.**
Skotlande, Scotland, 5.
Slauony, Slavonia, 5.
Soboak, Shobek, 63.
Soboym, Zeboiim, 63.
Sodom, 61, 63.
Soma, Naxos, 9 n.
Sophie, St. Sophia, church of, 5, 11.
Soudan of Babyloyne, Sultan of Cairo, 25, 27, 29, 31, 33, 47, 53, 57, 123.
— criticizes Christians, 77, 79.

Stageres, Stagira, in Chalcidice, 9.
Sti, Hesternit [*now* Sofia], 5.
Surrany, Syrians, 67 n.
Surry, Syrie, Cyrrye, Syria, 3, 7, 23, 27, 29, 45, 55, 65.
Synay, Mt. Sinai, 37, 39, 41.
Sypre, *see* **Cipre.**
Syrus, Cyrus the Great, 33 n.

Tagyna, an evil spirit, 69 n.
Talcas, 9 n.
Taprobane, Ceylon, 117 n.
Tartarye, Tartary, 3, 33, 123.
Temple of Jerusalem, 57, 59 n., 61.
Thomays, St. Thomas, 91 n., 93, 103, 117.
Tiberiadis, Se of, Sea of Tiberias, 65 n.
Tiberiadis, cete of, City of Tiberias, 65.
Tirus, Tyry, Tyre, 23 n., 25.
Trapasedye, Trebizond, 79.
Tray, Troy, 9 n.
Tresbria, Lesbos, 9 n.
Trinor, Hormuz, in the Persian Gulf, 87.
Tripolle, Tripoli, 29.
Turkye, Turkey, 3, 15, 29, 55.
Turritigia, Critige, 9 n.
Tytus, Titus, 59 n., 61.

Vngarye, *see* **Hongery.**
Vrye, Uriah, the good warrior, 47.

Vale Perlious, Valley Perilous, 103 n., 105, 107.
Vaspasianus, Vespasian, 59.
Venyse, Venice, 37, 87.

Walis, Wales, 5.
West Se, the Mediterranean, 39 n.

Yngelond, England, 5, 27.
Ypateia, Scarpanto [*now* Karpathos], 9 n.
Ypocras, Hippocrates, 17 n.
— daughter of, 17, 19, 21.
Ysrael, the Hebrew nation, 37, 39, 61.

Early English Text Society

OFFICERS AND COUNCIL

Honorary Director
PROFESSOR NORMAN DAVIS, M.B.E.
Merton College, Oxford

J. A. W. BENNETT
PROFESSOR BRUCE DICKINS, F.B.A.
A. I. DOYLE
PROFESSOR P. HODGSON
MISS P. M. KEAN
N. R. KER, F.B.A.

C. T. ONIONS, C.B.E., F.B.A.
PROFESSOR J. R. R. TOLKIEN
PROFESSOR D. WHITELOCK, F.B.A.
PROFESSOR R. M. WILSON
PROFESSOR C. L. WRENN

Honorary Secretary
R. W. BURCHFIELD
40 Walton Crescent, Oxford

Bankers
THE NATIONAL PROVINCIAL BANK LTD.
Cornmarket Street, Oxford

THE Subscription to the Society, which constitutes full membership, is £2. 2s. a year for the annual publications, from 1921 onwards, due in advance on the 1st of JANUARY, and should be paid by Cheque, Postal Order, or Money Order crossed 'National Provincial Bank Limited', to the Hon. Secretary, R. W. Burchfield, 40 Walton Crescent, Oxford. Individual members of the Society are allowed, after consultation with the Secretary, to select other volumes of the Society's publications instead of those for the current year. The Society's Texts can also be purchased separately from the Publisher, Oxford University Press, through a bookseller, at the prices put after them in the List, or through the Secretary, by members only, for their own use, at a discount of 2d. in the shilling.

The Early English Text Society was founded in 1864 by Frederick James Furnivall, with the help of Richard Morris, Walter Skeat, and others, to bring the mass of unprinted Early English literature within

the reach of students and provide sound texts from which the New English Dictionary could quote. In 1867 an Extra Series was started of texts already printed but not in satisfactory or readily obtainable editions. At a cost of nearly £35,000, 159 volumes were issued in the Original Series and 126 in the Extra Series before 1921. In that year the title *Extra Series* was dropped, and all the publications of 1921 and subsequent years have since been listed and numbered as part of the Original Series. Since 1921 some ninety volumes have been issued. In this prospectus the Original Series and Extra Series for the years 1867–1920 are amalgamated, so as to show all the publications of the Society in a single list. In 1955 the prices of all volumes issued for the years up to 1936 and still available, were increased by one-fifth.

LIST OF PUBLICATIONS

Original Series, 1864–1963. Extra Series, 1867–1920
(One guinea per annum for each series separately up to 1920, two guineas from 1921)

O.S. 1. Early English Alliterative Poems, ed. R. Morris. (*Out of print*.)   1864
    2. Arthur, ed. F. J. Furnivall. (*Out of print*.)   ,,
    3. Lauder on the Dewtie of Kyngis, &c., 1556, ed. F. Hall. (*Out of print*.)   ,,
    4. Sir Gawayne and the Green Knight, ed. R. Morris. (*Out of print, see* O.S. 210.)   ,,
    5. Hume's Orthographie and Congruitie of the Britan Tongue, ed. H. B. Wheatley. 5s.   1865
    6. Lancelot of the Laik, ed. W. W. Skeat. (*Out of print*.)   ,,
    7. Genesis & Exodus, ed. R. Morris. (*Out of print*.)   ,,
    8. Morte Arthure, ed. E. Brock. (*Reprinted* 1961.) 25s.   ,,
    9. Thynne on Speght's ed. of Chaucer, A.D. 1599, ed. G. Kingsley and F. J. Furnivall. (*Out of print*.)   ,,
   10. Merlin, Part I, ed. H. B. Wheatley. (*Out of print*.)   ,,
   11. Lyndesay's Monarche, &c., ed. J. Small. Part I. (*Out of print*.)   ,,
   12. The Wright's Chaste Wife, ed. F. J. Furnivall. (*Out of print*.)   ,,
   13. Seinte Marherete, ed. O. Cockayne. (*Out of print, see* O.S. 193.)   1866
   14. King Horn, Floriz and Blauncheflur, &c., ed. J. R. Lumby, re-ed. G. H. McKnight. (*Reprinted* 1962.) 30s.   ,,
   15. Political, Religious, and Love Poems, ed. F. J. Furnivall. (*Out of print*.)   ,,
   16. The Book of Quinte Essence, ed. F. J. Furnivall. (*Out of print*.)   ,,
   17. Parallel Extracts from 45 MSS. of Piers the Plowman, ed. W. W. Skeat. (*Out of print*.)   ,,
   18. Hali Meidenhad, ed. O. Cockayne, re-ed. F. J. Furnivall. (*Out of print*.)   ,,
   19. Lyndesay's Monarche, &c., ed. J. Small. Part II. (*Out of print*.)   ,,
   20. Richard Rolle de Hampole, English Prose Treatises of, ed. G. G. Perry. (*Reprinted* 1920.) 7s.   ,,
   21. Merlin, ed. H. B. Wheatley. Part II. (*Out of print*.)   ,,
   22. Partenay or Lusignen, ed. W. W. Skeat. 7s. 6d.   ,,
   23. Dan Michel's Ayenbite of Inwyt, ed. R. Morris. (*Out of print*.)   ,,
   24. Hymns to the Virgin and Christ; The Parliament of Devils, &c., ed. F. J. Furnivall. (*Out of print*.)   1867
   25. The Stacions of Rome, the Pilgrims' Sea-voyage, with Clene Maydenhod, ed. F. J. Furnivall. (*Out of print*.)   ,,
   26. Religious Pieces in Prose and Verse, from R. Thornton's MS., ed. G. G. Perry. 6s. (*See under* 1913.)   ,,
   27. Levins' Manipulus Vocabulorum, a rhyming Dictionary, ed. H. B. Wheatley. 14s.   ,,
   28. William's Vision of Piers the Plowman, ed. W. W. Skeat. A-Text. (*Reprinted* 1956.) 20s.   ,,
   29. Old English Homilies (1220–30), ed. R. Morris. Series I, Part I. (*Out of print*.)   ,,
   30. Pierce the Ploughmans Crede, ed. W. W. Skeat. (*Out of print*.)   ,,
E.S. 1. William of Palerne or William and the Werwolf, re-ed. W. W. Skeat. (*Out of print*.)   ,,
    2. Early English Pronunciation, by A. J. Ellis. Part I. (*Out of print*.)   ,,
O.S. 31. Myrc's Duties of a Parish Priest, in Verse, ed. E. Peacock. (*Out of print*.)   1868
   32. Early English Meals and Manners: the Boke of Norture of John Russell, the Bokes of Keruynge, Curtasye, and Demeanor, the Babees Book, Urbanitatis, &c., ed. F. J. Furnivall. (*Out of print*.)   ,,
   33. The Book of the Knight of La Tour-Landry, ed. T. Wright. (*Out of print*.)   ,,
   34. Old English Homilies (before 1300), ed. R. Morris. Series I, Part II. (*Out of print*.)   ,,
   35. Lyndesay's Works, Part III: The Historie and Testament of Squyer Meldrum, ed. F. Hall. (*Out of print*.)   ,,
E.S. 3. Caxton's Book of Curtesye, in Three Versions, ed. F. J. Furnivall. (*Out of print*.)   ,,
    4. Havelok the Dane, re-ed. W. W. Skeat. (*Out of print*.)   ,,
    5. Chaucer's Boethius, ed. R. Morris. (*Out of print*.)   ,,
    6. Chevelere Assigne, re-ed. Lord Aldenham. (*Out of print*.)   ,,

The Original and Extra Series of the 'Early English Text Society'

O.S. 36.	Merlin, ed. H. B. Wheatley. Part III. On Arthurian Localities, by J. S. Stuart Glennie. (*Out of print.*)	1869
37.	Sir David Lyndesay's Works, Part IV, Ane Satyre of the thrie Estaits, ed. F. Hall. (*Out of print.*)	,,
38.	William's Vision of Piers the Plowman, ed. W. W Skeat. Part II. Text B. (*Reprinting.*)	,,
39.	The Gest Hystoriale of the Destruction of Troy, ed. D. Donaldson and G. A. Panton. Part I. (*Out of print.*)	,,
E.S. 7.	Early English Pronunciation, by A. J. Ellis. Part II. (*Out of print.*)	,,
8.	Queene Elizabethes Achademy, &c., ed. F. J. Furnivall. Essays on early Italian and German Books of Courtesy, by W. M. Rossetti and E. Oswald. (*Out of print.*)	,,
9.	Awdeley's Fraternitye of Vacabondes, Harman's Caveat, &c., ed. E. Viles and F. J. Furnivall. (*Out of print.*)	,,
O.S. 40.	English Gilds, their Statutes and Customs, A.D. 1389, ed. Toulmin Smith and Lucy T. Smith, with an Essay on Gilds and Trades-Unions, by L. Brentano. (*Reprinted 1963.*) 55s.	1870
41.	William Lauder's Minor Poems, ed. F. J. Furnivall. (*Out of print.*)	,,
42.	Bernardus De Cura Rei Famuliaris, Early Scottish Prophecies, &c., ed. J. R. Lumby. (*Out of print.*)	,,
43.	Ratis Raving, and other Moral and Religious Pieces, ed. J. R. Lumby. (*Out of print.*)	,,
E.S. 10.	Andrew Boorde's Introduction of Knowledge, 1547, Dyetary of Helth, 1542, Barnes in Defence of the Berde, 1542-3, ed. F. J. Furnivall. (*Out of print.*)	,,
11.	Barbour's Bruce, ed. W. W. Skeat. Part I. 14s.	,,
O.S. 44.	The Alliterative Romance of Joseph of Arimathie, or The Holy Grail: from the Vernon MS.; with W. de Worde's and Pynson's Lives of Joseph: ed. W. W. Skeat. (*Out of print.*)	1871
45.	King Alfred's West-Saxon Version of Gregory's Pastoral Care, ed., with an English translation, by Henry Sweet. Part I. (*Reprinted 1958.*) 30s.	,,
46.	Legends of the Holy Rood, Symbols of the Passion and Cross Poems, ed. R. Morris. (*Out of print.*)	,,
47.	Sir David Lyndesay's Works, ed. J. A. H. Murray. Part V. (*Out of print.*)	,,
48.	The Times' Whistle, and other Poems, by R. C., 1616; ed. J. M. Cowper. (*Out of print.*)	,,
E.S. 12.	England in Henry VIII's Time: a Dialogue between Cardinal Pole and Lupset, by Thom. Starkey Chaplain to Henry VIII, ed. J. M. Cowper. Part II. (*Out of print,* Part I is E.S. 32, 1878.)	,,
13.	A Supplicacyon for the Beggers, by Simon Fish, A.D. 1528-9, ed. F. J. Furnivall, with A Supplication to our Moste Soueraigne Lorde, A Supplication of the Poore Commons, and The Decaye of England by the Great Multitude of Sheep, ed. J. M. Cowper. (*Out of print.*)	,,
14.	Early English Pronunciation, by A. J. Ellis. Part III. (*Out of print.*)	,,
O.S. 49.	An Old English Miscellany, containing a Bestiary, Kentish Sermons, Proverbs of Alfred, and Religious Poems of the 13th cent., ed. R. Morris. (*Out of print.*)	1872
50.	King Alfred's West-Saxon Version of Gregory's Pastoral Care, ed. H. Sweet. Part II. (*Reprinted 1958.*) 30s.	,,
51.	Þe Lifiade of St. Juliana, 2 versions, with translations; ed. O. Cockayne and E. Brock. (*Reprinted* 1957.) 25s.	,,
52.	Palladius on Husbondrie, englisht, ed. Barton Lodge. Part I. 12s.	,,
E.S. 15.	Robert Crowley's Thirty-One Epigrams, Voyce of the Last Trumpet, Way to Wealth, &c., ed. J. M. Cowper. (*Out of print.*)	,,
16.	Chaucer's Treatise on the Astrolabe, ed. W. W. Skeat. (*Out of print.*)	,,
17.	The Complaynt of Scotlande, with 4 Tracts, ed. J. A. H. Murray. Part I. (*Out of print.*)	,,
O.S. 53.	Old-English Homilies, Series II, and three Hymns to the Virgin and God, 13th-century, with the music to two of them, in old and modern notation, ed. R. Morris. (*Out of print.*)	1873
54.	The Vision of Piers Plowman, ed. W. W. Skeat. Part III. Text C. (*Reprinted 1959.*) 35s.	,,
55.	Generydes, a Romance, ed. W. Aldis Wright. Part I. 3s. 6d.	,,
E.S. 18.	The Complaynt of Scotlande, ed. J. A. H. Murray. Part II. (*Out of print.*)	,,
19.	The Myroure of oure Ladye, ed. J. H. Blunt. (*Out of print.*)	,,
O.S. 56.	The Gest Hystoriale of the Destruction of Troy, in alliterative verse, ed. D. Donaldson and G. A. Panton. Part II. (*Out of print.*)	1874
57.	Cursor Mundi, in four Texts, ed. R. Morris. Part I, with 2 photolithographic facsimiles. (*Reprinted* 1961.) 25s.	,,
58.	The Blickling Homilies, ed. R. Morris. Part I. (*Out of print.*)	,,
E.S. 20.	Lovelich's History of the Holy Grail, ed. F. J. Furnivall. Part I. (*Out of print.*)	,,
21.	Barbour's Bruce, ed. W. W. Skeat. Part II. (*Out of print.*)	,,
22.	Henry Brinklow's Complaynt of Roderyck Mors and The Lamentacyon of a Christen Agaynst the Cytye of London, made by Roderigo Mors, ed. J. M. Cowper. (*Out of print.*)	,,
23.	Early English Pronunciation, by A. J. Ellis. Part IV. (*Out of print.*)	,,
O.S. 59.	Cursor Mundi, in four Texts, ed. R. Morris. Part II. (*Out of print.*)	1875
60.	Meditacyuns on the Soper of our Lorde, by Robert of Brunne, ed. J. M. Cowper. 3s.	,,
61.	The Romance and Prophecies of Thomas of Erceldoune, ed. J. A. H. Murray. 12s. 6d.	,,
E.S. 24.	Lovelich's History of the Holy Grail, ed. F. J. Furnivall. Part II. (*Out of print.*)	,,
25.	Guy of Warwick, 15th century Version, ed. J. Zupitza. Part I. (*Out of print.*)	,,
O.S. 62.	Cursor Mundi, in four Texts, ed. R. Morris. Part III. 18s.	1876
63.	The Blickling Homilies, ed. R. Morris. Part II. (*Out of print.*)	,,
64.	Francis Thynne's Embleames and Epigrams, ed. F. J. Furnivall. 8s. 6d.	,,
65.	Be Domes Dæge (Bede's *De Die Judicii*), &c., ed. J. R. Lumby. (*Out of print.*)	,,
E.S. 26.	Guy of Warwick, 15th-century Version, ed. J. Zupitza. Part II. (*Out of print.*)	,,
27.	The English Works of John Fisher, ed. J. E. B. Mayor. Part I. (*Out of print.*)	,,
O.S. 66.	Cursor Mundi, in four Texts, ed. R. Morris. Part IV, with 2 autotypes. (*Out of print.*)	1877
67.	Notes on Piers Plowman, by W. W. Skeat. Part I. (*Out of print.*)	,,

The Original and Extra Series of the 'Early English Text Society'

E.S. 28. Lovelich's Holy Grail, ed. F. J. Furnivall. Part III. (*Out of print.*) 1877
    29. Barbour's Bruce, ed. W. W. Skeat. Part III. 25*s.*   "
O.S. 68. Cursor Mundi, in 4 Texts, ed. R. Morris. Part V. 30*s.* 1878
    69. Adam Davie's 5 Dreams about Edward II, &c., ed. F. J. Furnivall. 6*s.*   "
    70. Generydes, a Romance, ed. W. Aldis Wright. Part II. 5*s.*   "
E.S. 30. Lovelich's Holy Grail, ed. F. J. Furnivall. Part IV. (*Out of print.*)   "
    31. The Alliterative Romance of Alexander and Dindimus, ed. W. W. Skeat. (*Out of print.*)   "
    32. Starkey's England in Henry VIII's Time. Part I. Starkey's Life and Letters, ed. S. J. Herrtage. 9*s.* 6*d.*   "
O.S. 71. The Lay Folks Mass-Book, four texts, ed. T. F. Simmons. (*Out of print.*) 1879
    72. Palladius on Husbondrie, englisht, ed. S. J. Herrtage. Part II. 6*s.*   "
E.S. 33. Gesta Romanorum, ed. S. J. Herrtage. (*Reprinted 1962.*) 55*s.*   "
    34. The Charlemagne Romances: 1. Sir Ferumbras, from Ashm. MS. 33, ed. S. J. Herrtage. (*Out of print.*)   "
O.S. 73. The Blickling Homilies, ed. R. Morris. Part III. (*Out of print.*) 1880
    74. English Works of Wyclif, hitherto unprinted, ed. F. D. Matthew. (*Out of print.*)   "
E.S. 35. Charlemagne Romances: 2. The Sege off Melayne, Sir Otuell, &c., ed. S. J. Herrtage. (*Out of print.*)   "
    36. Charlemagne Romances: 3. Lyf of Charles the Grete, ed. S. J. Herrtage. Part I. 19*s.*   "
O.S. 75. Catholicon Anglicum, an English-Latin Wordbook, from Lord Monson's MS., A.D. 1483, ed., with Introduction and Notes, by S. J. Herrtage and Preface by H. B. Wheatley. (*Out of print.*) 1881
    76. Ælfric's Metrical Lives of Saints, in MS. Cott. Jul. E VII, ed. W. W. Skeat. Part I. (*Out of print.*)   "
E.S. 37. Charlemagne Romances: 4. Lyf of Charles the Grete, ed. S. J. Herrtage. Part II (*Out of print*)   "
    38. Charlemagne Romances: 5. The Sowdone of Babylone, ed. E. Hausknecht. (*Out of print.*)   "
O.S. 77. Beowulf, the unique MS. autotyped and transliterated, ed. J. Zupitza. (*Re-issued as No. 245. See under 1958.*) 1882
    78. The Fifty Earliest English Wills, in the Court of Probate, 1387–1439, ed. F.J. Furnivall. (*Out of print.*)   "
E.S. 39. Charlemagne Romances: 6. Rauf Coilyear, Roland, Otuel, &c., ed. S. J. Herrtage. 18*s.*   "
    40. Charlemagne Romances: 7. Huon of Burdeux, by Lord Berners, ed. S. L. Lee. Part I. (*Out of print.*)   "
O.S. 79. King Alfred's Orosius, from Lord Tollemache's 9th-century MS., ed. H. Sweet. Part I. (*Reprinted 1959.*) 30*s.* 1883
    79 b. Extra Volume. Facsimile of the Epinal Glossary, ed. H. Sweet. (*Out of print.*)   "
E.S. 41. Charlemagne Romances: 8. Huon of Burdeux, by Lord Berners, ed. S. L. Lee. Part II. (*Out of print.*)   "
    42. Guy of Warwick: 2 texts (Auchinleck MS. and Caius MS.), ed. J. Zupitza. Part I. (*Out of print.*)   "
O.S. 80. The Life of St. Katherine, B.M. Royal MS. 17 A. xxvii, &c., and its Latin Original, ed. E. Einenkel. (*Out of print.*) 1884
    81. Piers Plowman: Glossary, &c., ed. W. W. Skeat. Part IV, completing the work (*Out of print.*)   "
E.S. 43. Charlemagne Romances: 9. Huon of Burdeux, by Lord Berners, ed. S. L. Lee. Part III. (*Out of print.*)   "
    44. Charlemagne Romances: 10. The Foure Sonnes of Aymon, ed. Octavia Richardson. Part I. (*Out of print.*)   "
O.S. 82. Ælfric's Metrical Lives of Saints, MS. Cott. Jul. E VII, ed. W. W. Skeat. Part II. 20*s.* 1885
    83. The Oldest English Texts, Charters, &c., ed. H. Sweet. (*Reprinted 1957.*) 42*s.*   "
E.S. 45. Charlemagne Romances: 11. The Foure Sonnes of Aymon, ed. O. Richardson. Part II. (*Out of print.*)   "
    46. Sir Beves of Hamtoun, ed. E. Kölbing. Part I. (*Out of print.*)   "
O.S. 84. Additional Analogs to 'The Wright's Chaste Wife', O.S. 12, by W. A. Clouston. 1*s.* 1886
    85. The Three Kings of Cologne, ed. C. Horstmann. 20*s.* 6*d.*   "
    86. Prose Lives of Women Saints, ed. C. Horstmann. 14*s.*   "
E.S. 47. The Wars of Alexander, ed. W. W. Skeat. (*Out of print.*)   "
    48. Sir Beves of Hamtoun, ed. E. Kölbing. Part II. (*Out of print.*)   "
O.S. 87. The Early South-English Legendary, Laud MS. 108, ed. C. Horstmann. (*Out of print.*) 1887
    88. Hy. Bradshaw's Life of St. Werburghe (Pynson, 1521), ed. C. Horstmann. 12*s.*   "
E.S. 49. Guy of Warwick, 2 texts (Auchinleck and Caius MSS.), ed. J. Zupitza. Part II. (*Out of print.*)   "
    50. Charlemagne Romances: 12. Huon of Burdeux, by Lord Berners, ed. S. L. Lee. Part IV. (*Out of print.*)   "
    51. Torrent of Portyngale, ed. E. Adam. (*Out of print.*)   "
O.S. 89. Vices and Virtues, ed. F. Holthausen. Part I. (*Out of print.*) 1888
    90. Anglo-Saxon and Latin Rule of St. Benet, interlinear Glosses, ed. H. Logeman. (*Out of print.*)   "
    91. Two Fifteenth-Century Cookery-Books, ed. T. Austin. (*Out of print.*)   "
E.S. 52. Bullein's Dialogue against the Feuer Pestilence, 1578, ed. M. and A. H. Bullen. (*Out of print.*)   "
    53. Vicary's Anatomie of the Body of Man, 1548, ed. 1577, ed. F. J. and Percy Furnivall. Part I. (*Out of print.*)   "
    54. The Curial made by maystere Alain Charretier, translated by William Caxton, 1484, ed. F. J. Furnivall and P. Meyer. (*Out of print.*)   "
O.S. 92. Eadwine's Canterbury Psalter, from the Trin. Cambr. MS., ed. F. Harsley, Part II. (*Out of print.*) 1889
    93. Defensor's Liber Scintillarum, ed. E. Rhodes. 20*s.*   "
E.S. 55. Barbour's Bruce, ed. W.W. Skeat. Part IV. 6*s.*   "
    56. Early English Pronunciation, by A. J. Ellis. Part V, the present English Dialects. (*Out of print.*)   "
O.S. 94. Ælfric's Metrical Lives of Saints, MS. Cott. Jul. E VII, ed. W. W. Skeat. Part III. 30*s.* 1890
    95. The Old-English Version of Bede's Ecclesiastical History, re-ed. T. Miller. Part I, 1. (*Reprinted 1959.*) 30*s.*   "
E.S. 57. Caxton's Eneydos, ed. W. T. Culley and F. J. Furnivall. (*Reprinted 1962.*) 30*s.*   "
    58. Caxton's Blanchardyn and Eglantine, c. 1489, ed. L. Kellner. (*Reprinted 1962.*) 42*s.*   "
O.S. 96. The Old-English Version of Bede's Ecclesiastical History, re-ed. T. Miller. Part I, 2. (*Reprinted 1959.*) 30*s.* 1891
    97. The Earliest English Prose Psalter, ed. K. D. Buelbring. Part I. (*Out of print.*)   "

4

The Original and Extra Series of the 'Early English Text Society'

E.S.	59. Guy of Warwick, 2 texts (Auchinleck and Caius MSS.), ed. J. Zupitza. Part III. (*Out of print.*)	1891
	60. Lydgate's Temple of Glas, re-ed. J. Schick. (*Out of print.*)	,,
O.S.	98. Minor Poems of the Vernon MS., ed. C. Horstmann. Part I. (*Out of print.*)	1892
	99. Cursor Mundi. Preface, Notes, and Glossary, Part VI, ed. R. Morris. (*Reprinted* 1962.) 25s.	,,
E.S.	61. Hoccleve's Minor Poems, I, from the Phillipps and Durham MSS., ed. F. J. Furnivall. (*Out of print.*)	,,
	62. The Chester Plays, re-ed. H. Deimling. Part I. (*Reprinted* 1959.) 25s.	,,
O.S.	100. Capgrave's Life of St. Katharine, ed. C. Horstmann, with Forewords by F. J. Furnivall. (*Out of print.*)	1893
	101. Cursor Mundi. Essay on the MSS., their Dialects, &c., by H. Hupe. Part VII. (*Reprinted* 1962.) 25s.	,,
E.S.	63. Thomas à Kempis's De Imitatione Christi, ed. J. K. Ingram. (*Out of print.*)	,,
	64. Caxton's Godeffroy of Boloyne, or The Siege and Conqueste of Jerusalem, 1481, ed. Mary N. Colvin. (*Out of print.*)	,,
O.S.	102. Lanfranc's Science of Cirurgie, ed. R. von Fleischhacker. Part I. 24s.	1894
	103. The Legend of the Cross, &c., ed. A. S. Napier. (*Out of print.*)	,,
E.S.	65. Sir Beves of Hamtoun, ed. E. Kölbing. Part III. (*Out of print.*)	,,
	66. Lydgate's and Burgh's Secrees of Philisoffres ('Governance of Kings and Princes'), ed. R. Steele. (*Out of print.*)	,,
O.S.	104. The Exeter Book (Anglo-Saxon Poems), re-ed. I Gollancz. Part I. (*Reprinted* 1958.) 30s.	1895
	105. The Prymer or Lay Folks' Prayer Book, Camb. Univ. MS., ed. H. Littlehales. Part I. (*Out of print.*)	,,
E.S.	67. The Three Kings' Sons, a Romance, ed. F. J. Furnivall. Part I, the Text. (*Out of print.*)	,,
	68. Melusine, the prose Romance, ed. A. K. Donald. Part I, the Text. (*Out of print.*)	,,
O.S.	106. R. Misyn's Fire of Love and Mending of Life (Hampole), ed. R. Harvey. (*Out of print.*)	1896
	107. The English Conquest of Ireland, A.D. 1166–1185, 2 Texts, ed. F. J. Furnivall. Part I. 18s.	,,
E.S.	69. Lydgate's Assembly of the Gods, ed. O. L. Triggs. (*Reprinted* 1957.) 25s.	,,
	70. The Digby Plays, ed. F. J. Furnivall. (*Out of print.*)	,,
O.S.	108. Child-Marriages and -Divorces, Trothplights, &c. Chester Depositions, 1561–6, ed. F. J. Furnivall. (*Out of print.*)	1897
	109. The Prymer or Lay Folks' Prayer Book, ed. H. Littlehales. Part II. (*Out of print.*)	,,
E.S.	71. The Towneley Plays, ed. G. England and A. W. Pollard. (*Re-issued* 1952.) 30s.	,,
	72. Hoccleve's Regement of Princes, and 14 Poems, ed. F. J. Furnivall. (*Out of print.*)	,,
	73. Hoccleve's Minor Poems, II, from the Ashburnham MS., ed. I. Gollancz. (*Out of print.*)	,,
O.S.	110. The Old-English Version of Bede's Ecclesiastical History, ed. T. Miller. Part II, 1. (*Reprinted* 1963.) 30s.	1898
	111. The Old-English Version of Bede's Ecclesiastical History, ed. T. Miller. Part II, 2. (*Reprinted* 1963.) 30s.	,,
E.S.	74. Secreta Secretorum, 3 prose Englishings, one by Jas. Yonge, 1428, ed. R. Steele. Part I. 24s.	,,
	75. Speculum Guidonis de Warwyk, ed. G. L. Morrill. 12s.	,,
O.S.	112. Merlin. Part IV. Outlines of the Legend of Merlin, by W. E. Mead. 18s.	1899
	113. Queen Elizabeth's Englishings of Boethius, Plutarch, &c., ed. C. Pemberton. (*Out of print.*)	,,
E.S.	76. George Ashby's Poems, &c., ed. Mary Bateson. (*Out of print.*)	,,
	77. Lydgate's DeGuilleville's Pilgrimage of the Life of Man, ed. F. J. Furnivall. Part I. (*Out of print.*)	,,
	78. The Life and Death of Mary Magdalene, by T. Robinson, c. 1620, ed. H. O. Sommer. 6s.	,,
O.S.	114. Ælfric's Metrical Lives of Saints, ed. W. W. Skeat. Part IV and last. (*Out of print.*)	1900
	115. Jacob's Well, ed. A. Brandeis. Part I. 12s.	,,
	116. An Old-English Martyrology, re-ed. G. Herzfeld. 20s.	,,
E.S.	79. Caxton's Dialogues, English and French, ed. H. Bradley. 12s.	,,
	80. Lydgate's Two Nightingale Poems, ed. O. Glauning. 0s.	,,
	81. The English Works of John Gower, ed. G. C. Macaulay. Part I. (*Reprinted* 1957.) 40s.	,,
O.S.	117. Minor Poems of the Vernon MS., ed. F. J. Furnivall. Part II. 18s.	1901
	118. The Lay Folks' Catechism, ed. T. F. Simmons and H. E. Nolloth. 6s.	,,
	119. Robert of Brunne's Handlyng Synne, and its French original, re-ed. F. J. Furnivall. Part I. (*Out of print.*)	,,
E.S.	82. The English Works of John Gower, ed. G. C. Macaulay. Part II. (*Reprinted* 1957.) 40s.	,,
	83. Lydgate's DeGuilleville's Pilgrimage of the Life of Man, ed. F. J. Furnivall. Part II. (*Out of print.*)	,,
	84. Lydgate's Reason and Sensuality, ed. E. Sieper. Part I. (*Out of print.*)	,,
O.S.	120. The Rule of St. Benet in Northern Prose and Verse, and Caxton's Summary, ed. E. A. Kock. 18s.	1902
	121. The Laud MS. Troy-Book, ed. J. E. Wülfing. Part I. 18s.	,,
E.S.	85. Alexander Scott's Poems, 1568, ed. A. K. Donald. (*Out of print.*)	,,
	86. William of Shoreham's Poems, re-ed. M. Konrath. Part I. (*Out of print.*)	,,
	87. Two Coventry Corpus Christi Plays, re-ed. H. Craig. (*See under* 1952.)	,,
O.S.	122. The Laud MS. Troy-Book, ed. by J. E. Wülfing. Part II. 24s.	1903
	123. Robert of Brunne's Handlyng Synne, and its French original, re-ed. F. J. Furnivall. Part II. (*Out of print.*)	,,
E.S.	88. Le Morte Arthur, re-ed. J. D. Bruce. (*Reprinted* 1959.) 30s.	,,
	89. Lydgate's Reason and Sensuality, ed. E. Sieper. Part II. (*Out of print.*)	,,
	90. English Fragments from Latin Medieval Service-Books, ed. H. Littlehales. (*Out of print.*)	,,
O.S.	124. Twenty-six Political and other Poems from Digby MS. 102, &c., ed. J. Kail. Part I. 12s.	1904
	125. Medieval Records of a London City Church, ed. H. Littlehales. Part I. (*Out of print.*)	,,
	126. An Alphabet of Tales, in Northern English, from the Latin, ed. M. M. Banks. Part I. 12s.	,,
E.S.	91. The Macro Plays, ed. F. J. Furnivall and A. W. Pollard. (*Out of print.*)	,,
	92. Lydgate's DeGuileville's Pilgrimage of the Life of Man, ed. Katherine B. Locock. Part III. (*Out of print.*)	,,
	93. Lovelich's Romance of Merlin, from the unique MS., ed. E. A. Kock. Part I. (*Out of print.*)	,,
O.S.	127. An Alphabet of Tales, in Northern English, from the Latin, ed. M. M. Banks. Part II. 12s.	1905
	128. Medieval Records of a London City Church, ed. H. Littlehales. Part II. 12s.	,,

The Original and Extra Series of the 'Early English Text Society'

O.S. 129.	The English Register of Godstow Nunnery, ed. A. Clark. Part I. 12s.	1905
E.S. 94.	Respublica, a Play on a Social England, ed. L. A. Magnus. (*Out of print. See under* 1946.)	,,
95.	Lovelich's History of the Holy Grail. Part V. The Legend of the Holy Grail, ed. Dorothy Kempe. (*Out of print*.)	,,
96.	Mirk's Festial, ed. T. Erbe. Part I. 14s.	,,
O.S. 130.	The English Register of Godstow Nunnery, ed. A. Clark. Part II. 18s.	1906
131.	The Brut, or The Chronicle of England, ed. F. Brie. Part I. (*Reprinted* 1960.) 25s.	,,
132.	John Metham's Works, ed. H. Craig. 18s.	,,
E.S. 97.	Lydgate's Troy Book, ed. H. Bergen. Part I, Books I and II. (*Out of print*.)	,,
98.	Skelton's Magnyfycence, ed. R. L. Ramsay. (*Reprinted* 1958.) 30s.	,,
99.	The Romance of Emaré, re-ed. Edith Rickert. (*Reprinted* 1958.) 15s.	,,
O.S. 133.	The English Register of Oseney Abbey, by Oxford, ed. A. Clark. Part I. 18s.	1907
134.	The Coventry Leet Book, ed. M. Dormer Harris. Part I. 18s.	,,
E.S. 100.	The Harrowing of Hell, and The Gospel of Nicodemus, re-ed. W. H. Hulme. (*Reprinted* 1961.) 30s.	,,
101.	Songs, Carols, &c., from Richard Hill's Balliol MS., ed. R. Dyboski. (*Out of print*.)	,,
O.S. 135.	The Coventry Leet Book, ed. M. Dormer Harris. Part II. 18s.	1908
135 b.	Extra Issue. Prof. Manly's Piers Plowman and its Sequence, urging the fivefold authorship of the Vision. (*Out of print*.)	,,
136.	The Brut, or The Chronicle of England, ed. F. Brie. Part II. (*Out of print*.)	,,
E.S. 102.	Promptorium Parvulorum, the 1st English-Latin Dictionary, ed. A. L. Mayhew. 25s. 6d.	,,
103.	Lydgate's Troy Book, ed. H. Bergen. Part II, Book III. (*Out of print*.)	,,
O.S. 137	Twelfth-Century Homilies in MS. Bodley 343, ed. A. O. Belfour. Part I, the Text. (*Reprinted* 1962.) 25s.	1909
138.	The Coventry Leet Book, ed. M. Dormer Harris. Part III. 18s.	,,
E.S. 104.	The Non-Cycle Mystery Plays, re-ed. O. Waterhouse. (*Out of print*.)	,,
105.	The Tale of Beryn, with the Pardoner and Tapster, ed. F. J. Furnivall and W. G. Stone. (*Out of print*.)	,,
O.S. 139.	John Arderne's Treatises on Fistula in Ano, &c., ed. D'Arcy Power. 18s.	1910
139 b, c, d, e, f,	Extra Issue. The Piers Plowman Controversy: b. Dr. Jusserand's 1st Reply to Prof. Manly; c. Prof. Manly's Answer to Dr. Jusserand; d. Dr. Jusserand's 2nd Reply to Prof. Manly; e. Mr. R. W. Chambers's Article; f. Dr. Henry Bradley's Rejoinder to Mr. R. W. Chambers. (*Out of print*.)	,,
140.	Capgrave's Lives of St. Augustine and St. Gilbert of Sempringham, ed. J. Munro. (*Out of print*.)	,,
E.S. 106.	Lydgate's Troy Book, ed. H. Bergen. Part III. (*Out of print*.)	,,
107.	Lydgate's Minor Poems, ed. H. N. MacCracken. Part I. Religious Poems. (*Reprinted* 1961.) 40s.	,,
O.S. 141.	Earth upon Earth, all the known texts, ed., with an Introduction, by Hilda Murray. (*Out of print*.)	1911
142.	The English Register of Godstow Nunnery, ed. A. Clark. Part III. 12s.	,,
143.	The Prose Life of Alexander, Thornton MS., ed. J. S. Westlake. 12s.	,,
E.S. 108.	Lydgate's Siege of Thebes, re-ed. A. Erdmann. Part I, the Text. (*Reprinted* 1960.) 24s.	,,
109.	Partonope, re-ed. A. T. Bödtker. The Texts. (*Out of print*.)	,,
O.S. 144.	The English Register of Oseney Abbey, by Oxford, ed. A. Clark. Part II. 12s.	1912
145.	The Northern Passion, ed. F. A. Foster. Part I, the four parallel texts. 18s.	,,
E.S. 110.	Caxton's Mirrour of the World, with all the woodcuts, ed. O. H. Prior. (*Out of print*.)	,,
111.	Caxton's History of Jason, the Text, Part I, ed. J. Munro. 18s.	,,
O.S. 146.	The Coventry Leet Book, ed. M. Dormer Harris. Introduction, Indexes, &c. Part IV. 12s.	1913
147.	The Northern Passion, ed. F. A. Foster, Introduction, French Text, Variants and Fragments, Glossary. Part II. 18s.	,,
	[An enlarged reprint of O.S. 26, Religious Pieces in Prose and Verse, from the Thornton MS., ed. G. G. Perry. 6s.]	,,
E.S. 112.	Lovelich's Romance of Merlin, ed. E. A. Kock. Part II. (*Reprinted* 1961.) 30s.	,,
113.	Poems by Sir John Salusbury, Robert Chester, and others, from Christ Church MS. 184, &c., ed. Carleton Brown. 18s.	,,
O.S. 148.	A Fifteenth-Century Courtesy Book and Two Franciscan Rules, ed. R. W. Chambers and W. W. Seton. (*Reprinted* 1963.) 25s.	1914
149	Lincoln Diocese Documents, 1450-1544, ed. Andrew Clark. 18s.	,,
150.	The Old-English Rule of Bp. Chrodegang, and the Capitula of Bp. Theodulf, ed. A. S. Napier. 15s.	,,
E.S. 114.	The Gild of St. Mary, Lichfield, ed. F. J. Furnivall. 18s.	,,
115.	The Chester Plays, re-ed. J. Matthews. Part II. (*Reprinted* 1959.) 25s.	,,
O.S. 151.	The Lanterne of Light, ed. Lilian M. Swinburn. (*Out of print*.)	1915
152.	Early English Homilies, from Cott. Vesp. D. XIV, ed. Rubie Warner. Part I, Text. (*Out of print*.)	,,
E.S. 116.	The Pauline Epistles, ed. M. J. Powell. (*Out of print*.)	,,
117.	Bp. Fisher's English Works, ed. R. Bayne. Part II. 18s.	,,
O.S. 153.	Mandeville's Travels, ed. P. Hamelius. Part I, Text. (*Reprinted* 1960.) 25s.	1916
154.	Mandeville's Travels, ed. P. Hamelius. Part II, Notes and Introduction. (*Reprinted* 1961.) 25s.	,,
E.S. 118.	The Earliest Arithmetics in English, ed. R. Steele. 18s.	,,
119.	The Owl and Nightingale, 2 Texts parallel, ed. G. F. H. Sykes and J. H. G. Grattan. (*Reprinted* 1959.) 20s.	,,
O.S. 155.	The Wheatley MS., ed. Mabel Day. 36s.	1917
E.S. 120.	Ludus Coventriae, ed. K. S. Block. (*Reprinted* 1961.) 30s.	,,
O.S. 156.	Reginald Pecock's Donet, from Bodl. MS. 916, ed. Elsie V. Hitchcock. 42s.	1918
E.S. 121.	Lydgate's Fall of Princes, ed. H. Bergen. Part I. (*Out of print*.)	,,

The Original and Extra Series of the 'Early English Text Society'

E.S. 122.	Lydgate's Fall of Princes, ed. H. Bergen. Part II. (*Out of print.*)	1918
O.S. 157.	Harmony of the Life of Christ, from MS. Pepys 2498, ed. Margery Goates. (*Out of print.*)	1919
158.	Meditations on the Life and Passion of Christ, from MS. Add., 11307, ed. Charlotte D'Evelyn. (*Out of print.*)	,,
E.S. 123.	Lydgate's Fall of Princes, ed. H. Bergen. Part III. (*Out of print.*)	,,
124.	Lydgate's Fall of Princes, ed. H. Bergen. Part IV. (*Out of print.*)	,,
O.S. 159.	Vices and Virtues, ed. F. Holthausen. Part II. 14s.	1920
	[A re-edition of O.S. 18, **Hali Meidenhad**, ed. O. Cockayne, with a variant MS., Bodl. 34, hitherto unprinted, ed. F. J. Furnivall. (*Out of print.*)]	,,
E.S. 125.	Lydgate's Siege of Thebes, ed. A. Erdmann and E. Ekwall. Part II. (*Out of print.*)	,,
126.	Lydgate's Troy Book, ed. H. Bergen. Part IV. 18s.	,,

O.S. 160.	The Old English Heptateuch, MS. Cott. Claud. B. IV, ed. S. J. Crawford. (*Out of print.*)	1921
161.	Three O.E. Prose Texts, MS. Cott. Vit. A. xv, ed. S. Rypins. (*Out of print.*)	,,
162.	Facsimile of MS. Cotton Nero A. x (Pearl, Cleanness, Patience and Sir Gawain), Introduction by I. Gollancz. (*Reprinted* 1955.) 100s.	1922
163.	Book of the Foundation of St. Bartholomew's Church in London, ed. N. Moore. (*Out of print.*)	1923
164.	Pecock's Folewer to the Donet, ed. Elsie V. Hitchcock. (*Out of print.*)	,,
165.	Middleton's Chinon of England, with Leland's Assertio Arturii and Robinson's translation, ed. W. E. Mead. (*Out of print.*)	,,
166.	Stanzaic Life of Christ, ed. Frances A. Foster. (*Out of print.*)	1924
167.	Trevisa's Dialogus inter Militem et Clericum, Sermon by FitzRalph, and Bygynnyng of the World, ed. A. J. Perry. (*Out of print.*)	,,
168.	Caxton's Ordre of Chyualry, ed. A. T. P. Byles. (*Out of print.*)	1925
169.	The Southern Passion, ed. Beatrice Brown. (*Out of print.*)	,,
170.	Walton's Boethius, ed. M. Science. (*Out of print.*)	,,
171.	Pecock's Reule of Cristen Religioun, ed. W. C. Greet. (*Out of print.*)	1926
172.	The Seege or Batayle of Troye, ed. M. E. Barnicle. (*Out of print.*)	,,
173.	Hawes' Pastime of Pleasure, ed. W. E. Mead. (*Out of print.*)	1927
174.	The Life of St. Anne, ed. R. E. Parker. (*Out of print.*)	,,
175.	Barclay's Eclogues, ed. Beatrice White. (*Reprinted* 1961.) 35s.	,,
176.	Caxton's Prologues and Epilogues, ed. W. J. B. Crotch. (*Reprinted* 1956.) 30s.	,,
177.	Byrhtferth's Manual, ed. S. J. Crawford. (*Out of print.*)	1928
178.	The Revelations of St. Birgitta, ed. W. P. Cumming. (*Out of print.*)	,,
179.	The Castell of Pleasure, ed. R. Cornelius. (*Out of print.*)	,,
180.	The Apologye of Syr Thomas More, ed. A. I. Taft. (*Out of print.*)	1929
181.	The Dance of Death, ed. F. Warren. (*Out of print.*)	,,
182.	Speculum Christiani, ed. G. Holmstedt. (*Out of print.*)	,,
183.	The Northern Passion (Supplement), ed. W. Heuser and Frances Foster. (*Out of print.*)	1930
184.	The Poems of John Audelay, ed. Ella K. Whiting. (*Out of print.*)	,,
185.	Lovelich's Merlin, ed. E. A. Kock. Part III. 30s.	,,
186.	Harpsfield's Life of More, ed. Elsie V. Hitchcock and R. W. Chambers. (*Reprinted* 1963.) 45s.	1931
187.	Whittinton and Stanbridge's Vulgaria, ed. B. White. (*Out of print.*)	,,
188.	The Siege of Jerusalem, ed. E. Kölbing and Mabel Day. 18s.	,,
189.	Caxton's Fayttes of Armes and of Chyualrye, ed. A. T. Byles. 25s. 6d.	1932
190.	English Mediæval Lapidaries, ed. Joan Evans and Mary Serjeantson. (*Reprinted* 1960.) 20s.	,,
191.	The Seven Sages, ed. K. Brunner. (*Out of print.*)	,,
191A.	On the Continuity of English Prose, by R. W. Chambers. (*Reprinted* 1957.) 14s.	,,
192.	Lydgate's Minor Poems, ed. H. N. MacCracken. Part II, **Secular Poems**. (*Reprinted* 1961.) 40s.	1933
193.	Seinte Marherete, re-ed. Frances Mack. (*Reprinted* 1958.) 30s.	,,
194.	The Exeter Book, Part II, ed. W. S. Mackie. (*Reprinted* 1958.) 25s.	,,
195.	The Quatrefoil of Love, ed. I. Gollancz and M. Weale. (*Out of print.*)	1934
196.	A Short English Metrical Chronicle, ed. E. Zettl. (*Out of print.*)	,,
197.	Roper's Life of More, ed. Elsie V. Hitchcock. (*Reprinted* 1958.) 20s.	,,
198.	Firumbras and Otuel and Roland, ed. Mary O'Sullivan. (*Out of print.*)	,,
199.	Mum and the Sothsegger, ed. Mabel Day and R. Steele. 14s.	,,
200.	Speculum Sacerdotale, ed. E. H. Weatherly. (*Out of print.*)	1935
201.	Knyghthode and Bataile, ed. R. Dyboski and Z. M. Arend. (*Out of print.*)	,,
202.	Palsgrave's Acolastus, ed. P. L. Carver. (*Out of print.*)	,,
203.	Amis and Amiloun, ed. MacEdward Leach. (*Reprinted* 1960.) 30s.	,,
204.	Valentine and Orson, ed. Arthur Dickson. (*Out of print.*)	1936
205.	Tales from the Decameron, ed. H. G. Wright. 20s.	,,
206.	Bokenham's Lives of Holy Women (Lives of the Saints), ed. Mary S. Serjeantson. (*Out of print.*)	,,
207.	Liber de Diversis Medicinis, ed. Margaret S. Ogden. (*Out of print.*)	,,
208.	The Parker Chronicle and Laws (facsimile), ed. R. Flower and A. H. Smith. 84s.	1937
209.	Middle English Sermons from MS. Roy. 18 B. xxiii, ed. W. O. Ross. (*Reprinted* 1960.) 42s.	1938
210.	Sir Gawain and the Green Knight, ed. I. Gollancz. With Introductory essays by Mabel Day and M. S. Serjeantson. (*Reprinted* 1957.) 10s.	,,
211.	Dictes and Sayings of the Philosophers, ed. C. F. Bühler. (*Reprinted* 1961.) 45s.	1939

7

The Original and Extra Series of the 'Early English Text Society'

212. **The Book of Margery Kempe**, Part I, ed. S. B. Meech and Hope Emily Allen. (*Reprinted* 1961.) 42s. — 1939
213. **Ælfric's De Temporibus Anni**, ed. H. Henel. (*Out of print.*) — 1940
214. **Morley's Translation of Boccaccio's De Claris Mulieribus**, ed. H. G. Wright. (*Out of print.*) — "
215. **English Poems of Charles of Orleans**, Part I, ed. R. Steele. (*Out of print.*) — 1941
216. **The Latin Text of the Ancrene Riwle**, ed. Charlotte D'Evelyn. (*Reprinted* 1957.) 31s. 6d. — "
217. **Book of Vices and Virtues**, ed. W. Nelson Francis. (*Out of print.*) — 1942
218. **The Cloud of Unknowing and the Book of Privy Counselling**, ed. Phyllis Hodgson. (*Reprinted* 1958.) 40s. — 1943
219. **The French Text of the Ancrene Riwle**, B.M. Cotton MS. Vitellius. F. VII, ed. J. A. Herbert. (*Out of print.*) — "
220. **English Poems of Charles of Orleans**, Part II, ed. R. Steele and Mabel Day. (*Out of print.*) — 1944
221. **Sir Degrevant**, ed. L. F. Casson. (*Out of print.*) — "
222. **Ro. Ba.'s Life of Syr Thomas More**, ed. Elsie V. Hitchcock and Mgr. P. E. Hallett. (*Reprinted* 1957.) 35s. — 1945
223. **Tretyse of Loue**, ed. J. H. Fisher. (*Out of print.*) — "
224. **Athelston**, ed. A. McI. Trounce. (*Reprinted* 1957.) 15s. — 1946
225. **The English Text of the Ancrene Riwle**, B.M. Cotton MS. Nero A. XIV, ed. Mabel Day. (*Reprinted* 1957.) 25s. — "
226. **Respublica**, re-ed. W. W. Greg. 18s. 6d. — "
227. **Kyng Alisaunder**, ed. G. V. Smithers. Vol. I, Text. (*Reprinted* 1961.) 35s. — 1947
228. **The Metrical Life of St. Robert of Knaresborough**, ed. J. Bazire. (*Out of print.*) — "
229. **The English Text of the Ancrene Riwle**, Gonville and Caius College MS. 234/120, ed. R. M. Wilson. With Introduction by N. R. Ker. (*Reprinted* 1957.) 25s. — 1948
230. **The Life of St. George by Alexander Barclay**, ed. W. Nelson. (*Reprinted* 1960.) 28s. — "
231. **Deonise Hid Diuinite**, and other treatises related to *The Cloud of Unknowing*, ed. Phyllis Hodgson. (*Reprinted* 1958.) 30s. — 1949
232. **The English Text of the Ancrene Riwle**, B.M. Royal MS. 8 C. 1, ed. A. C. Baugh. (*Reprinted* 1958.) 20s. — "
233. **The Bibliotheca Historica of Diodorus Siculus translated by John Skelton**, ed. F. M. Salter and H. L. R. Edwards. Vol. I, Text. 42s. — 1950
234. **Caxton: Paris and Vienne**, ed. MacEdward Leach. 30s. — 1951
235. **The South English Legendary**, Corpus Christi College Cambridge MS. 145 and B.M. M.S. Harley 2277, &c., ed. Charlotte D'Evelyn and Anna J. Mill. Text, Vol. I. 35s. — "
236. **The South English Legendary**. Text, Vol. II. 35s. — 1952
[E.S. 87. **Two Coventry Corpus Christi Plays**, re-ed. H. Craig. Second Edition. (*Out of print.*)] — "
237. **Kyng Alisaunder**, ed. G. V. Smithers. Vol. II, Introduction, Commentary, and Glossary. 37s. 6d. — 1953
238. **The Phonetic Writings of Robert Robinson**, ed. E. J. Dobson. 28s. — "
239. **The Bibliotheca Historica of Diodorus Siculus translated by John Skelton**, ed. F. M. Salter and H. L. R. Edwards. Vol. II. Introduction, Notes, and Glossary. 15s. — 1954
240. **The French Text of the Ancrene Riwle**, Trinity College, Cambridge, MS. R. 14. 7, ed. W. H. Trethewey. 45s. — "
241. **Þe Wohunge of ure Lauerd**, and other pieces, ed. W. Meredith Thompson. 32s. — 1955
242. **The Salisbury Psalter**, ed. Celia Sisam and Kenneth Sisam. 84s. — 1955–56
243. **George Cavendish: The Life and Death of Cardinal Wolsey**, ed. Richard S. Sylvester. (*Reprinted* 1961.) 35s. — 1957
244. **The South English Legendary**. Vol. III, Introduction and Glossary, ed. Charlotte D'Evelyn. 25s. — "
245. **Beowulf** (facsimile). With Transliteration by J. Zupitza, new collotype plates, and Introduction by N. Davis. 70s. — 1958
246. **The Parlement of the Thre Ages**, ed. M. Y. Offord. 28s. — 1959
247. **Facsimile of MS. Bodley 34** (Katherine Group). With Introduction by N. R. Ker. 42s. — "
248. **Þe Liflade ant te Passiun of Seinte Iuliene**, ed. S. R. T. O. d'Ardenne. 30s. — 1960
249. **Ancrene Wisse**, Corpus Christi College, Cambridge, MS. 402, ed. J. R. R. Tolkien. With an Introduction by N. R. Ker. 30s. — "
250. **Laȝamon's Brut**, ed. G. L. Brook and R. F. Leslie. Vol. I, Text (first part). 70s. — 1961
251. **Facsimile of the Cotton and Jesus Manuscripts of the Owl and the Nightingale**. With Introduction by N. R. Ker. 42s. — 1962
252. **The English Text of the Ancrene Riwle**, B.M. Cotton MS. Titus D. XVIII, ed. Frances M. Mack, and Lanhydrock Fragment, ed. A. Zettersten. (*At press.*) 35s. — "
253. **The Bodley Version of Mandeville's Travels**, ed. M. C. Seymour. (*At press.*) 35s. — 1963
254. **Ywain and Gawain**, ed. Albert B. Friedman and Norman T. Harrington. (*At press.*) 35s. — "

The following is a select list of forthcoming volumes. Other texts are under consideration:
Sir Eglamour of Artois, ed. Frances E. Richardson.
Sir Thomas Chaloner: The Praise of Folie, ed. Clarence H. Miller.
Laȝamon's Brut, ed. G. L. Brook and R. F. Leslie, Vols. II and III.
Ælfric: Catholic Homilies, First Series, ed. P. Clemoes.
The Paston Letters, ed. N. Davis.
The English Text of the Ancrene Riwle, edited from all the extant manuscripts:
 Bodleian MS. Vernon, ed. G. V. Smithers.
 B.M. Cotton MS. Cleopatra C. VI, ed. E. J. Dobson.
 Magdalene College, Cambridge, MS. Pepys 2498, ed. A. Zettersten.
The York Plays, re-ed. Arthur Brown.
The Macro Plays, re-ed. Mark Eccles.
The Cely Letters, ed. A. H. Hanham.

April 1963

Publisher
LONDON: THE OXFORD UNIVERSITY PRESS, AMEN HOUSE, E.C. 4

The manufacturer's authorised representative in the EU for product safety is
Oxford University Press España S.A. of el Parque Empresarial San Fernando de
Henares, Avenida de Castilla, 2 – 28830 Madrid (www.oup.es/en or product.
safety@oup.com). OUP España S.A. also acts as importer into Spain of products
made by the manufacturer.

www.ingramcontent.com/pod-product-compliance
Ingram Content Group UK Ltd.
Pitfield, Milton Keynes, MK11 3LW, UK
UKHW022151230426
12049UKWH00003BA/43